Practical Ruby for System Administration

André Ben Hamou

Apress®

Practical Ruby for System Administration

Copyright © 2007 by André Ben Hamou

ISBN-13 (pbk): 978-1-59059-821-4

ISBN-10 (pbk): 1-59059-821-0

Printed and bound in the United States of America 9 8 7 6 5 4 3 2 1

Lead Editor: Jonathan Gennick
Technical Reviewer: Dee Zsombor
Editorial Board: Steve Anglin, Ewan Buckingham, Gary Cornell, Jonathan Gennick, Jason Gilmore, Jonathan Hassell, Chris Mills, Matthew Moodie, Jeffrey Pepper, Ben Renow-Clarke, Dominic Shakeshaft, Matt Wade, Tom Welsh
Project Manager: Denise Santoro Lincoln
Copy Edit Manager: Nicole Flores
Copy Editor: Nicole Flores
Assistant Production Director: Kari Brooks-Copony
Production Editor: Ellie Fountain
Compositor: Susan Glinert
Proofreader: April Eddy
Indexer: Broccoli Information Management
Artist: Kinetic Publishing Services, LLC
Cover Designer: Kurt Krames
Manufacturing Director: Tom Debolski

Distributed to the book trade worldwide by Springer-Verlag New York, Inc., 233 Spring Street, 6th Floor, New York, NY 10013. Phone 1-800-SPRINGER, fax 201-348-4505, e-mail orders-ny@springer-sbm.com, or visit http://www.springeronline.com.

For information on translations, please contact Apress directly at 2855 Telegraph Avenue, Suite 600, Berkeley, CA 94705. Phone 510-549-5930, fax 510-549-5939, e-mail info@apress.com, or visit http://www.apress.com.

The source code for this book is available to readers at http://www.apress.com in the Source Code/Download section.

For François.

Contents at a Glance

Contents

About the Author

 **ANDRÉ BEN HAMOU** went to Imperial College in 1999 ostensibly to study physics but tried not to let that get in the way of his inner geek, joining the Department of Computing's system support group to patch up its ailing Mac network. Over the course of the next five years he learned some stuff, including how to program in a few languages, how to analyze complexity, why magnets have two ends (red and blue), why loose coupling is important in system design, which cocktail bar is easily the best in London, on how many levels Macs are just brilliant, why cucumbers and tumble dryers do not mix, how to use a tape loader without losing an appendage, how to deploy databases without crying, how to model the quantum mechanics of an infinite potential well, and why the lid of a blender should always be secured before use.

Of all these revelations, however, one that particularly sticks out was coming to appreciate the mind-altering brilliance of the Ruby programming language. He has been addicted ever since, bringing it with him to his current job as chief geek for Freedom 255, a major UK ISP.

André enjoys walking, talking, and taking abusive liberties with the English language. He lives with his imaginary cat on the south coast of England. Send muffin recipes to andre@bluetheta.com.

About the Technical Reviewer

DEE ZSOMBOR has been a grateful Ruby programmer since 2004, when he escaped the painful entrapment of curly-brace programming languages. As a longtime OSS advocate, he saw the opportunity to put his convictions to the ultimate test by cofounding PrimalGrasp LLC (`http://primalgrasp.com`), a spicy software shop. PrimalGrasp proved to be a fabulous experience, following the spirit of "small is beautiful." Nowadays Dee develops with Ruby, JavaScript, and Erlang, and makes occasional contributions to the Rails framework. He enjoys mountain biking, reading, experimenting with graphics and, when time permits, swimming.

Acknowledgments

My experiences at Imperial College were life-changing. I'd like to thank Duncan White, on whose shoulder many an aspiring admin has perched, and who also has a supply of the most bizarre tomatoes ever to emerge from an English garden. For introducing me to Ruby in the first place, I consider myself indebted to Mike Wyer, one of the smartest sysadmins I ever met and certainly one of the most masterful administrators of clue to users. I also have to thank Tim Southerwood, not only for demonstrating that administrators can still be mirthful and well-balanced individuals even after years of service (hope for us all), but also for revealing that noodles come in flavors that could blow the side off a nuclear submarine.

Other university buddies to thank include Adam Langley for the maths, the geek-a-thons, the sparkling intellect, and the chocolate cake; Mark Thomas, whose decency, friendship, and acumen could always be relied upon; Nick Maynard, for being good enough to laugh at my jokes (particularly the bad ones) and for working on so many iterations of the host status monitoring project without tearing out my jugular; Phil Willoughby, who can spot a flaw in a design at a thousand paces and whose cynical sense of humor always made me chuckle; Paul Jolly, for the great debates and for providing a working environment with so many inside jokes that it was impossible to be stressed (lart, slap, clue, sneeze, stretch, lart, wibble); Ian McCubbin, who was the only person I knew whose body could simulate the effect of amphetamines, without pause, for weeks at a time; and James Moody, for the truly delightful lack of sugarcoating in his approach and for shielding the rest of us from unspeakable torment by being a Windows administrator of considerable skill (a rare beast indeed).

On a personal level, I'd like to thank Aidan Bowen, who is one of the finest blends of boss and good friend I've ever known (and who was kind enough to allow me to use examples from my daily work in this book). I'm also thankful that I have the pleasure of knowing Alexi Tingey, Andrew Smith, and Michael Allan, because friends this good are one of nature's most enduring miracles. I must thank mum as well for being so many things that I both admire and love at the same time.

It is also important to thank the wonderful people at Apress whose skill, experience, and patience have made this book possible. You guys rock.

Finally, I want to express my gratitude to and respect for Yukihiro Matsumoto for the creation and nurturing of the Ruby language. Together with a brilliant and dedicated community, Matz has given me a career, a hobby, and something to enthuse about, and for that I will always be thankful.

Introduction

It turns out that writing a book is pretty easy. Writing a book that is relevant to anyone but yourself—now that's far more difficult than I'd imagined. I love the elegance, simplicity, and power of Ruby, and I use it every day to make systems function at the ISP where I work. You would have thought that this combination of facts would make it straightforward to distill a few salient chapters on the matter. It doesn't. Indeed it took me nearly a month of trying to build a skeleton structure for the book before I realized that the problem was one of context.

You see, the target audience for this book is obviously system administrators, but that's about as helpful in narrowing the focus as asking a telephone company to connect you to Bob in Venezuela. We are an incredibly diverse bunch unified by a few common traits (if Slashdot is any measure). We are geeky, by which I mean that we love technology and structure for their own sake and get a kick out of problem solving. We always have too many plates spinning and not enough time to tend to them properly. We are asked to do everything from retrieving a lost e-mail to building a bespoke CMS from scratch, and it's always needed yesterday, such that this sort of thing happens far too often:

> *It's 8:52 on Monday morning and Jo comes running in. Before she's halfway into the room she's already blurting out, "The MD needs content mirroring on our mail servers implemented by close of business today or we're all getting sued!"*

It's in situations like this that it hits you: who in the name of sanity is Jo, and how does she keep getting past security?

Looking at our jobs from an engineering perspective, the notion of rapid deployment is so deeply ingrained in the daily routine that many if not most system administrators learn an interpreted language in short order. The question is, which one should you choose?

I used and trusted Perl for a good few years before I switched to Ruby. The reason I switched was inadvertently summarized by Shakespeare (thanks, Will). While the Bard was talking about life, he might well have been describing any of my nontrivial Perl scripts when he referred to a tale told by an idiot, full of sound and fury, signifying nothing.

Programs should be beautiful, not give you retina-detaching levels of eyestrain. As Eric Raymond put it, "Ugly programs are like ugly suspension bridges: they're much more liable to collapse than pretty ones, because the way humans (especially engineer-humans) perceive beauty is intimately related to our ability to process and understand complexity. A language that makes it hard to write elegant code makes it hard to write good code."

In short, administrators need a language that is as easy to think in as possible, is terse without being cryptic, has a syntax that usually makes the "right" way to build something the same as the "rapid" way to do so, and reads like executable metacode. Let's face it—these criteria leave only two mainstream languages standing: Ruby and Python. For my money, Python comes very close but only Ruby hits the mark.

When I started to use Ruby, I did what I suspect quite a few have done in the past. I wrote in Ruby and thought in Perl. This does not make for convincing scripts (in much the same way that I would have difficulty persuading you I was Carmen Miranda merely by stapling a banana to my head). What with having to unlearn bad habits resulting from all the bookkeeping one does in Perl, I only wish I'd appreciated the benefits of using Ruby earlier.

With all that said, I am in a position to explain the approach I've taken with this book. This is the book I wish someone had handed me six years ago when I first looked over someone's shoulder at some Ruby and decided I had better things to do. It is not even remotely a definitive Ruby language reference (although the first chapter tries to get you up to speed, assuming you've done a fair bit of programming). It is not a recipe book for 101 different ways to create an LDAP client. It doesn't have whole chapters with themes like "this is how you create a user on Linux, and Windows, and Solaris, and Mac OS X, and how you delete them, etc." It is also not microwave safe, nor should it be used as a floatation aid.

What I've tried to do is balance very conceptual, water cooler–style discussions with some strategically placed examples, focusing on the core technologies and techniques available to a Ruby-wielding administrator. My motivation for this approach is the conviction that, as geeks, we never read DVD player instruction manuals. I suspect this is because we prefer to have a general model of an abstract player in our head together with experience of what some common buttons look like. By organizing our thinking like this, we are more adaptable in dealing with unfamiliar systems—what Scott Adams refers to as "the knack."

In the demanding world of system administration, you have to be able to read and write code at speed. You need to have the knowledge of how to open a socket, lock a file, or coerce a file format. Fundamentally, you need to be able to crack open a crazy and overflowing toolkit to meet new and unexpected challenges. It is my hope that this book will provide you with a couple of extra wrenches to add to your collection.

Before we begin, for those who don't know it, here's a completely accurate history of Ruby.

A COMPLETELY ACCURATE HISTORY OF RUBY

In olden days, life was harder. Men were real men, women were real men, and even certain protozoa were real men. Everything was fields, and mastodons bellowed to each other across primeval swamps. It was an age of character, of salt-of-the-earth, brine-in-the-veins, chocolate-covered-spleen-with-sprinkles people.

Among all this hardship, something subversive glimmered in the hearts of humankind. A vibrant red glow in the darkness, filled with daring promise and gleeful abandon. A change was coming. It could be smelled on the wind as the sort of fruity bouquet of dismembered chestnuts.

In a small settlement on the frozen edge of the Arctic Circle, a boy was born to a family of chartered accountant trapeze artists. His birth was attended by a wise old halibut that had foreseen this event and was filled with great rejoicing. And it came to pass that as the Matz grew, a scarlet radiance began to invest his very being.

Toiled, he did, working with the deep magic inherited from those who had gone before. He cast algorithmic spells combining the dry and dusty with the spry and trusty until a shining crimson gem was hewn. Ruby was born.

An emergency, strokey-beard-type meeting of the establishment was hastily convened to decide upon the best way to cope with this upstart. It was obvious that anything that made life easy and enjoyable for so many was in flagrant violation of the puritanical ethic that prevailed. If the line between work and fun were blurred, the universe wouldn't make sense any more.

One by one, the senior wizards of the age began to fall under Ruby's winsome spell, first approaching it with caution, then with interest, and finally with cheerful addiction. The orthodoxy hit back with a blistering antihype campaign, reminding the faithful of the importance of what had gone before. The Ruby-ists returned a volley of anti-antihype, threatening complete recursive collapse.

Finally, balance was reached. The upstart had become an incumbent, and everywhere signs of its positive influence were to be found. A whole new generation of acolytes was riding the rails of power to weave highly structured webs of data and capability. Apprentice wizards found that they could do more and go further than they had thought possible. The future was exciting again and nothing would be the same.

CHAPTER 1

■ ■ ■

What Ruby Can Do for You

As I mentioned in the book's introduction, Ruby is my language of choice. It is the tool I instinctively reach for first when solving system administration problems. To recap, it has principally achieved this place in my affections by

- Making it simple to write nicely readable code

- Emphasizing convention over configuration, so a little effort goes a long way

- Offering seamless mechanisms for interfacing with C libraries

- Having syntax, extension, and execution conventions that very often make coding the "right" way and the "quick" way the same thing

- Adopting object-oriented principles so completely that extremely powerful metaprogramming techniques become readily available

Of course, this enthusiasm could be the result of some sort of massive, sugar-induced hyperbolic fit (a kilo of chocolate muffins can sometimes have this effect on me). Thus, I devote this first chapter to both introducing Ruby and hopefully making the case that it is everything I say it is. In addition, since I imagine that a very large portion of the audience for this book comes from a Perl background, I use Perl to draw attention to the syntactic and logical improvements that Ruby makes over many such traditional languages.

Furthermore, please don't worry if this chapter feels like a 200 mph whirlwind tour of the language—that's exactly what it is meant to be. The next chapter will rewind a little and get down to the everyday basics of using Ruby.

Hello World

Why don't we jump straight in with the example we all know and love? Here's the Ruby to dump the phrase "hello world" in the terminal:

```
$ ruby -e 'puts "hello world"'
hello world
```

As you might have guessed, the -e flag instructs the Ruby interpreter to execute whatever script follows (inside the single quotes in this case). For more on the command line options of the Ruby interpreter, do a man ruby. Anyone who's ever programmed in C will recognize the `puts` command. It is shorthand for "put string" (the string being the collection of characters inside the double quotes).

RI: THE RUBY REFERENCE

Before we delve too deeply into Ruby's built-in methods, classes, and other such foppery, it is essential that you be comfortable using the rather spiffy command line Ruby reference tool called `ri` that ships as part of the standard Ruby distribution. This is one of the best ways to learn about what the various parts of the core and standard Ruby libraries do. Want to know what the `String` class does? Simply invoke `ri String`. What if you know you want the reference for `puts` but can't remember which module/class it belongs to? A simple `ri puts` will list the possibilities.

If you are dealing with a class that has both a class method and an object method named the same thing, asking for `ri SomeClass.some_method` is ambiguous. `ri` will warn you of this if you attempt it and show you the alternatives, which are disambiguated through a conventional punctuation meme:

- `SomeClass::some_method` for class methods

- `SomeClass#some_method` for object methods

Make sure that you get into the habit of using such lookups anytime I mention a new class or method you don't recognize or you want to learn more about.

Now only the most extreme of masochists and some of my best friends use one-liners for all their scripting needs. A script is more usually kept in its own little text file. So create a plain text file called `hello.rb` in your editor of choice that looks like this:

```
#!/usr/bin/env ruby -w
puts "hello world"
```

I'm going to assume that, as a system administrator, you are familiar with the purpose of the first line in designating which interpreter to use for the rest of the file and how to make the file executable with a quick `chmod u+x hello.rb`.

The `-w` is quite important. It can be loosely thought of as "warnings mode" but is more properly defined as an instruction to go into verbose mode. The practical upshot of this is to display lots of warnings if you do something suspect. I always have this flag in my scripts unless forced to remove it by badly written libraries that vomit hundreds of warnings when used (yes, these sorts of libraries exist even in the much-vaunted Ruby universe, demonstrating the inescapable ubiquity of truly awful programmers).

All of that said, now that you have an executable file with some valid Ruby in it and a proper *shebang* line (i.e., the #! syntax) at the beginning, you can treat it as though it were like any other executable:

```
$ ./hello.rb
hello world
```

■Tip If your platform doesn't support the #!/usr/bin/env convention, then don't forget that the script can be run by passing it to the Ruby interpreter manually: <path_to_ruby_interpreter> -w hello.rb.

Let the rejoicing begin. Our first Ruby script is written and does what it's supposed to—nothing that is of any conceivable use whatsoever.

One approach to executing Ruby code that I haven't covered is the interactive Ruby shell irb, which is another standard part of the Ruby distribution. Because Ruby is interpreted rather than compiled, it can be executed one line at a time. Thus invoking the irb utility presents you with a command prompt at which you can start typing Ruby code. Pressing Enter wakes up the interpreter, which picks up where it left off and executes your code. It even shows you the inspected version of the last thing evaluated.

```
$ irb
irb(main):001:0> word = "lobotomy"
=> "lobotomy"
irb(main):002:0> word.reverse
=> "ymotobol"
```

Type **exit** or press Ctrl+D to quit the interpreter. Additionally, if your distribution was compiled with readline support, you will be able to use the up and down arrow keys to cycle through your command history or press Ctrl+A/Ctrl+E to jump to the start/end of the line. You'll find out pretty quickly if your irb doesn't have such support (like the build that comes with Mac OS X), as odd escape characters will appear when you try to perform any of these actions.

Make sure you have a terminal open with irb running when browsing code in this book. This will allow you practice as you go without having to create, save, and execute scripts. So equipped, we can embark on a headlong tour of the language.

Ruby in a Nutcracker

Ruby is an object-oriented (OO) programming language—a *very* object-oriented programming language. It is often surprising for those new to Ruby (but experienced in other languages that claim to be object oriented) just how pure Ruby's OO credentials are. To understand what this means and how it affects our approach to programming, it is first necessary to engage in a quick summary of object orientation.

Objects at Rest: The Theory of Object Orientation

Although experience may vary, I suspect that by the time most programmers get to their tenth-ever program, they have already started to fathom the power of abstraction. Simply put, *abstraction* is the ability to treat something as a black box, not caring about its internal workings. When throwing a stick for your dog, you probably don't keep a model of how her nervous system works going in your head. For the purpose of the game, she is simply a dog and all the complexity of being a slobbering pet with a vast array of biological mechanisms under the surface is irrelevant.

You do not have to care about her inner workings as long as she responds to certain commands and gives particular responses. In this sense, your view of her obeys the fundamental goal of OO design: *encapsulation*. If in some ultrabizarre parallel universe it was impossible to play catch with her without direct control of her nervous system (like some kind of puppet master), the game would be fearsome in its complexity. On the other hand, if you could cope with this breach of encapsulation, you could make her perform feats that might not otherwise be possible in our universe.

Having beaten that metaphor to death, I hope that the parallels in programming are apparent. I have heard it argued that the art of programming is inherently the art of managed complexity. Instead of having programs that exist as one gargantuan list of commands and data, we should break them up into logical chunks with well-defined interfaces because

- It becomes easier to get an overview of the functionality of the program and thus understand its mechanics.

- It allows the programmer to concentrate only on the code necessary to achieve one small piece of functionality at a time.

- Having well-defined interfaces between the chunks makes for easier proofreading and testing to catch logical and semantic mistakes.

- Encapsulation of both operations and data means less repetition of complex stretches of code (i.e., the code becomes less "noisy").

Appreciating these points, we can now talk about an *object* in the formal sense. An object is an entity that adheres to the preceding principles (see Figure 1-1). It has some internal set of data that we have no direct access to and provides a set of methods for us to use in interacting with it. An object is an *instance* of a *class*. That is to say that any given object is of a certain class (a dog, a vegetable, etc.) and that it has been produced or brought to life in some way.

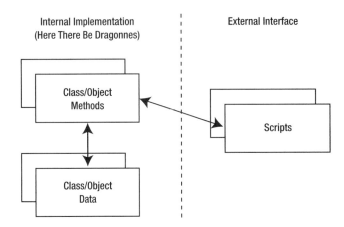

Figure 1-1. *The strict demarcation of object data through the use of methods*

Any language that claims to be OO has some mechanism for defining a class to have certain methods, constants, and data. These items can exist both at the class level and at the object level. What do I mean by this? If you think of a class as a factory that knows how to build objects of a certain type, then it makes sense that it will have at least one method of its own. This method is often called new in OO languages and is simply that which constructs an object of the pertinent class. Thus new would be a *class method* and, if it produced a car, drive would be an example of an *object method.*

In addition, every OO language I've ever used allows for the concept of a subclass. If we were modeling a fruit bowl, we might suddenly realize that whereas both oranges and apples can rot, only oranges really need to be peeled before consumption. Thus we might create a fruit class that implements the rot method and then orange and apple subclasses, of which only the former will have the additional peel method that neither its parent nor sibling implements (see Figure 1-2). This idea of a class family is another important example of how object-oriented programming encourages you to write as little code as possible and reuse it as often as is appropriate.

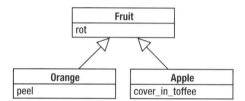

Figure 1-2. *Fruity method inheritance*

Informally, if a language implements functions and has some means for structuring data, then it is possible to adopt these programming patterns, whether the language claims to be OO or not. Indeed, as I wrote more and more C, I found myself creating libraries that followed these principles. Where I got into a mess, it was almost always because I had broken the encapsulation for the sake of expediency or (even worse) performance. I had experienced one of those moments of frustration when you look at the code you've written and decide it will be too time consuming/complex/bothersome to stick to the carefully defined interfaces. So I pulled on my latex gloves and penetrated the exterior.

If you've done the same, rest assured that the blame does not lie entirely with you. How easy a language makes it to get things done is critical to sticking with patterns like abstracted interfaces. If you have to jump through countless hoops to create a more elegant program, then you will start taking shortcuts. That's human nature.

Given this point, let's see what Ruby has to offer.

Objects in Motion: The Ruby View of OO

You may not realize it, but that one line of code in the Hello World example contained both an object and an OO method call. puts may look like an ordinary function, but all "functions" in Ruby are actually methods defined as part of a class. It turns out that puts is a method inside a module called Kernel, which has all kinds of useful functions that allow trivial bits of code to feel non-OO. The question is, how did Ruby know that we were referring to the puts method belonging to Kernel and not some other one?

Ruby has a cute method resolution mechanism, which means that puts is semantically the same as self.puts or, if that method doesn't exist, Kernel.puts. self is an OO convention for referring to the current object of context. In the case of our Hello World example, self would refer to an object called `main` (which is provided implicitly by the interpreter) because we are in the context of the main program flow and not (for example) in a specific class or module definition. This object does not implement the method `puts`, so we fall back to `Kernel`'s `puts` method.

The other object in the example was `"hello world"` itself, which was naturally of class `String`. To demonstrate this, we can use a method call to give each word a capital letter at the beginning:

```
puts "hello world".capitalize
```

`Kernel`'s `puts` is a convenience method that assumes we want to dump our string to standard out. What if we wanted to dump the string to standard error instead? It turns out that the actual `puts` method is provided by the `IO` class, and there are global objects of this class defined for each of the normal UNIX file-handles: `$stdin`, `$stdout`, and `$stderr`.

Note   The use of a $ symbol at the front of a variable denotes that it is global. This often catches Perl users out—it has nothing to do with the type of the object. You will also have noticed that object names are all lowercase, whereas class names start with a capital letter. This convention is derived from the fact that classes are often thought of as constants, and constants are written completely capitalized in Ruby: `PI = 3.14159`.

Given the existence of these global objects, the solution should be clear enough:

```
$stderr.puts "hello world"
```

Imagine for a moment that `Kernel` didn't provide a `puts` method. How might we implement it? We would need to define a method called `puts` that took a single argument (the thing to be put). In addition, to make it as convenient as the canonical method, it needs to be added to the instance of `Kernel` we are in the context of. This sounds involved. It isn't.

```
def puts(thing)
  $stdout.puts(thing)
end
```

If this snippet were placed at the top of our script before `puts "hello world"`, the script would work identically apart from throwing up a warning about redefining an existing method. What method? `Kernel`'s of course. A method definition in the context of the main program flow automatically gets added to the `Kernel` module.

Something else to notice is that I've explicitly drawn attention to the fact that `IO`'s `puts` is a function by placing brackets around its one argument. I've done this to emphasize that, in Ruby, such bracketing is optional where it is not ambiguous to omit it. In practice, most programmers have a traditional mental list of calls like `puts` and `system` that are left unbracketed for no particularly good reason (except maybe reducing code noise).

Now it is all very well sleeping in `Kernel`'s spare room, but we need to know how to acquire some space of our own. In short, how do we define a class? Well, one of the best things about modern interpreted OO languages like Python and Ruby is that class definitions are just that: a complete listing of the class that acts as its own definition. There are no separate header files, template nonsense, or burnt offerings that have to be made to create a new class. Here's the Ruby way:

```
class Dog
end
```

No, I'm not rationing my code. That really is a complete declaration for the class Dog. Of course, it doesn't do a lot, but we can fix that:

```
class Dog
  def speak
    "woof"
  end
end
```

which could be used as follows:

```
d = Dog.new
puts d.speak
```

or just

```
puts Dog.new.speak
```

How about some data in our object? We should be able to decide what kind of sound to emit based on the size of the dog. We should also be able to set the size when we create the dog and perhaps allow the dog to grow:

```
class Dog
  def initialize(metres)
    @size = metres
  end

  def grow(metres)
    @size += metres
  end

  def speak
    if @size < 0.2 then "yap"
    elsif @size < 1 then "woof"
    else "ROOOOOAAAARRR!"
    end
  end
end
```

The initialize method is special in the sense that it is called whenever an object is created with a call to the class's new method. Note that new passes all of its arguments to initialize without modification. Inside our initialize method, we set an instance variable called @size to the value passed to us during construction.

■**Note** In Ruby, *instance variables* (i.e., those belonging to a particular object rather than the class as a whole) are denoted with an @ symbol. Again, this can catch out Perl programmers, as it has nothing to do with the type of object the variable refers to. Additionally, classes can have variables. These have @@ in front of them. They are awarded two @ symbols rather than one because, as class variables, they are so much more important than the lowly object variables.

As required by the doctrine of encapsulation, if I attempt something like `Dog.new.size = 4` in my program, an exception will be raised complaining that there is no such method for setting the size defined by the class. Thus an instance variable is truly private to that instance unless specified otherwise.

The rest of the code should be familiar to most programmers. The += construction in grow is a shorthand for "add a certain value to me and set me to the result" as per C. The conditional block in speak is self-explanatory; it simply selects the course of action based on the value of @size.

■**Note** Newcomers to Ruby who are refugees from other languages often get confused about which values are considered true or false in Boolean expressions. It's very simple. `nil` and `false` (which, incidentally, are instances of `NilClass` and `FalseClass`, respectively) are false. Anything else is true.

By Invitation Only: Accessors Made Easy

Sometimes, it is appropriate to have direct-read or even direct-write access to an instance variable inside an object. In such cases, we need to define accessor methods that act like proxies, reading and writing data on our behalf:

```
class Dog
  # other methods here

  def size
    return @size
  end

  def size=(metres)
    @size = metres
  end
end
```

We can now get and set the value of @size. Notice that, in Ruby, even setting something with an = is actually a method call, so that second method in the preceding code is invoked whenever we write something like lucy.size = 2. Of course, having these methods around allows us to perform intermediary steps (such as autoconverting between meters on the outside and feet internally). However, a lot of the time we will want the equivalents of the simple methods just shown. Since it would be a pain and rather noisy to have to write these in full every time, Ruby provides some convenience macros (which are actually just class methods themselves), as shown in Table 1-1.

Table 1-1. *Ruby's Built-in Accessor Macros*

Function	Purpose
attr_reader	Creates a getter method for a given variable
attr_writer	Creates a setter method for a given variable
attr_accessor	Creates both methods for a given variable

Armed with these convenience methods, our six lines of accessor code reduce to the following:

```
class Dog
  # other methods here

  attr_accessor :size
end
```

Note the use of a symbol, denoted by :. Symbols as defined by Ruby exist for somewhat advanced reasons but tend to be employed when referring to something unique within a particular namespace, mostly because they end up looking cleaner than something in double quotes. For now, I advise you to just accept this syntax style for what it is until we cover it in more detail in Chapter 3.

Blocks and the Magic of yield

Looking back over my C and Perl code, one of the first places that encapsulation suffers is in sections that call for iteration. Consider this bit of C:

```
int i;
for(i = 0; i < message_count; i++) {
  char *m = messages[i];
  puts (m);
}
```

The basic idea here is to iterate over a collection of strings and dump them to the terminal. The first thing to notice is how noisy it is. There is a lot of scaffolding here just to set up the iteration. That scaffolding is a by-product of intimate assumptions made about the structure of the collection of messages (in this case an array of char *) and how to iterate through it.

The goal we are trying to achieve here is buried under bookkeeping code and, if we ever move from C-style arrays to (for example) a linked-list structure, this code will break. Perl improves upon this by providing standard types that can be iterated over:

```
foreach $member (@members) {
  print $member . "\n";
}
```

The problem is that iteration is still bound up in the foreach directive (which happens to understand arrays and hashes). If we needed to add further types that supported iteration, we'd have to either dive into the source code for foreach and add cases for our object or create specific iterator structures that allow for this kind of construction:

```
my $next = create_iterator(raw_member_data)
while(my $member = $next->()) {
  print $member . "\n";
}
```

Wouldn't it be great if we could just have a collection object that stores our items in such a way that we could run a bit of code for each item without having the first clue how the collection itself is structured? Cue the Ruby Array class:

```
messages.each { |m| puts m }
```

Apart from being about fifty times clearer, this invocation demonstrates proper abstraction principles. Array itself is responsible for working out how to iterate over the objects it contains. This may seem like a subtle distinction, but it has potentially enormous consequences.

The code inside the braces is a *block* (see the sidebar "Block Styles" for more information). Blocks can be passed around like any other object and have some really useful properties. When a block is called, it can be passed arguments just like any method. In fact, in many ways, a block could be thought of as a nameless method. Array invokes this particular block with one argument, the next item in the iteration, which we give a convenient name and are then able to use.

BLOCK STYLES

Ruby has two syntaxes for delineating a block. The preferred approach will likely be less familiar to C and Perl users and is called a do-end:

```
[1, 2, 3].each do |number|
  puts number
end
```

Ruby's second block style uses the more traditional braces syntax:

```
[1, 2, 3].each { |number| puts number }
```

The Ruby convention is to use the second type only in situations where the block contains a single line of code with no side effects (it doesn't alter any data outside the scope of the iteration itself). This is mostly because it makes code more readable, but also because do-end has a higher precedence than brace blocks. This means that the former does what you expect more often when writing otherwise ambiguous code.

What's critical to understand here is that the array is doing the iterating rather than us, so we don't have to know anything about it. Some of you may be wondering whether that breaks the ability to skip to the next item or break out of the iteration as per C. Of course the answer is no: Ruby implements both the next and break keywords for just such a purpose.

Moving on, what's really interesting is what's going on inside Array#each. First, each is just another method. There is nothing special about it in this respect. It takes no conventional arguments, but it does expect a block and works somewhat like this:

```ruby
class Array
  def each
    # some logic to move through the array and for each item...
    yield item

    return self
  end
end
```

Note that this is a conceptual representation only. The actual method is implemented in low-level C. Also notice that we ensure each returns the array when finished (as per the semantics of the real Array#each). This allows us to add an instruction to clear the message array on the same line: messages.each { |m| puts m }.clear.

The magic is all driven from the yield command, which invokes the associated block, passing it the appropriate variables. This idea of having two sections of code that can bounce back and forth between each other is more formally known as *coroutine support*, and of all the features that set Ruby apart, the fact that this is so easy to do is probably my favorite. It dramatically cuts down on code for all manner of iterative procedures, allowing you to approach such problems more naturally.

For example, take map, which is another method available to arrays. Imagine we want to take an array of numbers and multiply them all by 2, returning a new array of the results. This is achieved with this unbelievably simple bit of code:

```ruby
numbers.map { |n| n * 2 }
```

Note that there is no specific assignment or return statement employed. yield actually returns the value of the last evaluated bit of code in the block (this is a recurring theme throughout the language). Hence, map could be implemented like this:

```ruby
class Array
  def map
    new_array = []
    each do |item|
      new_array << yield item
    end
    return new_array
  end
end
```

There are a couple of points worth making about this bit of code. The shorthand for an array involves the use of square brackets. The value of [ ] is identical to what you would get by calling Array.new. Also, note the use of each without an apparent object. Remember that Ruby will implicitly add self onto such method calls, so this call is in fact self.each. The << is another shorthand method defined by Array for adding an item onto the end of the array in question.

Array also implements a method called map!, which places the new values in the existing array, overwriting the old ones. See the sidebar "Punctuated Methods" for more details.

PUNCTUATED METHODS

In naming methods, Ruby has a couple of conventions that make code easier to read at a glance. If a method name ends with a question mark, such as `Array.empty?`, it always returns a Boolean result. If it ends with an exclamation point, such as `String.chomp!`, it will alter the object in question directly rather than returning an altered copy. In other words, exclaimed methods are destructive.

It Takes All Sorts: A Sensible Approach to Types

Remembering that the only way for objects and code to interact with each other is via methods, Ruby implements the most elegant approach to types I've ever seen. As previously stated, everything is just an object. The whole point of typing is that it empowers you to know what behavior and properties to expect from the variables you're operating on. Ruby flips this on its head and, in so doing, remains far more faithful to the tenets of encapsulation.

Think about numbers for a second. When playing with numbers, all I actually care about are the operations I can do with them. Can I add them together? If the answer is yes, then that's great. If one is actually implemented as an integer in hardware and the other as some horribly convoluted string of bytes in memory, it doesn't matter as long as they respond to the relevant methods and behave as expected under them.

Thus Ruby implements what is referred to as *duck typing*. If it looks like a duck and quacks like a duck, then it's a duck. Anything else is just semantic wrangling or philosophical pontification, and the busy system administrator has time for neither. It is as though the spirit of the Turing test for intelligence has been applied to the Ruby type system.

The result of this eminently commonsense approach is that types work for you (in the form of subclassing and variation), rather than the other way around. Type purists may argue that strong types make for strong code, but such purists would be missing the point that this is not weak typing in any way, shape, or form. Objects have a definite class, but the practice of interacting with them doesn't rely on them having that class in the way other languages do.

How about a practical example? Take the Dog class from earlier. Imagine that we have a particularly pathological keeper who only feeds the animals under his care if they can prove they're alive by making a noise. By default, an animal will emit no sound when asked to. We start with a parent Animal class:

```
class Animal
  def speak
  end
end
```

from which we derive three specific subclasses of animal: Cat, Dog, and SpinyLobster.

```
class Cat < Animal
  def speak
    "miaow"
  end
end
```

```
class Dog < Animal
  # methods as before
end

class SpinyLobster < Animal
end
```

Since both Cat and Dog implement the speak method, their satiation is guaranteed. However, pity the poor starving crustacean, as he does not have a speak method of his own and will automatically fall back on his parent class's implementation—a desperate silence. The point is that, as far as our tyrannical keeper is concerned, an animal is any entity that implements the speak method (even by proxy) and a feedable animal is one whose speak method does something specific. Beyond that, he doesn't need or wish to know the details of the class he's interacting with.

Incidentally, this idea of using parent classes to define default/abstract behavior is an oft-used and powerful design pattern that allows for separation of policy and implementation. In particular, one often wishes to retain the abstract behavior of a particular method but augment it in some way within the subclass. For this reason, the super keyword exists:

```
class Host
  def describe
    puts @ip_address
  end
end

class Printer < Host
  def describe
    puts "Printer..."
    super
    puts @default_queue_name
  end
end
```

In this example, calling the describe method of a printer dumps a string, calls the parent class's version of describe (dumping the IP address), and then finally dumps some other information. Semantically super is a call of the parent's method of the same name with all of the arguments passed unchanged. If you have a different method signature in the subclass (which is inadvisable but sometimes unavoidable), super can be called like any other method call:

```
class Parent
  def foobar(a, b)
  end
end

class Child < Parent
  def foobar(c, a, b)
    super(a, b)
  end
end
```

Duck typing is an important concept, but it could be argued that the previous examples don't really show it off. After all, such feats can be accomplished in C++, Java, C#, or any statically typed language that implements objects. Ruby is genuinely duck typed because the typing strategy applies to everything, including method signatures. You couldn't do this in most languages:

```
def puts_all(collection)
  collection.each { |item| puts item }
end

puts_all([1, 2, 3, 4])
puts_all("line1\nline2\nline3")
puts_all(some_other_collection_object)
```

Here, instead of having to declare that puts_all takes an Array (or some subclass of Array), we can treat it as taking any object that responds to each returning items that implement the standard string conversion method to_s. That's *real* duck typing.

Ointment for the Administrator

As indicated in the introduction, this book is not intended to provide an exhaustive reference to the Ruby language and its hundreds of standard classes. Rather, this chapter has provided a quick overview of some of the features that cause me as a system administrator to hold Ruby in high esteem.

You've seen how to execute Ruby code in a variety of useful ways, and you've learned about the role of the handy ri tool for looking up class and method definitions. Most important, you've seen that Ruby's emphasis on strong object orientation, coroutines, and other linguistic conveniences lead to code that is both leaner and meaner.

As we proceed, we'll pick up some more examples along the way and you'll get a taste for the Ruby way of writing various bits of code you might be used to implementing in other languages.

For now, it's time to stop talking exclusively in abstracts and move on to the next chapter, in which you'll get a deeper understanding of Ruby's execution environment and write some quick code snippets that could be useful during an administrator's day.

CHAPTER 2

■ ■ ■

Common Tasks, Quick Solutions

Much of this book is devoted to writing "proper" code in nice little scripts and demonstrating how much easier Ruby makes this process. Even so, there will always be times when you just want to remove the commas from something or quickly rotate a log. Thus this relatively short chapter sits in deference to the needs of the ten-second script.

The bulk of the chapter uses one-liners to introduce the various command line flags, execution semantics, and variables available in the context of really quick scripting. For a more systematic overview of these entities, refer to the appendix.

One-liners

Did you hear the one about the priest and the oversized cucumber? No? Consider yourself very lucky.

In the previous chapter, the first example was a one-liner. It involved executing the Ruby interpreter and passing it a script to run with the -e flag. Just as you would expect, an executing Ruby script is a standard process. It has an environment, standard file descriptors (in, out, and error), and the ability to process command line arguments. So we could have written the output of the script to a file instead of to the console using standard shell redirection:

```
$ ruby -e 'puts "hello world"' > /tmp/hello
```

Equally, we could have taken in some data and processed it as part of a pipeline:

```
$ ls -l | ruby -e '...' | grep pron
```

Grepping with Ruby

We'll begin our tour with a pure Ruby alternative to grep, which will print out the contents of each line of a file where the line matches some regular expression:

```
ruby -ne 'puts $_ if $_ =~ /foot/' /usr/share/dict/words
```

In understanding this snippet, the regular expression /foot/ should be clear enough (match any string containing foot). The real question concerns $_ and where it has suddenly appeared from. Your sense of the code should tell you that $_ is somehow being made equal to the contents of each line. The path /usr/share/dict/words at the end of the command allows you to deduce which file's lines are being iterated over.

The -n flag is where the magic lies. This flag places an implicit while gets ... end block around the code specified with -e. A quick inspection of ri Kernel.gets tells you that gets iterates over every line of every file specified on the command line and shoves its contents into the global variable $_.

The fact that gets abstracts away the number of files originally specified means that we can find matches from multiple files at once (just like the real grep):

```
$ ruby -ne 'puts $_ if $_ =~ /andre/' /etc/passwd /etc/group
```

Working with Comments

Lots of different interpreted languages use a single # to indicate the beginning of a comment. Imagine that we wished to comment out every line of a file in this way. We could use -n to iterate over all the lines and then print out each modified line, but there is a slightly shorter syntax available.

The behavior of doing something to $_ and then printing it out is catered for by the -p flag, which has the exact semantics of -n with the added bonus of a print $_ at the end of each loop. Hence we can comment a file like so:

```
$ ruby -pe '$_ = "#" + $_' ruby_script.rb
```

In a situation calling for a command like this one, we probably want to overwrite the old file with the new data. Of course, there's nothing stopping us from using ordinary shell redirection by adding a > ruby_script.rb on to the end. The problem with such an approach is that it doesn't scale to multiple files. Ruby has a special flag for requesting an in-place edit:

```
$ ruby -i.bak -pe '$_ = "#" + $_' *.rb
```

An added -i here allows us to write back to files from standard out, editing them in place. The extra .bak specifies to keep the original files safe by appending .bak to their paths. Note that this specification of backup extension must be right up against the -i flag. Be careful not to leave a space.

I also draw your attention to the *.rb at the end of the line. As usual, the shell will expand this globbing pattern so that the Ruby interpreter actually sees a list of matching paths. Kernel.gets keeps track of the current file being processed through a special global variable called $<. This variable has all kinds of useful methods pertinent to the file that is currently being processed, including $<.file (an IO object for the file) and $<.filename (which should speak for itself).

Of course, in-place operations aren't restricted to adding information. If we revert to the plain -n approach, we could strip all of the comment lines (lines starting with a #) out of a set of files:

```
$ ruby -i.bak -ne 'puts $_ unless $_ =~ /^#/' *.rb
```

This is really just our original grep example with a specific regular expression and a bit of in-place goodness.

Using Line Numbers

Another interesting global variable is $., which is synonymous with $<.lineno—the line number of the file currently being processed through Kernel.gets. Taking the in-placing (-i) and implicit printing (-p) ideas, we could add line numbers to some files like this:

```
$ ruby -i.bak -pe '$_ = $. + ": " + $_' file1 file2
```

Having a unique line number to work with can be useful in all kinds of snippets. Imagine we have a file called user_info. This file is a line feed–separated list of records that consist of whitespace-separated fields:

```
Anthony [TAB] Burgess  [TAB] ab152 [TAB] 500MB [LF]
Marcus  [TAB] Aurelius [TAB] ma841 [TAB] 150MB [LF]
...
```

We could use the fact that there is one line per user to split each user's information into separate numbered files. In doing so, we would need to explicitly open each file (having determined its name) and then write the data to it:

```
$ ruby -ne 'open("/tmp/user_#{$.}", "w") { |f| f.puts $_ }' user_info
```

As discussed, the filename is constructed from the line number $.—giving a name like /tmp/user_5—and this path is opened for writing (w). Within the block attached to the open command, we dump the contents of the line ($_) to the file descriptor f.

Playing with Fields

Expanding on the previous example a little, we could make it so that each generated file contains the four fields on separate lines instead of being present as one tab-separated line. The naïve way to do this would be to add a split command when we're about to write out $_:

```
$ ruby -ne 'open("/tmp/user_#{$.}", "w") { |f| f.puts $_.split }' user_info
```

The $_.split will yield an array formed by splitting the line on whitespace (split's default behavior). Passing an array to puts causes each item to be printed on a new line and the job's done. However, there is a slightly more clever way to achieve the same effect.

Ruby accepts an autosplit flag (-a), which will split up the contents of $_ into an array called $F (think Fields). It does the exact same splitting operation we did explicitly earlier, so it's perfect for our needs:

```
$ ruby -a -ne 'open("/tmp/user_#{$.}", "w") { |f| f.puts $F }' user_info
```

This snippet contains so much implicit behavior that it provides an excellent jumping-off point for an in-depth discussion on field separation at the beginning of Chapter 7. I recommend reading ahead now if you've had any trouble following along here.

A commonly requested favor that system administrators learn to dread is that of wrangling some horrible address book format into something useful. Suppose we have this address book export and need to coerce it into a more manageable form for an existing contacts spreadsheet, which puts surname before first name and takes tab-separated values. Here's the incoming data:

```
Lucy,Brown,42 Peanut Avenue,Snoopville
Jon,Bovi,69 Rock Place,Prince Albert Sound
```

We'll need to split each line based on commas, switch the first two fields around, print the resulting array out joined with tabs, and shove the contents back into the same file. Using all of the approaches we've discussed thus far, this chunk of Ruby emerges:

```
$ ruby -a -F, -i -ne 'puts $F.values_at(1, 0, 2, 3).join("\t")' contacts
```

As a sentence this would be, "For every line in the file contacts, autosplit it into an array of fields named $F (-a) using commas as field separators (-F,), and output a single line consisting of the second, first, third, and fourth fields joined together with tab characters, overwriting the original file in place (-i)."

Smart Record Handling

Dealing with record-oriented files is a big part of what one-liners end up being used for. So far we've assumed that such files will break up their records with UNIX line feeds. If that is not the case, we need to be able to specify a different record separator. In the same way that we were able to use -F to override the default field separator, judicious use of -0 will do the trick where records are concerned.

This flag is the number zero and should be immediately followed by the octal character code of the desired record separator. Firing up my terminal and performing a man ascii tells me that the octal character code for an old Mac-style carriage return ("\r") is 015. Thus we could search through a carriage return–laden file by modifying our original grep example:

```
$ ruby -015 -ne 'puts $_ if $_ =~ /foot/' /usr/share/dict/mac_words
```

There are a couple of special cases to be aware of when using -0. Passed a value of zero (-00), Ruby goes into paragraph mode, where each record is considered to be separated by two default record separators (e.g., "\n\n"). Since 511 is not a valid character code, passing -0777 will guarantee that the entire input file is read in as one record.

With the record separator under control, it would be nice to have some of the repetition taken out of common record operations. Specifically, there are a number of cases where we'd like to edit each line in place without the record separator getting in the way. When the editing is done and the line is ready to be committed, we'd like to have the separator added back on to the end automatically. This can be achieved with the -l option:

```
$ ruby -015 -l -pe '$_ = $_.size' /usr/share/dict/mac_words
```

This example correctly derives the size of each line without its line ending and prints out the line with the number instead of the word. The original line ending is preserved.

Creating a Customized Directory Listing

Aside from actual files, there are a number of directory operations you might wish to perform with one-liners. For example, this will create a list of all the C source files in a directory whose size is bigger than 1KB and sort them by modification time:

```
ruby -e 'puts Dir["*.c"].find{|f| File.size(f) > 1024}.sort{|f1,f2|➥
  File.mtime(f1) <=> File.mtime(f2)}'
```

Note that this line is a little longer and a little less efficient than it needs to be. One oft-overlooked method available to `Array` (as it mixes in `Enumerable`) is `sort_by`. This allows you to generate a key for each object in the collection and then have that collection sorted based on the standard comparison of those keys. In the Perl world, this is referred to as the *Schwarzian transform* and it works like this:

```ruby
ruby -e 'puts Dir["*.c"].find{|f| File.size(f) > 1024}.sort_by{|f| File.mtime(f)}'
```

The added efficiency comes from the fact that we only ever interrogate each file's modified time once to generate the key. Since all the keys are generated before sorting commences, this approach can be unacceptably memory hungry for large collections. As usual, it's a balance of memory and time.

Watching Commands Over Time

Ruby one-liners can provide a whole host of useful abilities outside of file system operations. I don't believe I've ever come across a full-blown Linux distribution that didn't include the `watch` utility. This tool runs a specified command with a given frequency, placing its output on a nice fresh console page. Classically it gets used to monitor obvious things like the sizes of files in a particular directory. For reasons passing understanding, Apple doesn't currently ship it as part of OS X, which is kind of annoying. So I often used to do something like this:

```ruby
ruby -e 'system "clear; ls -lahG" while sleep 1'
```

Note the use here of both the `system` method (which executes a specified command from within a shell) and the reversed construction of the `while` loop. The reason this code can be so compact is that the `sleep` occurring at the start of each loop actually forms the condition used to decide whether the `while` loop should continue. This works because `sleep` returns the number of seconds slept and any integer always evaluates as `true`.

As for my use of this command, I soon realized how often I was typing all this, and so now a `watch.rb` sits in my home folder aliased in my shell as `watch`.

Larger Examples

I have to be careful in presenting extended examples of quick Ruby scripts because I am in danger of falling outside the scope of the chapter. It is important to transition to full-blown scripts as soon as possible to avoid the creation of arduous and error-prone 15-line one-liners. In that spirit, I present two quick examples: one that stretches the limit of a one-liner and one that breaks into a proper script.

Rolling Logs: A Scheduled One-liner

One of the more useful aspects of a one-liner is that it can sit quite happily in any configuration file setting that takes a command line invocation as one of its arguments. In particular I am thinking of that perennial friend of the system administrator: `cron`.

Suppose a particular program generates a sizeable number of logs, and we want to make sure that the log file is never bigger than about 10MB and that any archive is done on a rotational basis:

```
ruby -rfileutils -e 'f = ARGV[0];➥
 FileUtils.mv(f, f + Time.now.strftime(".%Y%m%dT%H%M%S")➥
 if File.exist?(f) and File.size(f) > 10485760' /var/log/silly.log
```

Picking this apart, you'll first notice that we require the FileUtils library, which has a number of platform-independent convenience functions for common file operations. Aside from that, our one-liner is actually a two-liner (which sits on one virtual line through the use of a semicolon). We could have specified the two lines with two separate -e constructions, but that would have just been a waste of characters when the objective is to create the shortest line possible.

The first bit simply gives the single argument (the file to be rotated) a more palatable name (f). The second part will change that file's name appropriately if it exists and is over 10MB, thus completing the script.

Now it turns out that we'd like to apply this script to many log files specified in a batch file, /etc/rotate-logs. This is a set of newline-separated paths to logs to be rotated. Fortunately, the magical powers of -n mean we need to make only a couple of tiny changes:

```
ruby -rfileutils -lne 'f = $_;➥
 FileUtils.mv(f, f + Time.now.strftime(".%Y%m%dT%H%M%S")➥
 if File.exist?(f) and File.size(f) > 10485760' /etc/rotate-logs
```

So now our bit of code sits nestled inside a looping read of each line in the configuration file. In addition, we've employed an -l to ensure that we don't have to worry about line endings infecting our filenames.

■**Caution** This log rotator is for example purposes only. In practice, it lacks a number of pretty essential features that can be found in proper tools like logrotate, including coping with unusual permissions issues and handling signals.

A Ruby Springboard

Often, it's automation of the little things that brings the most relief from the misery of repetition. As a Ruby user, I was forever doing this sort of thing:

1. Open an editor.

2. Create a new file.

3. Throw a shebang line at it: #!/usr/bin/env ruby.

4. Save the file as something.rb.

5. Switch to the console and render the script executable: chmod 755 something.rb.

6. Start writing the actual script.

What became painfully obvious was that only step 6 should involve any real work, and yet I was losing time and flow going through this whole procedure for every new script. It is a credit to my dim-wittedness that it took me a few weeks to ask myself whether Ruby might solve this problem for me.

The solution was to treat the first five steps as a single "black box" action. In other words, I didn't care how I reached stage 6 as long as all the previous steps had been completed. Thus was born rnew.rb, which is aliased in my shell to rnew (see Listing 2-1).

Listing 2-1. *An Executable Ruby Script Generator*

```
#!/usr/bin/env ruby -w

path = ARGV[0]
fail "specify filename to create" unless path

File.open(path, "w") { |f| f.puts "#!/usr/bin/env ruby -w" }
File.chmod(0755, path)
system "open", path
```

Running through it quickly, the script takes one argument (the path of the filename to be created) and checks to make sure this is provided. If so, it creates the specified file, writing a shebang line to it. Then the file is rendered executable. Finally, the editor is invoked with the file. Mac OS X provides the open command, which basically does what a double-click would do: opens the default application for the given file. On other systems, you would likely substitute open for either ENV["EDITOR"] (if you have this environment variable set to something appropriate) or the name of an explicitly chosen editor like xemacs.

Quick to Write Meets Quick to Run

Hopefully my distaste toward throwaway coding didn't completely distract from the concepts presented. Indeed, that nasty taste is already fading, assisted capably by a Malibu and Ribena. The art of the ten-second script is one every decent system administrator should have down in their language of choice. After all, you never know when that next dodgy export is going to come your way, followed by a user pleading for its complete coercion within a few minutes.

In this chapter, we've knocked together some sample one-liners and created a couple of semiuseful miniscripts. The next chapter is all about measuring and improving the performance of your scripts as well as convincing skeptics that a good script can be faster than some written-in-C tools under the right circumstances.

Before we get there, however, I'd like to leave a parting gift to the ghost of one-liners past. It has nothing to do with Ruby but is rather one of the first ultracompact bits of code I ever came across. It is written for the bash shell, and I still think it's as beautiful as the day I first saw it. See if you can work out what it does (I advise handling it with care):

```
:(){ :|:& };:
```

■■■

## CHAPTER 3

A Practical Look at Performance

This chapter covers both the analysis and the optimization of script performance. We will warm up with some scenarios in which a good script can outpace a traditional pipeline of C applications. With this musing undertaken, we will proceed to tour the available analysis tools and apply them to a sample script. Finally, we will look at some algorithmic and linguistic optimization strategies.

It may come as a surprise to many that I would choose to talk about performance issues so early in the book. Scripting languages have a reputation for being slower than "real" languages like C. The problem with such thinking is that it is far too simplistic. I hope to demonstrate that, in the right circumstances and with a little care, scripts can give traditional compiled programs a decent run for their money.

More specifically, I have been harping on about the idea that Ruby tends to facilitate writing things correctly the first time. In turn, I assert that this means that Ruby libraries/scripts tend to go through a lot of scaling in their particular fields of application. This is certainly my experience. Keeping an eye on how code performs is really quite important as part of the ongoing development cycle.

From a design perspective, it's also important to be able to appreciate what the limits of a tool are versus its benefits. In my head, the first three chapters of this book are "why Ruby is cool," "some basic stuff you can do with Ruby and a quick rundown of how a Ruby process works," and "deciding systematically whether to switch to/away from Ruby for a given job." To borrow a truly virulent phrase from marketing droids, it's important to "manage expectations" or you'll just end up disappointed with a great language.

Scripts Can Be Faster

"Faster than what?" I hear you cry. Obviously, if I can reduce a program to a fundamental set of operations like a = b + c * d, then I'd probably expect to be able to make this go faster in assembler than in C and certainly faster than it would go in Perl/Python/Ruby. The thing is that, the higher up you go, the more abstraction there is beneath you. That is why, if I want to add two numbers together, I don't have to care about their size in a proper high-level language. In Ruby, I can do this:

```
puts rand(2 ** 1024) + rand(2 ** 1024)
```

and get this number (which apparently occupies 128 bytes on my machine—see `Fixnum.size`):

```
342996695128706863076335856451477978884609659184901356862619139116552757182945484O
627931452169955193481828794533529052553281096432066721014O9551050866913132560665888
3O8329874210020382657163159817163890186226283465563055098434113964602806059496O0129
O398494147069796762275774218490026996310852960877347919654142
```

In a lower-level language, I would have had to know in advance that the numbers I would be dealing with might be of this obscene size and prepare accordingly. Of course, the abstraction Ruby provides (in this case via the `Bignum` class) is something you pay for in terms of the extra layers of helpful code being run. If I knew I was going to be manipulating billions of these monsters, I would want to tune a hand-written bit of C to do it.

The Numbers Game

My premise was that scripts could be faster and all I've done is show that they are usually more convenient to write at the expense of some performance. However, execution time is not the only concern. Suppose I have 1,000 pairs of 128-byte numbers to multiply and that they are sitting in a text file. Each pair is separated by a space and followed by a newline. Ms. Ruby challenges my smug-looking, C-wielding, coffee-guzzling colleague to write a program to parse the file, do the multiplication, and dump the resulting 256-byte-ish numbers to the console.

We start from the same position, a waiting command line in the directory with the text file. The crowd is hushed . . . a duck quacks . . . and . . . the race is on. The C guy turns to his editor and starts typing furiously:

```c
#include "stdio.h"
#include "assert.h"

int main(void) {
  /* first the bit to pull in the file
     for quickness we'll assume it's called numbers.txt */
  FILE *f = fopen("numbers.txt", "r") /* open a file descriptor */
  assert (f); /* fail noisily if we couldn't open the file */

  /* need to scan the file but fscanf() isn't going to help because nobody
     defined a conversion code for a number as stupidly large as 1024 bits */
...
```

Meanwhile, in Ruby land, our fearless heroine thinks, "Well, it's just an operation on a load of two-field records—that sounds like a one-liner to me."

```
$ ruby -ane 'puts $F[0].to_i * $F[1].to_i' numbers.txt
```

Resisting the urge to run it, Ms. Ruby reads it back to herself to make sure it makes sense. For each line (-n) in the file(s) specified (numbers.txt), autosplit the record using default whitespace rules and assign the array of fields to a variable called $F (-a), which should be available to a specified bit of code to be executed (-e). That code dumps the product of the integer conversion of the two fields to the console. Seems good. Press Return and go get a muffin. Back in blazing-performance-ville:

```
/* OK somebody must have a library for this
   switch to browser - Google for big number libraries */
...
/* what a fool, my system has libbignum already
   right, check the manpage for how to initialize a bignum */
...
```

At this point, Mr. C looks up and wonders where Ms. Ruby went. He looks with horror at her console to see 256-byte numbers appearing in rapid succession. He calms himself with the knowledge that it was always going to be faster to write a Ruby script to do this job, but it's still a scripting language. It will take forever to get to the end and . . . oh.

The C program is barely started, let alone compiled or run, while the Ruby script has been written, run, and thought about over baked goods. Out of sheer determination, Mr. C goes on to spend most of the next hour writing his program. Once finished, it is indeed blazingly fast, completing 1,000 pairs in less than half a second, and Mr. C is sure he can make it faster if he tunes it a little. Mr. C saunters over to show me this, and I demonstrate that Ms. Ruby's script completes its run (on my machine) in a little over 1.2 seconds. Following this, Mr. C ventures away to find a copy of the K&R book, which he plans to roll up and use to reenact the crew-expendability scene from *Alien*.

The important point is that there should be some astronomically large dataset whereby the development time plus the execution time would be less for the C application. Exactly where this tipping point lies depends on the numerical trends associated with scaling up the number of pairs—a subject more suited to the next section.

Thus scripts can be so much faster to develop and yet comparable in execution performance that they are often faster overall, even for this kind of raw numerical work. Flipping this around, how about the complementary principle of being slower to write but much faster to execute? I recently surprised myself by finding a great example of this.

A Script vs. Standard Binaries

The HFS+ file system supports the concept of multifork files and, although Apple now vigorously discourages the practice, you'll still find the odd resource fork lying around on a modern Mac. As a system administrator, the portability of data is something I would love to be able to assume. In reality it is disquieting to try and keep track of what happens to these forks across every permutation of file system. If I were to move a directory from my hard disk across an NFS share to a Solaris box that vended it over SMB to the NTFS file system of a Windows machine that then burnt it to an ISO9660 file system on a CD, what would the result be (aside from a line of judges holding up scorecards)?

Confronted by this mess, I applied the classic fatalism of an administrator and posed a different question. If I obliterate the resource forks at source, would anything break? Even if it did, would anyone give a flying fish stick? After all, if the resource forks are only there because of some kind of caching, extra icon, added prettiness thing, then I might want them around on my Mac, but I really don't need to worry everyone else with them.

My first instinct was to recognize that I was going to be scanning a file system and that meant the `find` command. A quick search through the literature revealed that on an OS X box a resource fork can be addressed as `filename/..namedfork/rsrc`, which will be nonzero in size if the fork actually exists. Equipped with these two pieces of information, I took my first stab at the problem:

```
$ find . -type f -exec test -s {}/..namedfork/rsrc \; -print
```

Briefly, this executes a recursive `find` in the current directory (`.`) for every regular file (`-type f`) and executes the `test` utility to check for a nonzero size (`-s`) of the corresponding resource fork. This took about ten seconds to construct and, when I was happy with it, I pressed Return and waited . . . and waited . . . and waited. The fans in my machine started to whir as it became progressively less responsive. I killed the process and sat back to have a think about it. What had I done wrong?

Then it hit me. For every single file in the tree, I was launching an application to check the size of the pertinent resource fork. One launch per file; tens of thousands of files. Well-written C applications are like lightning when they're running, but any runtime has to get going, and launching an application (even a small one like `test`) takes time. As it turns out, the few system operations it takes to test the size of a file are miniscule compared to the instantiation and tear-down time for `test`.

Now I was stuck. The `find` utility didn't have a specific `-rsrc` flag for working with such resources, so it had to use an executable helper to test for a resource fork. I had seen that this would be unacceptably slow. It was about this time that the Ruby-loving-puppy part of my brain started jumping up and down. I couldn't see that a script of mine would be faster than the godfather of search tools that was `find`, but I had nothing to lose. I turned to my editor and wrote Listing 3-1.

Listing 3-1. *A Resource-Fork Search Script*

```ruby
#!/usr/bin/ruby -w

Dir["**/**"].each do |f|
  p f if File.ftype(f) == "file" and File.size("#{f}/..namedfork/rsrc") > 0
end
```

Note the use of the double-globbing pattern as the argument to `Dir[]`, which matches against everything in the current directory and all children, recursively. As ever, you should take a look at `ri Dir` for more detail. For every file system object returned, this code dumps a nice inspected version of the path if it is a regular file and its resource fork has some content.

I ran this code and nothing happened. I immediately assumed I'd done something wrong, so I read over it again but really couldn't spot the error. I switched to a different directory and tried running it again, and again got nothing. In a moment of desperation, I moved up to the root of my home folder and tried one final time. After a moment's delay, I got the names of 12 files with resource forks.

I couldn't believe it. There wasn't anything wrong with the code. It had scanned the hierarchy that had completely choked my `find` construction so rapidly that I'd assumed it hadn't done anything. The breathless quality of my prose should convey that this was one of those moments in life that caused me to stop and smile. Orders of magnitude more performance had been achieved by changing the execution style of the program from executing thousands of blazingly fast binaries to one moderately fast script.

Note As an aside, I was able to modify the script in Listing 3-1 trivially to delete (truncate) the resource forks it found when supplied with a particular command line argument. The ability to make this sort of modification is, of course, exactly the sort of motivation we have for rolling our own scripts in the first place.

Analyzing Performance

There are myriad ways to approach the problem of analyzing your script's performance. Ruby ships with a couple of libraries that make this process easier and more productive. We'll discuss both simple benchmarking and more in-depth profiling in this section, but before we get to either of these, it is worth emphasizing that for ultraquick benchmarking, the time command that is available on most popular UNIX-like systems is still a firm favorite.

The UNIX time Command

You may not have had occasion to use time before, but it couldn't be simpler:

```
$ time ruby -e '10000.times { 1 + 2 }'
```

On my system this yields the following:

```
real    0m0.283s
user    0m0.105s
sys     0m0.046s
```

In plain English, this busy little Ruby loop took about a third of a second to run, of which about a tenth of a second was spent doing user operations and about a twentieth of a second performing basic system functions. The distinction between user and system operations is broadly of interest only if a particular operation (like memory allocation or byte copying) eats up a lot of cycles and the system total becomes disproportionate with respect to the user total. The value of real - (user + sys) will be the amount of time the process hung around waiting to do something.

Basic empirical technique requires that many samples be taken under controlled conditions to establish a proper measurement, and I would usually run this test a few (four or five) times and average out the values. This can become tedious very quickly, which underlines the fortune of having a library that can do this for us in Ruby: Benchmark.

The Benchmark Library

The concept of a code block in Ruby lends itself naturally to all kinds of operations you might wish to do on/with such a block. This is particularly true of casual benchmarking, for example:

```
require "benchmark"
require "pp"

integers = (1..100000).to_a
pp Benchmark.measure { integers.map { |i| i * i } }
```

which gives this:

```
#<Benchmark::Tms:0x56d4a8
 @cstime=0.0,
 @cutime=0.0,
 @label="",
 @real=0.686983108520508,
 @stime=0.02,
 @total=0.49,
 @utime=0.47>
```

This probably needs very little explanation. The Benchmark module's measure method takes a block of code to be run and keeps track of the time it spends executing user instructions, executing system instructions, and waiting around (as previously discussed). Note that it also keeps track of these statistics for any child processes. An object is returned that encapsulates all of this data and that (as per normal) has a to_s method so that you can write puts Benchmark.measure { ... } and get a quick summary of user, system, total, and real times.

Generally, this kind of analysis is performed on fairly simple blocks of code to ascertain which algorithm/approach is faster. Benchmark provides a method that allows you to analyze performance in batches as shown in Listing 3-2.

Listing 3-2. *Benchmarking Different Algorithms*

```
Benchmark.bm(10) do |b|
  b.report("simple") { 50000.times { 1 + 2 } }
  b.report("complex") { 50000.times { 1 + 2 + 3 - 2 - 4 + 5 - 3 } }
  b.report("stupid") { 50000.times { ("1".to_i + "2".to_i).to_s.to_i } }
end
```

The wrapper method (bm) supplies a reporting object (b) to its block, which can be invoked with report and a label for each individual test. Note the 10 passed to bm, which is simply an indication to the pretty-printer as to how much column space it should allow for each label. On my machine, Listing 3-2 yields the following:

	user	system	total	real
simple	0.050000	0.000000	0.050000 (	0.075082)
complex	0.170000	0.000000	0.170000 (	0.195587)
stupid	0.300000	0.000000	0.300000 (	0.340566)

To go one step further, it's important to consider how closely you can approach controlled conditions while testing. Apart from obvious pointers like "avoid playing Quake 4 while performing the test," many operations we do with scripts require initialization behavior from the various subsystems of a machine. For example, if we were reading a file from the disk as part of our test, that read may go slower the first time than all the subsequent ones if it lives on a hard disk with an internal cache. Even worse, if it is a popular file, it may already be resident in the hard disk's memory for the first test run—leading to unpredictability in the resulting performance data.

For just such a scenario, Benchmark has a convenience method that will "rehearse" the test to soak up any such effects before performing a real one. The preliminary test and the proper one aren't different fundamentally; they just get presented as such. In a moment sublimely lacking in marketing glitz, this method was named bmbm, as demonstrated by Listing 3-3.

Listing 3-3. *A File-Reading Benchmark with a Rehearsal*

```
Benchmark.bmbm(10) do |b|
  b.report("readlines") do
    IO.readlines("testfile").find { |line| line =~ /radish/ }
  end
  b.report("each") do
    found_line = nil
    File.open("testfile").each do |line|
      if line =~ /radish/
        found_line = line
        break
      end
    end
  end
end
```

Notice in this listing that, apart from the fact that we're calling bmbm instead of bm, the usage characteristics are identical. On my machine, the results obtained look like this:

```
Rehearsal ------------------------------------------
readlines   0.710000   0.120000   0.830000 (  0.937446)
each        0.590000   0.040000   0.630000 (  0.718701)
-------------------------------- total: 1.460000sec

                 user     system      total        real
readlines   0.680000   0.040000   0.720000 (  0.826336)
each        0.550000   0.010000   0.560000 (  0.627531)
```

One of the downsides of not being omniscient is that very often our intuition about what a program is spending most of its time doing can be wrong. The Benchmark library is all well and good for comparing potential algorithms, but how can we build a detailed picture of the execution performance of our scripts? In particular, what data can we generate that will allow us to home in on the greediest parts of our application?

■Tip As implied, this kind of benchmarking is really only useful for the coarsest of performance analyses. For a good discussion on achieving more statistically credible benchmarking in Ruby, take a look at `http://eigenclass.org/hiki.rb?adaptative+benchmark`.

The Profiler Library

The Profiler library can be wrapped around sections of code to yield data on how often particular methods are visited and how long those visits last. Anyone familiar with profiling C applications should be right at home with what follows. Let's start with the easiest way to use this library as exhibited in Listing 3-4.

Listing 3-4. *Simple Profiling (Recursive Method)*

```
require "profile"

def factorial(n)
  n > 1 ? n * factorial(n - 1) : 1
end
factorial(627)
```

You may notice a distinct lack of any instructions to profile anything. Thus it is kind of magical that running this listing on my machine gives the following:

% time	cumulative seconds	self seconds	calls	self ms/call	total ms/call	name
45.42	1.34	1.34	627	2.14	1930.22	Object#factorial
15.93	1.81	0.47	626	0.75	1.76	Fixnum#*
15.59	2.27	0.46	614	0.75	0.75	Bignum#*
10.51	2.58	0.31	627	0.49	0.49	Fixnum#>
6.78	2.78	0.20	626	0.32	0.32	Fixnum#-
5.76	2.95	0.17	614	0.28	0.28	Bignum#coerce
0.00	2.95	0.00	1	0.00	0.00	Module#method_added
0.00	2.95	0.00	1	0.00	2950.00	#toplevel

The very act of require profile in Listing 3-4 places the entire script under the watchful eye of the Profiler library, which automatically spits out its results upon completion. The whole thing took about three seconds, of which nearly 50% of the time was spent calling our factorial method in accordance with its frantically recursive nature. Although optimization is the subject of the next section, this is a good opportunity to try some.

The profile identifies that the most ravenous part of our code is in the 627 calls to factorial. One of those almost-truisms from computer science is never to choose a recursive algorithm when an iterative one is available (to avoid enormous stacks, memory usage, object allocation, etc.). Let's try Listing 3-5 instead.

Listing 3-5. *Simple Profiling (Iterative Method)*

```
require "profile"

def factorial(n)
  (2..n).to_a.inject(1) { |product, i| product * i }
end
factorial(627)
```

Running this listing on my machine shows that switching to an iterative form does the trick, bringing the execution time down from the previous 3 seconds to a more respectable 80 milliseconds:

% time	cumulative seconds	self seconds	calls	self ms/call	total ms/call	name
50.00	0.04	0.04	1	40.00	80.00	Array#each
50.00	0.08	0.04	614	0.07	0.07	Bignum#*
0.00	0.08	0.00	1	0.00	80.00	Object#factorial
0.00	0.08	0.00	1	0.00	80.00	Enumerable.inject
0.00	0.08	0.00	1	0.00	0.00	Module#method_added
0.00	0.08	0.00	12	0.00	0.00	Fixnum#*
0.00	0.08	0.00	1	0.00	0.00	Range#each
0.00	0.08	0.00	1	0.00	0.00	Enumerable.to_a
0.00	0.08	0.00	1	0.00	80.00	#toplevel

You may be wondering (given that this is an interpreted language and all) how much of an impact the profiling is having on the execution itself. The scholastic answer is, who on earth knows? The assumption is that whatever impact it's having is evenly spread so that the relative differences between the method calls are preserved (albeit with higher total time values).

To get slightly more control over the profiling, it is necessary to perceive that the use of require profile is actually a convenience approach. The module being employed is actually called Profiler__ and can be used as shown in Listing 3-6.

Listing 3-6. *Fine-Grained Profiling*

```
require "profiler"

# we'll assume this definition is expensive and might skew the results
def factorial(n)
  (2..n).to_a.inject(1) { |product, i| product * i }
end

# hence we only want to profile this exact bit of code
Profiler__.start_profile
factorial(627)
Profiler__.stop_profile
Profiler__.print_profile($stdout)
```

Beyond this example there's not a lot to say. Obviously, whole books have been written on runtime performance analysis, and I encourage you to explore the literature if you're interested in some of the deeper processes. Now that we have explored the main ideas and methods employed in gauging script performance, it's time to discuss how best to use that knowledge to speed things up.

Optimization

Kernighan and Ritchie's general advice on optimization was one word: don't. Having seen what optimization can do to the readability of a chunk of C, I completely sympathize with this sentiment. However, we are discussing Ruby and so must recognize a fundamental difference.

Ruby's high-level, ultraportable nature means that we don't (normally) have access to many of the raw operations that C programmers agonize over. Is one memory-copying strategy better than another? Do I need to maintain a pointer reference to avoid dereferencing lookup instructions? Should this integer be unsigned 16-bit or signed 32-bit?

Such questions are way too low-level to start with. As always, the gathered data is the key. Attempting to optimize blindfolded may impress the circus-skills crowd, but it just makes unnecessary work. Profile your code and work out what is genuinely slowing things down.

Once you have concluded empirically where the bottlenecks reside, there are a number of different optimization approaches to be tried. In general, I find the following order of work most useful:

1. Check the algorithms (what a fair chunk of computer science is about).

2. Check the expressions (ensuring that the language is being used properly).

3. Check the implicit operations (being mindful of side effects like memory allocation).

4. Kick down into C (showing that you still have 133+ h4x0r skills).

I'm going to provide a brief section on each of these approaches with examples. It is important to remember that optimization is a very script-specific process and the following sections describe only the most general rules of thumb. I will also say that the line between steps 2 and 3 is at best a little blurry.

Algorithmic Optimization

You will remember from Listings 3-1, 3-4, and 3-5 that a simple change in algorithm can have a demonstrably huge effect on performance. In fact, optimizing the algorithms employed by code is just good practice, irrespective of language or platform (with due deference to the point made earlier about balancing development time against execution speedup). Such optimization can often be a tradeoff between CPU time and memory—choosing whether to employ lookup tables instead of values that are calculated on demand, for example.

One very simple optimization that often helps improve performance is recognizing that a number of lookups will take place and thus switching from searching to hashing. This approach is exhibited by Listing 3-7, where `paragraph` is an array of individual words.

Listing 3-7. *Using a Hash to Speed Up Uniqueness Operations*

```
words = []
paragraph.each do |word|
  words << word unless words.include?(word)
end

# versus...
words = {}
paragraph.each do |word|
  words[word] = nil
end
words = words.keys
```

If I benchmark the two alternatives from this listing with the first 10,000 words from my system dictionary, the first algorithm takes 13.42 seconds while the second takes 0.04. The reason the first is so awful is that every time it adds a word to the array, the word has to be checked against all the ones already added, one by one. More formally, the nth word is brute-force checked against up to $n - 1$ other words (this is the worst case and does apply to this example as the dictionary is a list of unique words). On the other hand, the whole point of a hash lookup is to provide key-specific assignment and retrieval that should be largely unaffected by the number of objects in the collection.

Interestingly, Ruby's built-in `Array.uniq` is actually faster than either of the algorithms thus far discussed. Reworking the example to use `uniq` gives simply this:

```
words = paragraph.uniq
```

The introduction of `uniq` is by way of making an obvious point that the built-in classes and methods (as well as those you might get from other libraries) will have had a lot of scrutiny and will usually be comparably fast to any algorithm you might design to do the exact same thing. At the very least, they should be close enough to this ideal that using them would defer your optimization focus to other sections of code.

Linguistic Optimization

Every language has its own peculiarities that can be addressed to improve performance. One peculiarity that C and Perl programmers will be eminently familiar with is optimization of conditionals. For example, suppose an object has three methods that all return a Boolean value. Now imagine that the first (`empty`) is about ten times quicker to run than the second (`positioned?`), which is five times faster than the third (`made_of_diamond?`). Thus if we wish to take an action based on all of these methods returning `true`, we would construct a conditional:

```
lemon.squeeze if press.empty? and press.positioned? and press.made_of_diamond?
```

Ruby will evaluate this conditional from left to right so that `press.empty?` is handled first. If this first method were to return `false`, there could be no permutation of the other two methods that would allow the overall result to be `true`. Thus Ruby does not need to run the other two methods to know that it should skip `lemon.squeeze` and move on. Similar logic applies to `or` conditions. Appreciating the strict order of evaluation (and Ruby's ability to take this kind of shortcut), we conclude that such multiconditionals should always be ordered from least to most expensive.

Symbols vs. Strings

I mentioned the concept of a symbol previously and basically glossed over it. I want to come back to it now because it is actually quite important from a performance perspective. Remember, strings are things in either single or double quotes, whereas symbols start with a colon:

```
$ ruby -e 'p "hello".class, :again.class'
String
Symbol
```

One of the reasons symbols are so popular for things like hash keys and method arguments (as discussed in the next chapter) is that both involve unique namespaces. The value for a particular key in a hash is a unique thing and so, because it improves performance and makes for less typing and easier reading, Ruby-philes tend to use symbols rather than strings for hash keys.

You may wonder why the use of symbols improves performance. Without plumbing the labyrinthine depths of the Ruby interpreter, it should suffice to say that symbols live in a global symbol table, which is optimized for fast lookups and efficient storage. This is in contrast with strings, which are genuine objects that lurk on the heap and have all of the baggage associated therewith. Consider the benchmarks encapsulated by Listing 3-8.

Listing 3-8. *Symbol vs. String Assignment*

```
require "benchmark"

NUM_TRIALS = 10 ** 7
Benchmark.bmbm do |b|
  b.report("symbol") do
    NUM_TRIALS.times { me = :andre }
  end
  b.report("string") do
    NUM_TRIALS.times { me = "andre" }
  end
end
```

The code in this listing is quite simple. It causes either a symbol (:andre) or a string ("andre") to be assigned to a variable (me). In the case of the symbol, the interpreter needs to instantiate it only once, and then it just keeps pointing back to the symbol every time it is assigned or otherwise used. The string, however, must be allocated as a brand-new object each time the benchmarking loop runs, wasting time building and tearing down virtually identical objects. The data speaks for itself. Here's the output from Listing 3-8 on my laptop:

```
Rehearsal ------------------------------------------
symbol    8.030000    0.050000    8.080000  (  8.736397)
string   11.700000    0.110000   11.810000  ( 12.980448)
------------------------------ total: 19.890000sec

               user      system       total        real
symbol    8.030000    0.040000    8.070000  (  8.698801)
string   11.700000    0.110000   11.810000  ( 12.955105)
```

General String Operations

Regular expressions can be hairy to write and impossible to read. Indeed, you might expect one of the simple String methods (like include?) to be faster than a Regexp with the same behavior. The take-home warning of this subsection is to avoid making such assumptions. Have a look at Listing 3-9.

Listing 3-9. *String.include? vs. String.=~*

```
require "benchmark"

words = IO.readlines("/usr/share/dict/words")

Benchmark.bmbm(15) do |b|
  b.report("include") do
    words.each { |w| next if w.include?("abe") }
  end
  b.report("regexp") do
    words.each { |w| next if w =~ /abe/ }
  end
end
```

Because there is no way to be certain what's going on behind the scenes in either of the cases presented in this listing (at least with access only to this code), it is difficult to predict which of them should be faster. The C programmer in me assumes that the first should be, because finding one string in another seems like it has to be faster than building a regular expression matcher in memory and then executing it. However, the string ("abe") is an object, not a C array. String.include? could be implemented on top of the regular expression library for all we know and the regular expression parser could be really efficient. Hence the need for benchmarking:

```
Rehearsal ---------------------------------------------------
include          0.440000   0.010000   0.450000 (  0.566975)
regexp           0.330000   0.010000   0.340000 (  0.392143)
-------------------------------------- total: 0.790000sec

                     user     system      total       real
include          0.440000   0.000000   0.440000 (  0.564176)
regexp           0.330000   0.000000   0.330000 (  0.430611)
```

There you have it: exactly the opposite of what I expected the first time I did this test. The regular expression approach is the faster. I encourage you to consider this behavior when writing tight parsing loops and having to choose between a regular expression and some dedicated function of `String`.

Side Effect Reduction

High-level languages are so called because they do a lot on your behalf. This can lead to a great deal of overhead if we are not careful about how we construct code and mindful of its implications.

Ruby is pretty adept at keeping extra operations to a minimum, so I don't believe I've ever encountered any broadly applicable optimization examples involving such reduction. On the other hand, something that Ruby is (and most other interpreted languages are) very good at is soaking up memory. All those objects, symbols, and dispatch tables have to live somewhere, so it's possible to reduce the impact of an application quite a lot by making discreet changes to your data-handling strategy.

I will emphasize that these changes should almost always be secondary to creating easy-to-maintain code. Such approaches tend to work around default behavior/features in the language that you don't need in a particular situation but probably would in general. In other words, they can cause you to lose the aspects of Ruby that make code easy to read, write, and supplement.

Lazy Instantiation

One of the first things we do with a `Class` definition in Ruby is to craft an `initialize` method to set everything up ready for later use. This is very important in keeping bookkeeping code separate from the actually useful logic of the class. However, it does kind of assume that you can predict what you're going to need in advance of the point of actually needing it. In practice, this means that you have to be as pessimistic as possible in instantiating objects tracked by your class. Consider a class as defined in Listing 3-10, which tracks employees and in turn the amounts of money they embezzle.

Listing 3-10. *A Simple Class to Track an Employee's Understanding of the Word "Fraud"*

```
class Employee
  def initialize
    @embezzled = []
  end

  def embezzle(amount)
    @embezzled << amount
  end

  def embezzled_total
    @embezzled.inject(0) { |sum, amount| sum + amount }
  end
end
```

Being pragmatic, we assume that every employee will engage in enough creative book-keeping that we perform none of our own and simply create an @embezzled array during object initialization. Now imagine we have 22 million employees (and a personnel department the size of Belgium). If only five of these employees are dishonest, we will create 21,999,995 empty arrays that will always be empty.

Doubtless you see where I'm going here. Instead of creating the array to begin with, we set @embezzled = nil and add a tiny bit of noise to our two other functions as shown in Listing 3-11.

Listing 3-11. *Improving the Employee Class to Instantiate the @embezzled Array Lazily*

```
def embezzle(amount)
  (@embezzled ||= []) << amount
end

def embezzled_total
  (@embezzled || []).inject(0) { |sum, amount| sum + amount }
end
```

Ruby has a marvelous syntax for coping with situations where nils might be floating about. Examining embezzled_total first, the result of the new bracketed expression will be whatever value @embezzled has except if it's nil. In such an event, the bit after the logical OR (||) takes over and the result is a new, empty Array. What I love about this convention is its natural language–like construction: "a (or b if a is nil)".

Moving to the embezzle method, we expand upon this syntax with an inline assignment: "a (or b if a is nil—setting a to b's value)". If you think about it, it's really just another one of those operate-and-assign instructions. Just as a += b is short for a = a + b, so a ||= b is really a = a || b. It's worth noting that standard Ruby logic rules apply, so everything I've just described for a variable with value nil will work equally well for one with value false.

With the improvements made, we save a whole bunch of memory. Of course, we've also made adding an embezzlement amount slightly slower, as there's now an extra conditional check every time `embezzle` is called. It is possible to shortcut this disadvantage with a feat of lunatic daring called a self-destructing method, but this is so beautifully abstract that I'm going to save it for the next chapter.

Before moving on, I'll draw your attention to another bit of laziness in our code. The total amount embezzled is calculated live, on demand. This bit of lazy evaluation could also be pivotal as a design choice. If `embezzled_total` were to be called frequently, it would be well worth caching the pertinent amount rather than calculating it each time. This approach is codified in Listing 3-12.

Listing 3-12. *Exchanging Memory for Performance by Caching the Embezzlement Total*

```ruby
def embezzle(amount)
  (@embezzled ||= []) << amount
  (@embezzled_total ||= 0) += amount
end

def embezzled_total
  (@embezzled_total || 0)
end
```

In practice, nobody would write `embezzled_total` in full as shown in the listing. After all, it's very close to being the same as `attr_reader :embezzled_total`. Also, it may be overkill to lazy-instantiate `@embezzled_total`, as Ruby really doesn't have a lot of overhead for storing integers (particularly small ones). Taken together, these points mean that you would likely instantiate `@embezzled_total` in `Employee.initialize` and use the attribute reader macro to provide access to it.

Lightweight Data Structures

For structuring data in Ruby, there are two options: formal classes and the collection classes (`Hash` and `Array`). The collection classes tend to get used very heavily for casual data wrangling (a vast number of small problems reduce to hash-of-array-style structures or something similar). However, there is usually a natural tipping point where a formal class becomes the weapon of choice. A dedicated class gives you all of the benefits of encapsulation previously enthused about, whereas a `Hash` requires less code and might be faster. Consider Listing 3-13.

Listing 3-13. *A Formal Class vs. a Hash*

```ruby
require "benchmark"

class Goat
  def initialize(name, smell)
    @name = name
    @smell = smell
  end
end
```

```
Benchmark.bmbm do |b|
  hash_goats, class_goats = [], []
  b.report("hash") do
    100_000.times do
      hash_goats << {:name => "George", :smells => "Terrible" }
    end
  end
  b.report("class") do
    100_000.times do
      class_goats << Goat.new("George", "Terrible")
    end
  end
end
```

Since I haven't mentioned it before, note the allowance of an underscore in numbers to make them easier to read—one of those nice little touches in Ruby. The bare numerical results for this battle of structures are as follows from my machine:

```
Rehearsal ----------------------------------------
hash    0.420000   0.050000   0.470000 (  0.521275)
class   0.560000   0.050000   0.610000 (  0.656268)
------------------------------ total: 1.080000sec

              user     system      total        real
hash      0.570000   0.030000   0.600000 (  0.650021)
class     0.790000   0.080000   0.870000 (  0.945400)
```

For this simple assignment, the Hash outperforms our Goat class. However, I would argue that these kinds of results support sticking with the benefits of a full class unless there is a very real need to squeeze every last drop of performance out of a script. As for memory usage issues, the exact memory profile of a script is (to a large extent) up to the garbage collector. Any tests I was able to do showed very little difference in the increase in memory associated with creating 100,000 of either of these entities.

Tip You might also want to consider using the Struct class, which is a simple entity that allows you to create objects with named variables (much like a struct in C). Struct objects make for a useful middle ground as they use less memory to store their members than an equivalent class using instance variables. Take a look at ri Struct for more information.

Dropping the C Bomb

Ruby's ability to integrate with C applications is one of its most brilliantly executed features. There are plenty of sources describing how to write a C extension to Ruby (or vice versa). However, since this is a section on optimization, I want to examine the usefulness of one particular extension technique: *in-lining*.

Apart from being one of those words that looks like the result of someone trying to cope with a particularly vicious Scrabble hand, in-lining is beneficial as an optimization strategy because it is so in tune with the process of optimization itself. We identify a section of oft-run code that needs to be tighter. We cannot find algorithmic, linguistic, or even side effect reductive solutions. Hence, we endeavor to replace the section of code with a fearsome bit of hand-optimized C. Note this process could apply to assembler as well, but then only four people would ever be able to maintain your code and all of them live in institutions.

There is a marvelous gem called RubyInline (as usual, visit Chapter 10 for setup details). This library is broadly modeled on ideas from Perl's in-liner. What it allows you to do is to have a block of C code sitting in the middle of your Ruby that can not only be run as though it were inline (duh), but also bind things like C function names directly to your code so you can call them as though they were Ruby methods. Take the set-bit counting algorithm described in Listing 3-14.

Listing 3-14. *Pure Ruby vs. In-lined C for a Given Algorithm*

```ruby
require "benchmark"
require "inline"

class Integer
  def count_set_bits(use_c = false)
    return csb(self) if use_c
    return 0 if self.zero?
    bits, x = 1, self
    bits += 1 while (x = x & (x - 1)).nonzero?
    bits
  end

  inline do |builder|
    builder.c "int csb(long x) {
      if (x == 0) return (x);
      int bits = 1;
      while ((x = x & (x - 1))) bits++;
      return (bits);
    }"
  end
end

Benchmark.bmbm do |b|
  b.report("ruby") { 100_000.times { 152363.count_set_bits } }
  b.report("c") { 100_000.times { 152363.count_set_bits(true) } }
end
```

The difference that writing the algorithm in C makes is really quite substantial:

```
Rehearsal --------------------------------------
ruby   1.940000   0.020000   1.960000 (  2.255809)
c      0.170000   0.000000   0.170000 (  0.189972)
---------------------------- total: 2.130000sec

           user      system      total       real
ruby   1.950000   0.020000   1.970000 (  2.521235)
c      0.170000   0.000000   0.170000 (  0.206750)
```

Obviously, system administrators don't tend to need to optimize this sort of algorithm very often, but timetabling or other sorts of constraint-based problems might benefit greatly from being able to in-line small chunks of C. In addition, some institutions will have prebuilt C/C++ libraries for doing some of their back-end work. Imagine how useful this approach would be in preserving that work while reaping the benefits of surrounding it in a modern language.

Ramming Speed

Hopefully, you've picked up a sense of the ability of a Ruby script to be truly performant even when compared with its more traditional, compiled brethren. We've looked at some of the major ways in which performance can be analyzed and bottlenecks found, and we've explored some of the techniques with which such problems can be alleviated.

The ability to write fast code is important, but it isn't what makes Ruby so compelling. The reason that Ruby adapts so well to almost any conceivable project is due to its linguistic dynamism. The versatility of metaprogramming is something that Ruby provides in abundance and can be of great use to the system administrator; thus it is the focus of the next chapter.

CHAPTER 4

■ ■ ■

The Power of Metaprogramming

So far, you'll have acquired an impression of the basics of Ruby—its flavor, if you will. For me, what really sets it apart is the way in which it facilitates *metaprogramming*. Of course, this is a somewhat nebulous statement if one hasn't properly defined what class of programming is worthy of such a prefix (see the sidebar "Meta . . . What?").

This is the last of the chapters that take a "did you know?" approach to the language itself, identifying features that will be useful in your day-to-day programming. The concepts presented in this chapter are not inherently system administration–specific, but they are key to writing clean, expressive Ruby code. Moreover, the techniques discussed here can allow for some truly powerful approaches to traditional system challenges (as you will see throughout the rest of the book).

In this chapter I discuss things like macros, dynamic methods, and domain-specific languages. All of these fit under the general umbrella of "code that does something with code." This is probably the most intuitively obvious definition of metaprogramming, and anyone who's ever used a #define statement in C to enable the writing of less noisy code will be eminently familiar with such concepts.

In addition to these customary metaprogramming techniques, this chapter also examines flexible method signatures, class extension methodologies, and even a few examples that really show off Ruby's near-gymnastic flexibility.

META . . . WHAT?

To be honest, this word "metaprogramming" has never been on very solid footing. Particularly over the last few years, it seems to have come to refer to any code construction concept that hasn't been widely used or seen before. So you pick a language like Perl, take everything Ruby does that's more expressive or dynamic, and call that metaprogramming. That said, Ruby continues to surprise me with just how small it can make my code. The ability to refactor a problem not just by juggling functions around, but by restructuring the language almost at will makes for often remarkable productivity increases.

Because I am a bear of very little brain, it has taken my forays into Ruby coding to truly recognize that any programming language is merely an abstraction in the same fashion as any library for that language. What we think of as keywords or primitives in a language are nothing more than defined and abstracted functionality.

> The reason that Ruby forces this conclusion home is that it genuinely blurs the boundary between what you think of as the language and what you refer to as a library. Ruby's pure object-oriented nature is what makes it possible to override and augment so much of its behavior. In other words, saying that "everything is just an object" is actually a profoundly liberating assertion. It means that the language requires very few primitives and that absolutely everything else can be tinkered with.

Flexible Method Signatures

One obvious benefit of Ruby's versatility is the approach it allows when constructing and calling methods. In this section, we'll take a look at how to simplify and generalize method signatures (argument patterns) with default values. We'll also see how such signatures may be further empowered through the use of parameter hashes. Finally, we'll examine an extremely powerful convention for dynamic method construction.

Default Values

One of the nicer features of C++ (and other languages) is the availability of method *polymorphism*. Specifically, methods can be defined that all share the same name but that have different signatures (one might take two integers while another takes three). Thus it is possible to define a method that adapts to the number and nature of its arguments. Polymorphism support also means that, if a method is discovered that would benefit from some extra parameter, the behavior of the method with this parameter can be "bolted on" so as to yield extra functionality without breaking any existing code.

Note In the particular case of C++ (due to its static nature), method signature changes require a recompilation and relinking of all dependent code. This can be a big hassle for large code bases.

In Ruby, such requirements are catered for a little differently. The feature of being able to add arguments without breaking code can be looked at in reverse. In the spirit of making Ruby code as terse as possible, methods are often designed to take as few parameters as the programmer can get away with. In order to avoid having this lead to a paucity of control, extra parameters can be defined along with default values. Thus the user of such a method need only specify values for such arguments when the default values must be overridden.

Imagine a scheduling class that is initialized with starting and finishing times and is able to determine whether a supplied time value is within the schedule's range. Casually, this class might be used as follows:

```
now = Time.now
schedule = Schedule.new(now - 3600, now + 3600)
schedule.current?(now) # => true
```

Before we try to build this class, take a look at the final line. For testing purposes, we might wish to be able to specify times in the past or future at which to test the currency of the schedule.

Hence Schedule.current? takes a parameter of the time at which the check is to be made. Overwhelmingly, however, we are just going to want to know whether the schedule is current now (as we do in the preceding code). It would be nice to be able to invoke current? without a parameter and still get the same functionality. This is achieved in Listing 4-1.

Listing 4-1. *A Class That Includes a Method Definition with a Default-Specified Parameter*

```
class Schedule
  def initialize(from, to)
    @from, @to = from, to
  end

  def current?(time = Time.now)
    @from <= time and time <= @to
  end
end
```

As you can see from this listing, setting a parameter equal to some value specifies a default value for that parameter. The value can be an object or an expression that returns an object. Note that the expression in Listing 4-1 to return the current time (Time.now) is evaluated at runtime each time the method is invoked, rather than via static substitution as seen in lesser languages. Obviously, we are not limited to one default-valued parameter. Listing 4-2 shows a method with two default-valued parameters.

Listing 4-2. *A Method with a Number of Default-Specified Parameters*

```
def rolecall(person1, person2 = "Dick", person3 = "Harry")
  "#{person1}, #{person2} and #{person3}"
end

rolecall("Tom") # => "Tom, Dick and Harry"
rolecall("George", 42) # => "George, 42 and Harry"
```

Not only does Listing 4-2 demonstrate the overriding of default values, but it also shows that required and optional parameters can coexist. If we tried to call rolecall with no parameters, an exception would be raised, as there is no way for the interpreter to cope with such a call given that at least one parameter is needed. In other words, rolecall has an *arity* of between one and three (it takes between one and three arguments).

Listing 4-2 also has a sneaky example of duck typing. Because Integer and its subclasses respond to the to_s method (which is implicitly called on the finally evaluated value of each #{...} block in the method), we were able to pass in a number as a person's name.

It should be evident that once a parameter is given a default value, all subsequent parameters to the method must also have one. Otherwise, the Ruby interpreter would have to guess whether an argument was overriding a default-valued parameter or specifying a value for its neighbor.

Whether or not this ability is particularly "meta" is debatable and really depends on the definition of a method. Administrators used to shell scripting will recognize that this is really nothing new (although being able to specify expressions as defaults rather than constants is somewhat novel).

Parameter Hashes

A more genuinely high-level time-saver is the idea of using a hash to pass optional parameters to a method. Ruby has a nice syntactic convention such that

```
cook("fish", "portions" => 2, "style" => "Cajun")
```

is semantically identical to

```
cook("fish", {"portions" => 2, "style" => "Cajun"})
```

More properly, if the last argument in a method call is a hash, then the curly brackets may be omitted to reduce the clutter a little. Of course, passing values in a hash allows for named parameters, a concept that's been repopularized by Objective-C (for one). In addition, the use of a hash means that the user can specify only those values that she wishes to override in cases where the method has some notion of default behavior.

We will construct a method definition that takes advantage of these concepts in just a moment. Before we do, I want to review the concept of a Symbol. As I have mentioned previously, symbols are often used as hash keys because they have both speed and style advantages. They are particularly appropriate in the case of parameter hashes, as the same old set of keys will tend to be used repeatedly. Thus it makes sense to use an entity that gets allocated only once and isn't subject to the performance hit of a dynamically allocated, mutable string. From here on, we'll discard the use of strings in favor of symbols wherever possible, as in Listing 4-3.

Listing 4-3. *A Skeleton Method That Uses Dynamic Parameters from a Hash*

```
def install_package(name, params = {})
  path = (params[:path] || "/")
  receipt = (params[:receipt] || true)
  # do something with the package name, path, and receipt flag
end
```

The first thing to note with this listing is that we didn't simply choose to have everything passed dynamically. Often, there is a logical subset of parameters without which the method makes absolutely no sense. Such parameters should be given pride of place in the method signature as arguments in their own right (as we did for name in Listing 4-3).

This method signature also uses the concept of a default for a parameter so that it really could be called like this:

```
install_package("Tux Racer")
```

which is in keeping with the optional nature of the rest of the arguments. Alternatively, the way this method is constructed allows us to override items like the default installation path:

```
install_package("Tux Racer", :path => "/games")
```

The "this or that" construction use in Listing 4-3 is great for casually constructed defaults. However, for reasons of modularity or even nonrepetition, we may wish to factor out the process of accumulating default values. For instance, we may end up with a series of methods that all need the same set of parameters with the same default values. If we don't want to step up to full-blown configuration classes (which have always struck me as atom bombs to crack walnuts), then we need to create a method that will ensure any unspecified setting in the parameter hash is created with its default.

More specifically, we have some cloud of settings that we want to merge into the parameter hash passed by the user. It turns out that the Hash class has an ideal method for this, as demonstrated in Listing 4-4 (see ri Hash.merge for more detail).

Listing 4-4. *An Outsourced Default-Setting Mechanism*

```
def package_defaults(params)
  {:path => "/", :receipt => true}.merge(params)
end

def install_package(name, params = {})
  params = package_defaults(params)
  # do something with name, params[:path], and params[:receipt]
end
```

Missing Method Dynamic Dispatch

Default-valued parameters are useful, and dynamic methods using parameter hashes are kind of neat. For genuinely impressive dynamism, though, we can turn to being able to call methods that don't exist.

Calling a method that doesn't exist isn't some Zen thing. We aren't talking about whether a method makes a noise like one hand clapping if it falls in the middle of a subroutine and there's no one around to debug it. Rather, we return to the idea that any method can be overridden. In particular, Object has a method called method_missing, which is invoked when a script calls a method that doesn't exist. Since everything inherits from Object, any class can override the behavior of this wonderful little method.

You may wonder what good it could possibly do to intercept what is essentially a cry of panic from a given object. The answer lies in the method signature for method_missing:

```
def method_missing(symbol, *args)
  # do something with the symbol or the arguments or both
end
```

The first argument (symbol) is unsurprisingly the name of the method that was called. Remember that there are very few undefinable methods in Ruby, so symbol can look like count= or []= as well as more humdrum examples like flush. The second argument (args) is used to soak up all arguments passed to the method in a single array.

Anyone who's used Rails will be familiar with its dynamic finders that allow you to do things like User.find_by_name("slartibartfast"). Although there is quite a lot of structured complexity behind these finders, they are essentially powered by a dynamic dispatch from the missing method routine—something like that shown in Listing 4-5.

Listing 4-5. *Skeleton Example of Dynamic Dispatch Through method_missing*

```
def method_missing(symbol, *args)
  if symbol.to_s =~ /^find_by_(\w+)$/
    fields = $1.split("_and_")
    # build a query based on the fields and values (args)
  else super
  end
end
```

The first thing to watch out for with the approach demonstrated in Listing 4-5 is assuming that a Symbol behaves exactly like a String on the grounds that they are intimately related. Listing 4-5 contains an explicit cast (to_s) before performing the regular expression match. This casting strategy copes with the subtle differences between symbols and strings without making any assumptions that might lead to code fragility.

The other point of interest here is the now-familiar use of super. In this context, the use of super means that having a method_missing override for specific method names won't interfere with the normal exception process for genuine miscalls. Once again the nature of object-oriented inheritance ensures the minimum amount of code noise for the maximum amount of flexibility.

Macros

It is interesting and probably highly irrelevant that if you place the emphasis on the second syllable of the word "macro" and give the "r" a bit of a roll, it sounds like a word in Arabic meaning "frowned upon" or "disapproved of." Plenty of very smart people disapprove of macros in general, not because they are inherently bad, but rather because the line between use and abuse is almost paper-thin. I'm not nearly as smart as those people, so I love macros unconditionally.

We've already seen that Ruby has methods like attr_accessor, which somehow imbues a class with a pair of methods for getting and setting a particular instance variable. This is a method that builds other methods, so I'm pretty comfortable calling it a macro. The fact that it is defined as part of the basic language might tempt us to think of it as a keyword (particularly given that it does something so fundamental to a class). However, recalling the discussion about Ruby's inherent blurring of such terms, a quick ri attr_accessor reveals that it's actually a method of Module.

Module Inclusion

This general idea of adding bundles of functionality to a class or even an instantiated object runs throughout the language and is fundamental to the operation of a *mix-in*. Ruby does not have multiple inheritance, so acquiring abstract behavior from multiple sources requires a different approach. A mix-in is most often a simple collection of functions that can be added to any class that obeys a method contract. That is to say that if your class implements certain basic methods, a whole range of behavior can be built on top of those methods. The quintessential example of this is the Enumerable module.

If you create a collection class that has an each method for iterating through the members, you can get a number of useful methods "for free" by including the Enumerable module. These include detect, each_with_index, include?, inject, and zip. In addition, if the objects in your collection implement the standard comparison method (<=>), Enumerable gives you max, min, and sort.

These methods may seem familiar as Array implements them all. It does so by including Enumerable and implementing each. Let's give this a try ourselves with Listing 4-6.

Listing 4-6. *Skeleton Implementation of an Enumerable Collection*

```
class Toybox
  include Enumerable
  def each
    yield toy while (toy = retrieve_toy)
  end
end
```

With a class definition like that in Listing 4-6, we could call toybox.include?(some_toy) without having to write the include? method explicitly. Enumerable will use our each function (the details of which I have left sketchy as they are unimportant) to iterate through the collection and search for the specified toy.

Now that we've tried one of Ruby's built-in modules, we'll take the next step and create one of our own. This module will generalize the concept of a contactable entity. This would be of use if you had two unrelated classes that modeled users of a system and servers with auto-mated mailboxes. In such a case, it is often difficult to factor out a superclass of both that would implement common functionality.

Superclasses factored out to implement common functionality tend to end up with names like Entity, which is really just another word for Object. Whenever I catch myself using such a name, I know it's time for a mix-in. In this instance, we'll create a module called Contactable with the contract shown in Table 4-1.

Table 4-1. *The Contract for the Contactable Module*

Requires	To Provide
email_address	send_email
fax_number	send_fax

We might assume that a User would have both an e-mail address and a fax number, but it is less likely that a Server would have the latter. We could make the first item of the requirements compulsory and the second optional. Assuming that integration of this module into the existing classes will happen at different times and that we want to break as little as possible, it would be easiest to make each requirement optional. Thus we will only attempt to do something for each method in the To Provide column if the corresponding requirement is met—a truly dynamic approach exemplified by Listing 4-7.

Listing 4-7. *A Mixable Module for Sending E-mails and Faxes*

```ruby
module Contactable
  def send_email(subject, message, attachments = {})
    return unless respond_to?(:email_address)
    address = email_address
    raise "e-mail address not set" unless address
    # build the e-mail and send it
  end

  def send_fax(message)
    return unless respond_to?(:fax_number)
    number = fax_number
    raise "fax number not set" unless number
    # build the fax and send it (beep beep)
  end
end
```

When the `Contactable` module is included in our two classes, they gain the two defined methods (`send_email` and `send_fax`). Note that we cache the returned value of `email_address` and `fax_number` within the functions. This is because these methods could be doing more than a simple retrieval operation. Assuming the worst in this respect keeps performance overheads to a minimum.

You may be interested to learn that `include` is a sort of macro in itself. It is a method of the `Module` class that takes one or more module names as arguments (we have only ever specified one). For each of these modules, it invokes `module.append_features(klass)` on the class in which it was invoked. In turn, `append_features` adds the constants, instance methods, and module variables of the module specified to the host class.

Object Extension

By itself, the `include` directive will not add class methods to a particular class. A different function defined by the `Object` class allows you to specifically add methods to any object. That method is called `extend`.

The `extend` method works very much like `include` in that it takes the set of instance methods (but not the constants or module variables) in a module and defines them in the context of the object from which `extend` was invoked. The code and output in Listing 4-8 highlight the difference between `include` and `extend`.

Listing 4-8. *Inclusion vs. Extension*

```ruby
module Extension
  def where_am_i
    p self
  end
end
```

```
class Rabbit
  include Extension
end

class Hat
end

# Objects
Hat.new.where_am_i        # => [Exception raised]
hat_extended = Hat.new
hat_extended.extend(Extension)
hat_extended.where_am_i  # => #<Hat:0x1087b44>
Rabbit.new.where_am_i     # => #<Rabbit:0x4bab4>

# Classes
Hat.where_am_i            # => [Exception raised]
Rabbit.where_am_i         # => [Exception raised]
```

Inclusion adds instance methods to a class, whereas extension actually bolts methods onto whatever is being extended, yielding new class methods if the entity being extended is a class. In other words, if we had written Hat.extend(Extension)—extending the class itself—we would have been able to call Hat.where_am_i (a class method).

If this manner of defining an empty class and then extending it seems a little cumbersome, remember that you can create classes using Class.new. This approach gets rid of the declarative style of class creation altogether and replaces it with this:

```
Hat = Class.new
```

which can even be extended inline as extend returns the object being extended:

```
Hat = Class.new.extend(Extension)
```

You're unlikely to use this style of class creation much, but it's handy to remember for those times when brevity conquers all. Speaking of which, recall that extend works on any object. This means that it is possible to mix-in methods to instantiated objects without affecting any of their brethren, as demonstrated in Listing 4-9.

Listing 4-9. *Using extend to Add Methods to Individual Objects*

```
module AdminFunctions
  def wipe_disk(mount_path)
    # wipe the specified disk
  end
end

class User
  def admin?
    # determine whether the user is an admin or not
  end
```

```
    def logon(name, password)
      # authenticate the user
      extend(AdminFunctions) if admin?
    end
end
```

Walking through this listing, a `User` object is defined to be instantiated without any of the methods available to an administrator. It is only by calling `logon` and being designated an administrator that the bundle of administrative functions is added to the given object and only to that object. As you can imagine, the ability to modify the functional makeup of a class or an object at runtime is extraordinarily powerful and opens up any number of previously obscure design patterns. For a particular example of this, take a look at the sidebar "Self-Destructing Methods."

SELF-DESTRUCTING METHODS

One particularly cute example of dynamic method declaration is that of method self-redeclaration. Inside a given method, the `def` construction is still valid and will run in the same context as its surrounding method. The method defined can be anything, including the method currently being run. Thus we can ensure that a particular function is only ever run once for any given object like this:

```
class Host
  def upgrade
    @version += 1
    def upgrade; end
  end
end
```

So `Host.upgrade` will increase the version number when first run but then redefine itself to do nothing if ever called again. Note the use of a semicolon to force an end-of-line, saving a little space. It is not difficult to imagine that you could implement an entire state machine using this technique.

Domain-Specific Languages (DSLs)

One of the reasons Rails was written in Ruby was that the possibilities so far discussed in this chapter all come together to make the language ideal for building other languages. The practical upshot of this can be seen in the number of macros available to an `ActiveRecord` subclass in Rails. Listing 4-10 is the definition for such a subclass called `User`, which relies on some of `ActiveRecord`'s macros to provide a shorthand for what might otherwise be a lot of code.

Listing 4-10. *A Sampling of the ActiveRecord Macros in Rails*

```
class User < ActiveRecord::Base
  acts_as_list
  belongs_to :company
  verifies_inclusion_of :office, :in => ["Geneva", "Paris", "Rome"]
end
```

The lines within the `User` class definition in this listing add commonly used functionality to the class but with so little noise that it is virtually impossible to misunderstand what they do (see Chapter 6 for further discussion of `ActiveRecord`). This idea of designing macros around a particular set of tasks pertinent to some problem domain is a really cool demonstration of how useful Ruby can be. As examined in Chapter 11, the Rake system is built around a task-oriented DSL that can easily be applied to the jobs associated with system administration.

The idea of a language designed to solve a problem is nothing new. If nothing else, this is a pretty reasonable definition of any programming language, including Ruby. What you will see is that Ruby is particularly suited to prototyping new languages for a few reasons:

- Few keywords mean greater freedom in the namespace.

- Brackets (and to a lesser extent braces) are considered syntactic sugar.

- Method definition, inclusion, and overriding are completely dynamic.

- Common types (arrays, hashes, strings, and numbers) have "obvious" forms.

By way of a demonstration, imagine a server configuration system built around Ruby. Somewhere in the back of our minds we have a shorthand language we'd like to use for specifying the capabilities of a given server. Broadly, we want to be able to name the server and then give it particular features like this:

```ruby
server "bitbucket.example.com" do |srv|
  srv.shares "/homes", :over => ["afp", "smb"], :as => "HOMES"
end
```

Where this example is concerned, we have the concept of a named server and at least one method that can be used to configure it (`shares`). In choosing how to implement the features of the DSL implied by our example, we should model these concepts with a class. Listing 4-11 does just that.

Listing 4-11. *A Simple Server Class That Satisfies the Needs of the DSL*

```ruby
class Server
  def initialize(hostname)
    @hostname = hostname
    @sharepoints = {}
  end

  def shares(path, params)
    (params[:over] || []).each do |protocol|
      proto_shares = (@sharepoints[protocol] ||= {})
      share_id = (params[:as] || "UNKNOWN")
      proto_shares[share_id] = path
    end
  end
end
```

Each server object tracks shares through a hash called @sharepoints. The shares method adds the pertinent details to this hash. Notice how the names of methods are chosen so that the DSL reads like standard English as much as possible. All that is left in this example is to provide the server method that sits at the root of each definition. This will need to be in the global namespace (i.e., available outside the confines of the Server class definition):

```
def server(hostname)
  yield Server.new(hostname)
end
```

This tiny snippet completes the DSL as specified, initializing one of our Server objects and passing it to the block supplied by the client script.

■**Tip** The approach of configuring services through code allows for the use of dynamic values as well as runtime validation/sanity checking. This often leads to a configuration process that is more powerful and more resilient, which is why I revisit it throughout the book.

Plug-in API: Macros for Adding Macros

Given that everything is just an object, and that methods can be added to objects dynamically, and that macros are just methods designed a certain way, it should be obvious that we can write code to add macros to an object dynamically. Indeed there is no limit to the recursion of this approach, except that which is imposed the moment that blood starts to gush from both ears.

Listing 4-10 mentions the acts_as_list macro available in Rails. I'm going to execute a brief tour of one way to write a Rails plug-in as a means to explore pluggable functionality more generally. For any plug-in, we ideally want it to be completely self-contained in such a way that it can be included in our classes with the utmost simplicity. In addition, that which is included should be limited to macros that create further functionality on an as-needed basis.

Recall that the include command actually runs Module.append_features. We can override this call to allow us to get all the advantages of a normal inclusion (the replication of constants in particular), while giving much tighter control of method creation. If our override's only unique step is to extend the class with an acts_as-style method, that method can then be defined to add further class and instance methods.

In Listing 4-12, we overhaul the Contactable module we were playing with earlier along theses lines.

Listing 4-12. *The Contactable Module Refactored As a Plug-in*

```
module Contactable
  def self.append_features(klass)
    super
    klass.extend(Macros)
  end
```

```
def Macros
  def acts_as_contactable
    extend ClassMethods
    include InstanceMethods
  end
end

module ClassMethods
  # none to speak of
end

module InstanceMethods
  # methods from listing 4-7 go here
  end
end
```

With the module defined in this way, inclusion into a class will only create the class method acts_as_contactable. This method will, of course, be available to the class and all of its subclasses. If one of the subclasses runs this method, it and it alone will be extended to include all of the class and instance methods defined. This approach has the virtue that it nicely compartmentalizes individual sections of code and gives a greater degree of flexibility and control over exactly how and when methods are added.

Heavy Meta

In this chapter we explored some of the metaprogramming concepts that Ruby facilitates. From flexible method signatures to macro design, we have touched on some of the approaches that Ruby-ists adopt that render their code quicker to design and maintain. Depending on your particular language background, some or none of these ideas may be familiar to you. If bits of it seem rather abstract, I can only ask you to stick with it, as I have used every one of the techniques described in this chapter in real code and the resulting scripts have benefited enormously.

As I said at the beginning, I really don't have a good definition of metaprogramming. About the best description I can come up with is that by which the US Supreme Court denotes pornography: I know it when I see it. There were lots of arcane examples of Ruby metaprogramming that I decided to leave out of this chapter because it was difficult to see how they might be of benefit to most system administrators. From a purely aesthetic perspective, however, I encourage you to search for such whimsies if you are in the mood for some dessert.

This chapter forms the last part of the general introduction to the language. The chapters that follow seek to apply what we have covered to more concrete topics affecting system administrators. In particular, the next chapter covers an activity that many, if not most, scripts spend their time doing: creating files.

CHAPTER 5

■■■

Building Files the Smart Way

One of the most brilliant design choices found in UNIX-style operating systems is the notion that "everything is just a file." In other words, if your programming language can do very basic reading/writing of files and a little string handling, you can drive the configuration and environment of every bit of software you care about.

In this chapter, we will explore the most common file-building methodologies and find out how to apply them the Ruby way. In particular, before getting down to writing a single byte, we'll discuss and create some safe file operations. Such operations are imperative in system maintenance and administration scripts. Thus we will deal with the safety issues before proceeding to discuss both program- and template-driven file creation.

Safety First

I remember one morning my coworkers and I were sitting around in the systems support room chatting about something (snack foods as the key to happiness if memory serves) when someone uttered those portentous words: "That's odd." Now, an experienced administrator will tell you that these two little gems, when spoken together, are the verbal equivalent of a small highland terrier yapping inexplicably 30 minutes before your city is leveled by an earthquake.

In this case, the doomsayer in question had noticed that the performance of his web browser had become a little erratic, seeming to operate in fits and starts. No sooner had he explained this than the guy behind me complained that his mail client had started timing out. It's at this point that we received our first phone call requesting support.

Two or three hours later, when the apocalypse had spent itself, we were finally in a position to understand what had gone wrong. You see, our DNS server was driven dynamically out of a database. Every few minutes, a little script would run to read the configuration and the zone files, compare them with what it thought they should say according to the contents of the database, and update them as necessary (refer to Figure 5-1). If an update did take place, the script would nudge the name-server daemon to get it to notice the new configuration.

In theory, a single run of the script was supposed to take far less time than the interval between such runs. In theory, it was unthinkable that more than one instance of the script would be running at once. In theory, tomatoes are fruit. So much for theory.

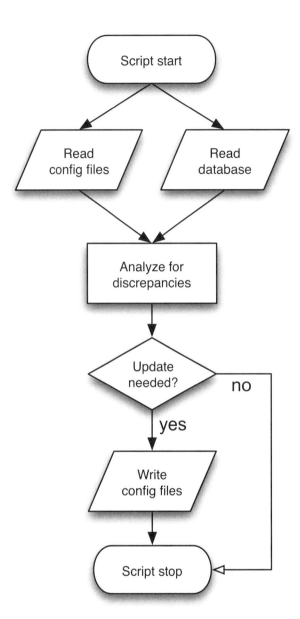

Figure 5-1. *The deceptively simple flow of the update script*

The first instance of the script (we'll call it A) started running and, probably due to abnormal load on the server, got about halfway through writing an updated configuration file when a second instance (B) was invited to the party. It read the half-written file and naturally concluded that there was a vast swath of zones missing from the server. Hence, B leapt into action and started writing a new configuration file on top of the now mostly complete one A had been committing to disk. As A finished, it nudged the name-server daemon to let it know it should reread its configuration files, which at this point (of course) were only halfway through being written by B. As if by magic, a good chunk of zones suddenly went AWOL.

Now people were having problems with web access, e-mail, and even network volumes, which all relied heavily on DNS resolution. This meant more hits of Refresh buttons and sides of computers. The abnormally large number of demands for name resolution in turn put increased load on the DNS server, which meant that within about 20 minutes there were four instances of this script competing with each other, completely obliterating the zone information on the server and pushing it to sustain maximum load. By the time one of our guys realized it was a DNS issue and could get a remote session on the machine, an entire Whitehall farce was going on in memory, all because of one little false assumption made by the scriptwriter.

The moral I took from this episode was an important one. When writing scripts that mess about with files on disk, concurrency issues must be considered from the very beginning. In other words, it is important to take explicit steps to enforce the kinds of mutually exclusive behavior required by the script in this story. Fortunately, Ruby makes it easy to do the right thing in this respect.

File Locking

All the mainstream operating systems implement some form of file locking and vend a pretty simple API for using it. In the context of a file, a *lock* is a flag that can be requested by a process that, in general terms, means "This lavatory is currently occupied—wait your turn." More specifically, there are two styles of locks supported by the UNIX locking mechanism.

A *shared* lock can be held by many processes at the same time. An *exclusive* lock can be held by only one process at a time. You are most likely to use exclusive locking day to day, as you generally want to just stake a claim to a file for the whole duration of the read/write portion of your script. This is the so-called coarse locking approach and, while lacking elegance, it is the most difficult to get wrong.

You might be wondering under what circumstances you'd use shared locking. The classic scenario employing this approach involves a file that lots of processes want to read from and occasionally write to. Each process acquires a shared lock while reading and then continues on its merry way until it has finished reading, releasing the lock when done. Of course, if the file isn't changing, it doesn't matter how many processes read from it simultaneously—it will always say the same thing. However, some process now decides to modify the file. This writing process should ask for an exclusive lock on the file and, since only one process can hold an exclusive lock on a particular file at any one time, it will have to wait until all of the shared locks have gone away. Thus shared locks are overwhelmingly a mechanism for ensuring read integrity, whereas exclusive locks ensure both read *and* write integrity.

Blocking Locks

The simplest kind of locking is that which blocks your program until the lock may be granted. Have a look at the code in Listing 5-1, which demonstrates a simple lock-write-unlock procedure.

Listing 5-1. *Safe File Writing Using a Lock*

```
File.open("/tmp/foo", "w") do |f|
  f.flock(File::LOCK_EX)
  f.puts "Locking is the key to ... pun interrupted"
  f.flock(File::LOCK_UN)
end
```

This code starts by attempting to open a file for writing and names the object representing access to that file f (a file handle). Personally, I always use this block-style invocation of File.open, as the block doesn't execute unless the file was successfully opened with the required access rights. Also, it makes something we're about to do much easier.

Once we have our file handle, we call the flock method with the argument File::LOCK_EX, requesting an exclusive lock on it (File::LOCK_SH would request a shared lock). At this point, if any other process has any kind of lock on the file, our script will block and wait for the other locks to be released. Once the file is clear of locks, our script can then write its little message into the file. As a final act of tidiness, we explicitly unlock the file again, indicating that we've finished with it.

Nonblocking Locks

Now what if we merely want to check whether there's a lock and do something different if we can't get immediate access to the file? The flock call allows us to request this behavior with an extra flag (File::LOCK_NB), as shown in Listing 5-2.

Listing 5-2. *Locking but Not Blocking*

```
File.open("/tmp/foo", "w") do |f|
  if f.flock(File::LOCK_EX | File::LOCK_NB)
    f.puts "I want to lock it all up in my pocket"
    f.flock(File::LOCK_UN)
  else warn "Couldn't get a lock - better luck next time"
  end
end
```

In this listing, we once again use the block form of File.open, but instead of the lock-write-unlock approach we used last time we do the following:

1. Try to acquire a lock without blocking

2. If successful, write and then unlock

3. If unsuccessful, throw up a warning

Note, incidentally, the use of the bitwise OR operator (|) when selecting the behavior of flock. This should be familiar to anyone who's done this sort of thing in C.

Abstracted Locking

The fact that, in general terms, we always seem to end up with a lock call at the beginning of the block and an unlock call at the end points to a possibility for abstraction. There are many ways to do what I'm about to (see the sidebar "Open Abuse" for an alternative approach). The following is probably the easiest to follow and provides a nice opportunity to show off the ability to add methods to built-in classes in Ruby.

What we want to do is define a method that acts as much like open as possible, but will implicitly give us an exclusively locked file to play with and automatically unlock it for us. Take a look at Listing 5-3.

Listing 5-3. *Extending the File Class to Include a Convenient Locked Writing Method*

```
class File
  def File.open_locked(*args)
    File.open(args) do |f|
      begin
        f.flock(File::LOCK_EX)
        result = yield f
      ensure
        f.flock(File::LOCK_UN)
        return result
      end
    end
  end
end
```

As previously explored, we can extend Ruby's built-in classes like any other class with a simple class declaration, inside which all definitions are in the context of that class. The method signature for open_locked uses the * construction. This simply means "gather up any arguments passed to this method and dump them in an array." In this case, the array is called args, but there is nothing special about that name.

The usefulness of the args variable we define becomes obvious in the next line, where we invoke File.open in its by now familiar block form. Essentially, we are ensuring that our function has an identical signature to the function we're mimicking by not giving the slightest hoot what that signature is. It also means that any future changes to the argument structure of File.open won't break this code.

The actual meat of the code contains the requisite lock-operate-unlock logic. Just as with File.open, any code using our method should present open_locked with a block of code that accepts a file handle. The difference, of course, is that this handle will be exclusively locked when passed by our method.

We expressly want any errors that would normally raise an exception to still do so unhindered, in keeping with our mimicry of File.open. The only minor difference is that, whatever may go wrong, if we've locked the file we must unlock it again. Hence the use of a begin... ensure...end block. As you might surmise, everything within the ensure part is run irrespective of whether an exception is in the process of being raised.

Our striving to impersonate `File.open` as much as possible is why we're also careful to preserve the `result` of the passed code block. Once again, this is how `File.open` behaves and it allows us to do this kind of thing:

```
raw_data = File.open_locked("/tmp/foo") { |f| f.read }
```

OPEN ABUSE

Instead of creating an open-like method we could specifically override open. This would mean that `File.open` itself would automatically lock and unlock files for us (just like our `open_locked` method). Playing with such an important method is probably something we want to do in a fairly careful manner, as it will affect a lot of subsequent code. On this basis, I want to emphasize that this example should be taken more as an academic "what if" than something you would choose to do in production code. `File.open` is just too fundamental to mess with in large projects without inviting trouble.

Grabbing an exclusive lock regardless of whether a read-only or read-write file handle has been requested would needlessly degrade performance. Thus we need to achieve two things that `open_locked` didn't. The first is to override `File.open` correctly so that we don't start causing warnings to appear and so that it is still available to us internally. After all, neither you nor I have the desire to completely reimplement file operations from scratch in any language if we don't have to. The second goal is to be a little smarter with the type of lock we ask for than our first attempt in Listing 5-3 (which you should read before this sidebar). Here's a solution:

```
class File
  class << self
    alias open_old open
  end

  def File.open(path, mode = "r", perm = 0644)
    File.open_old(path, mode, perm) do |f|
      begin
        f.flock(mode == "r" ? LOCK_SH : LOCK_EX)
        result = yield f
      ensure
        f.flock(File::LOCK_UN)
        return result
      end
    end
  end
end
```

Examining the features that make this different from the `open_locked` solution, we first have to discuss the aliasing process. Within the context of a class definition, a new alias to an existing instance method can be created with the `alias` keyword. The problem is that the method we are trying to overwrite is a class method, and so we have to use a somewhat advanced bit of syntax. The double chevron (`<<`) construction means that we wish to extend the class in the context of its class-level namespace (the double chevron actually means "extend the current implicit object"). Thus the aliasing is done at this level.

The rest of the code should be much easier to follow. This time we have to care about the parameters to open, as the type of lock will depend on the mode variable. Also, for quickness, we take certain liberties with the permissions setting just to give us something to pass to the original method without having to worry too much.

Process Locking

One cute trick I've seen employed quite a lot ensures that there is never more than one instance of a script running. First, pick a location on the disk that is appropriate for the storing of process running data. If your script is designed to run as a UNIX daemon, it will usually have a PID file associated with it that you create in /var/run/myscript.pid, so that is an obvious choice for this next step. Otherwise something in /tmp will do.

As early as possible in your script, get a handle to your chosen file and attempt to gain an exclusive lock on it in the manner discussed throughout this section. If you can't get the lock, you know another instance of your script is already lurking somewhere in memory and the new instance can bow out gracefully.

What if you forget to release the lock before your script exits, or the script crashes before it has an opportunity to unlock the file? Won't that leave you unable to run the script ever again? The beauty of this approach is that file locks are a property of the process requesting them (at least for our purposes). If the process goes away for whatever reason, the OS guarantees that the lock will be released.

Locking Considerations

Whether protecting files or processes, there are a couple of points to be aware of when employing file locks:

- UNIX-style systems treat file locking as advisory by default. The fact that you've been good and wrapped your file system calls in flocks in no way implies that another application will be blocked if it attempts to do an ordinary write to the file of interest without any flocking.

- Some file systems have inconsistent/nonexistent support for the flock call (NFS prior to Linux 2.6.12 in particular springs to mind), so you need to be conscious of where your code will be deployed.

Safe File Operations

This concern over regimented access to files is all very well, but it doesn't protect you from one other important class of file-integrity issue: *partial writes*. If your script crashes halfway through its operation, the OS will tidy up the locks and another process will be free to access the file you were writing. Unfortunately, if you didn't finish writing data to disk, you now have a serious problem.

You simply cannot guarantee that your script won't crash or run out of disk space or some such thing. We have to find a way to make sure that a configuration file, for example, only gets overwritten with a complete replacement or not at all. Also, it would be nice to achieve the kind of file-locking safety we had in the previous subsection so that when we write files we can guarantee that no other process is reading from them.

Abstracting Safe File Operations

As before, our approach will be to add a method to the built-in `File` class that mimics the behavior of `File.open` but that copes with our file-safety concerns transparently. The strategy for performing a safe write will be to write all data to a temporary file and then move it on top of the original only upon its closure.

This approach prevents partial writes, as a given file updated this way can be overwritten only when there is a complete replacement ready. In addition, the only file system operation that is as close to being atomic (indivisible—it either completes or it doesn't) as we can hope for is a move. Moving a file on disk actually does nothing of the sort; it simply changes the path associated with the file. This means that the code shown in Listing 5-4 will provide the safe writes we're looking for.

Listing 5-4. *Extending the File Class to Include an Anti–Partial Writes Method*

```
require "fileutils"
require "tempfile"

class File
  def File.open_safely(path)
    result, temp_path = nil, nil
    Tempfile.open("#{$0}-#{path.hash}") do |f|
      result = yield f
      temp_path = f.path
    end
    FileUtils.move(temp_path, path)
    result
  end
end
```

Let's unpick this carefully. The first thing to note is that we've included the functionality provided by the `FileUtils` module—this is necessary for the file move we'll be doing near the end. Additionally, we'll call on the services of the `Tempfile` class for creating the temporary file.

You should immediately notice a similarity of construction when comparing Listing 5-4 to Listings 5-2 and 5-3. We are essentially wrapping a block operation (albeit with a single postoperation step) in another block-accepting method (ours).

The definition of `open_safely` is simpler than that of `File.open` because it is a specifically write-only method. As such, it takes only one argument, namely the `path` of the file to be written. We use a numeric `hash` of this `path` together with the name of the invoking application ($0) to construct a unique path for the temporary file. `Tempfile.open` takes this base name and adds the application's PID and a unique index to it, and this forms the complete temporary filename. An example of a path produced via this method would be `/tmp/filesift-736474449.5189.1`.

`Tempfile.open` creates this file read-writeable by the user running the script only (mode 600). Thus we `yield` the handle to this file to the block our method was passed. The calling script can write data to its heart's content and then, once it returns, we note the `result` (for the same reasons discussed previously in the context of Listing 5-3).

We also make a note of the path allocated by `Tempfile`. We have to get this from within the temporary file block—we don't necessarily know this in advance, as the index on the end of the filename can be anything from 0 up to 9.

With the file written and the result secure, all that remains is to move the temporary file over the top of the original. This is accomplished through one of the nice convenience methods of the `FileUtils` module—in this case, `FileUtils.move`. You should take a look at `ri FileUtils` to see a complete list of the rather handy set of methods provided by this module.

The more astute among you may be wondering what happened to the locking code. Didn't we still want that kind of protection? Remember that we are creating a brand-new file—nothing else will be reading from or writing to it because no other process should have the vaguest clue that it exists. Once the move has happened, the original file will actually hang around if any other processes have file handles to it—implying read safety on an albeit out-of-date copy of the file. In other words, since the moving of the file is atomic and it doesn't destroy any currently occurring access to the old file, we get concurrency protections automatically.

Using the Abstraction

Given the functionality provided by the code in Listing 5-4, it would be useful to consider an example of its use. In particular, because this file-safety approach compensates for the broadest spectrum of potential mishaps, it is the one I use almost all the time.

A recent example of this was the building of /etc/passwd on a Linux box. As you will doubtless be aware, this file contains the definition of the set of users on such a machine together with pertinent information such as their UID, home directory, and default shell.

In this case, I was presented with a challenge to build this file based on the contents of a CSV export from a central management system. I will not show the steps taken to parse to CSV file, as this subject is covered extensively in Chapter 7. Instead, we enter the fray in Listing 5-5 with an array called `users` that is populated with one hash per user. In turn, each hash has all the data needed to construct dynamic bits of the appropriate line in /etc/passwd.

Listing 5-5. *Safely Writing /etc/passwd*

```
require "safe_file"  # this will be the code from Listing 5-4

FIELDS = [:login, :password, :uid, :gid, :name, :homedir, :shell]

File.open_safely("/etc/passwd") do |passwd|
  users.each do |user|
    passwd.puts user.values_at(*FIELDS).join(":")
  end
end
```

As you can see in this listing, there is not a lot of work involved in actually creating the file. For each user, the defined set of field names (`FIELDS`) is used to pick out the relevant fields from the hash containing the user's information. Note the use of * to unpack the array object into a list of arguments to be passed to `Hash.values_at`. The array thus generated is joined together with semicolons in accordance with the format used by /etc/passwd.

As we would demand from any decent abstraction, all the hard work of ensuring the file is written safely and completely (or not at all) is handled by the `open_safely` method we wrote in Listing 5-4. This leaves us to concentrate on getting the format of the file right.

The Pen Is Mightier Than the Words

Now that a snug feeling of safety permeates the way we interact with files on disk, it's time to create some. Conceivably, there are thousands of different formats of file you might wish to create in myriad bizarre ways. You'll understand then that it is a continuing surprise to me that there is basically only one big choice when setting out to design your file-writing scripts. You're either a builder or a templater (which is almost certainly not a real word).

This section is intended to provide a flavor of the sorts of file creation approaches available in Ruby. It does not go into detail about any particular technology; rather, it presents a conceptual overview of the kinds of subtasks system administrators often find themselves doing when generating files.

Mob the Builder: Program-Driven File Creation

The first approach is usually typified by writing a lot more code than data. Every time you write a script that does something like `puts "fish-sticks: 8"`, you are engaging in an excruciatingly simple form of the builder pattern. You are telling your script not only what to write, but also exactly when to write it.

When Ruby-ists talk of builders, however, they rarely include such trivialities. The accolade of "proper builder library" tends to be reserved for honking great kitchen-sinks of modules bristling with classes that allow you to use tiny drops of code to create vast oceans of data.

Builders tend to exist for document formats designed to hold highly structured data. The API usually gives you a means to construct a version of the document in memory that uses formal object relationships and other niceties of the language to track the structure. Once the data has been built up in this manner, there is often one big, thrilling write command that will give you a text/binary dump of the file in the appropriate format to reproduce the given data structure.

Building XML

Probably the best-known builder tools are the various XML building libraries. The need to write XML is becoming more and more essential all the time, as everyone and his monkey decide that it is the one true way to exchange data (more on this in Chapter 7). Hence, making it easy for poor system administrators is essential. Listing 5-6 is a quick example using the well-known Builder library (`http://builder.rubyforge.org`) to produce a tiny, headless XHTML document.

Listing 5-6. *Building an XHTML Document*

```
require "builder"

builder = Builder::XmlMarkup.new
page = builder.html do |html|
```

```
  html.head { |head| head.title("Users") }
  html.body { |body| body.a("bob", "href" => "b1") }
end
```

This listing demonstrates the use of Ruby structural formalisms (mostly blocks) to specify the construction of an XML document. We start by initializing a builder object that is responsible for doing the actual building. Note that the initialization step can be used to do things like specify an output file handle and default indentation policy. See the documentation for more detail.

Thus initialized, the page is constructed as the output of a set of nestled Builder commands. Note the ability to refer to the names of elements (head, body) without special quoting. Builder is using the method_missing approach discussed in Chapter 4 to provide an on-demand domain-specific language whereby any unknown method name is treated as an instruction to open a new child XML element with that name.

Simple string content is added by providing a single argument to one of these method calls, as seen in head.title("Users"). Any properties to go inside the tag are specified using a hash after this initial string, as demonstrated in the next line where an href is specified for the link. This is akin to the flexible method signature approach also discussed in Chapter 4.

Given the code as written in Listing 5-6, the output will look like this:

```
<html><head><title>Users</title></head><body><a href="b1">bob</a></body></html>
```

Building Images

Perhaps a better example of the way in which a builder can be helpful in abstracting away the complexity of a genuinely inscrutable file format is seen with an early Ruby interface to the popular GD (www.boutell.com/gd/) library. This library provides a mechanism for translating individual drawing commands into a rasterized image, and an example of just this is shown in Listing 5-7.

Listing 5-7. *Using GD to Build a GIF*

```
require "GD"

image = GD::Image.new(100, 100)      # create an empty canvas, 100 pixels square
red = image.colorAllocate(255, 0, 0) # define the color red as RGB(255, 0, 0)
image.rectangle(25, 25, 75, 75, red) # draw a red square in a particular place
image.gif STDOUT                      # dump the GIF of this drawing to standard out
```

What I love about this approach to drawing is that I don't have to give a flying walnut about how the GIF format works in order to produce one. It's like playing with Logo (http://el. media.mit.edu/Logo-foundation/) all over again. This kind of abstraction is often one of the biggest advantages of Builder libraries. Much more detail on this subject can be found in Chapter 9.

Building Repetitive Text Files

The other place you find a little code to generate a lot of data is when generating files with a lot of repetition. For example, I recently had to build a file that mapped every IP address in a certain subnet to a particular time of day. I leave it as an exercise for the reader's paranoia to decide why one might require the script shown in Listing 5-8.

Listing 5-8. *Building a File with Repetitive, Programmatically Defined Contents*

```
seconds_per_ip = 60 * 60 * 24 / 254.0

File.open("config.txt", "w") do |f|
  1.upto(254) do |d|
    seconds = (d - 1) * seconds_per_ip
    hrs = seconds / (60 * 60)
    mins = (seconds / 60) % 60
    secs = seconds % 60
    f.puts "1.2.3.#{d} " + sprintf("%.2i:%.2i:%.2i", hrs, mins, secs)
  end
end
```

This listing shouldn't be too difficult to follow. It opens a file, and then iterates through the set of numbers from 1 to 254, using those numbers to determine both the IP address and an appropriate time of day. Note again that, because of the block structure of the `File.open` invocation, the script will do no work if the file fails to open for writing—exactly as we'd want.

Building/Changing Text Files Using a Policy

The final pertinent example is where a script essentially acts as a conversion tool, taking a set of structured data and wrangling it into a different format or updating some of the values as they go past. This sort of script usually does a few things a lot of times, implying repetition of operations rather than data. Take as an example the code in Listing 5-9 that I use to scan all of my C source files in a given directory and check that the copyright notices are up to date.

Listing 5-9. *Using Ruby As a Line Editor to Update Copyright Notices*

```
Dir["*.[c|h]"].each do |path|
    lines = IO.readlines(path)

    line_number, first_year = nil, nil
    lines.each_with_index do |line, i|
        next unless line =~ /Copyright (\d+)/
        line_number, first_year = i, $1.to_i
        break
    end

    this_year = Time.now.year
    expected_notice = if first_year and first_year < this_year
        "// Copyright #{first_year}-#{this_year} Andre Ben Hamou"
```

```
    else "// Copyright #{this_year} Andre Ben Hamou"
    end

    if line_number
        next if lines[line_number].chomp == expected_notice
        lines[line_number] = expected_notice
    else lines.unshift(expected_notice)
    end

    puts "Updating #{path.inspect}"
    File.open(path, "w") { |f| f.puts lines }
end
```

This is not the most elegant of scripts, but it took about two minutes to write and has proven invaluable ever since. Because it demonstrates a number of useful Ruby-isms, I'm going to take a few moments to explain it, beginning with the very useful `Dir` class.

Anyone familiar with the command line will know about *globbing* patterns. These are the standard means for selecting files on the basis of patterns within file paths. So the invocation on the first line retrieves every path matching `anything.c` or `anything.h` as an array we can iterate through.

■**Tip** Going deeper into the `Dir` invocation at the top of Listing 5-9, you might be tempted to think that the use of square brackets in this manner is hard-coded into the language somehow. In fact, this operator and many others that have to be special in other languages can be overridden in Ruby. Simply use a method definition of the form `def [](key)` or `def []=(key, value)`.

For each of the paths generated, we read every line of the corresponding file into an array. For such trivial access to files, particularly where you will be fiddling with the contents on a line-by-line basis, you'll find yourself enjoying the convenience of `IO.readlines` quite a bit.

The next task of this script is to scan through the source file looking for the copyright notice. Note the use of `each_with_index`, which is available to any class that includes the behavior from the rather useful `Enumerable` module. We use this method because we're going to need to remember what line the copyright notice was on for later.

Within the line-iterating block, we use the facility of being able to state conditionals after the block of code they refer to (go back and look if you don't believe me). This convention makes that line very easy to read—an inherent good. It also means less nesting of code, as we only do the rest of the block if the line matches the regular expression.

If a match is found, we assume that it will be the only one, note its position and first stated year, and then break out of our iteration. After all, there is no more scanning to be done. Why waste time doing so?

A rather useful property of the Ruby way of doing things is that blocks, procedures, and other logical groupings of code almost always return the value of the last expression evaluated within them. In the previous section, the methods had an explicit `return` at the end of them to make it obvious to the beginner what was being returned. Had I removed this keyword and simply left the variable in question by itself, the code would have been semantically identical.

It turns out that we can treat an `if-elsif-else-end` block like this as well. So rather than waste code by having to explicitly assign the correct string to `expected_notice` in both branches of the conditional, we can think about it more abstractly. Specifically, we can assign the value of the last evaluated expression in the conditional to the variable. Pretty neat.

Following on from this, the script now tests to see whether any copyright notice was found in the source file. If so, and it was correct, we jump to the next file and start again. Note that the `next` in this case refers to the most local iteration we are doing, which is the walk through the path names. If the line needs updating, we overwrite it in memory. If no copyright notice was found, we shove the correct notice at the top of the set of lines.

If we're still executing the block at this point, then we've done something that requires updating the file on disk. We do so and dump a quick note to that effect for the operator. Mission accomplished.

Some of you may be familiar with source control systems that use placeholders in the comments so that scripts can insert copyright and other information. In other words, the source file is basically still a source file, but it contains little pockets of metainformation designed to be substituted for actual information. Such schemes are the very essence of the second file-creation concept: *templates*.

ThundERbolts and Lightning: Template-Driven File Creation

Already in this book, we have gained much utility from the Ruby feature for inserting dynamic values into strings. This pattern of having a moderate amount of static data with a few dynamic bits is most conducive to the template approach. Think about this code snippet:

```
nouns = ["mind", "body", "soul", "independence", "shock", "fishcakes"]
puts "Randomness is a state of #{nouns[rand(nouns.size)]}."
```

Here we define a list of (in)appropriate nouns for our sentence and then, just before printing it out, we insert a random noun as the last word. For simple substitutions, this is a great way to build what is after all a dynamic string (since at least one character is built programmatically). This is the template pattern in action.

Web developers who have been held hostage by PHP will recognize one of its few genuine strengths is that it allows you to do something like this:

```
<p>Today we celebrate the first, glorious anniversary of <? amusing_event ?>.</p>
```

The ability to in-line small chunks of code into other data is what made PHP so popular for rapid web development (and rightly so). It should come as no surprise that very early on the Ruby community decided it needed an equivalent system. Thus *Embedded Ruby* (ERb for short) was born.

Anyone who has constructed a site in Rails will be eminently familiar with the use of ERb. Ruby code gets wrapped in either a `<% code_here %>`-style block if you need to perform some logical operation that has no direct output for the page or a `<%= code_here %>` to specifically insert the string value of the last evaluation in the code block. As an example, I might want the title of my web page to include the time it was rendered. The following snippet achieves this:

```
<head>
  <title>15 Ways to Slice a Mango - <%= Time.now %></title>
</head>
```

It occurred to me almost as soon as I saw this style of file creation that it could be enormously useful for configuration files. Take my message-of-the-day file sitting at /etc/motd. I would quite like this file to be updated periodically with some dynamic information, but I have an overall layout that I like and don't want to have to re-create in code. So I have an ERb version that looks like this:

```
*** Welcome to <%= `/bin/hostname -s` %> ***

There are <%= `/usr/bin/who`.split("\n").size %> active sessions as of➥
  <%= Time.now %>.

Remember - nothing unreal exists so if you see Santa in here, give him a wave.
```

ERb can be invoked within a script as part of a more complex procedure (try unpicking the Rails view system if you have a spare week), but in this case we just want to parse the entire file and do the ERb substitution. If your system has a build of Ruby, it will almost certainly have the erb script installed. Mine does and so, every quarter of an hour, it runs erb /etc/motd.erb > /etc/motd.

You might well imagine a huge configuration file like the one for the SSH daemon whereby we want to set up defaults for the vast majority of settings but need a couple to be dynamically generated. Or how about belly-dancer files, which have static tops and tails but dynamic middles? They always bring a smile to my face.

■Note The main reason I've ended up disliking PHP has very little to do with fundamental problems in the language and far more to do with emotional baggage. It's the prospect of having to debug yet another 650KB monolithic dino dung-ball of PHP that has been driving most of a web site for a few years that brings me out in a cold sweat. The reason such carbuncles exist is that PHP put an emphasis on in-lining, and then lots of happy-go-lucky web designers got so used to thinking in these terms they didn't stop to consider the point at which the use of templates by themselves becomes hopelessly unwieldy. Let their mistake be our education.

When Flat Files Fall Flat

In this chapter, we took a detailed look at how to deal with files safely, based on the argument that proficiency in handling files defensively is essential due to the pervasive nature of file manipulation within a system administrator's daily work. Such file operation safety has been achieved both via canonical file locking and the use of temporary files to prevent partial writes. We also saw how to add methods providing such functionality to the core Ruby File class as part of a convenient abstraction.

We engaged in a high-level discussion of the most common approaches to creating files via building and templating. The Builder library example hopefully provided a sense of how complex XML might be built with simple Ruby. In addition, we saw that templating can make for an extremely easy-to-maintain mechanism when dealing with documents whose contents have extensive static sections.

The remarkably powerful convention of file-based configuration allows you to place all kinds of weird and wonderful abstractions on top of the basic business of configuring your applications and daemons. However, there rapidly comes a point where data needs to exist independently of a single computer. We have concentrated on writing files, but where is the data coming from?

More and more, new versions of software seem to be moving away from basic text files to database-held configuration. Conceivably, this could be a problem as no interface can be as commonly accessible as a simple file. However, as long as the interfaces are still well understood and supported, this design choice can offer some real advantages in terms of speed and functionality. The next chapter will shine a spotlight on such storage choices as we move from flat files to a cloud of data.

CHAPTER 6

■ ■ ■

Object Storage and Retrieval

Data, data, everywhere, but not a byte to eat. How we store, organize, and access data can determine the future success of software systems and thus the organizations that rely on them so heavily. Choosing poorly in these respects can doom us to a long, agonizing information death as complexity, inefficiency, and competing constraints spiral out of control.

This chapter explores the myriad choices available for keeping your 1s and 0s safe, easy to work with, and able to scale up to meet demand. In particular, the focus is on approaches that force us to do as little thinking as possible about the actual mechanics of object storage. Very often we are constrained by the data storage choices made by others. Occasionally, *we* get to make such choices from day one.

Thus the solutions presented here are a selection of those we might consider when we need to store real objects and their associated properties (including child objects in the case of collections). The assumption will be that a "good" solution for these kinds of problems is one where we are not making low-level decisions about how our objects should be serialized. We can just think in terms of something similar to an `object.commit` operation and its corresponding `object.retrieve`.

The strategies for object storage broadly divide into two camps: local disk and network aware. Of course, the ability to do things like mount a remote file system and operate on its files blurs the boundaries between these two camps a little. Nonetheless, these two approaches tend to lend themselves naturally to particular classes of problem, and so each one gets a section in this chapter.

In the local disk section, I discuss three potential approaches to object storage: pure Ruby, `Marshal`, and `YAML`. For the network-aware contingent, I discuss the possibilities engendered through `memcached` and finish off with a fairly in-depth discussion on the vexed subject of SQL and `ActiveRecord`.

Local Disk Storage

Most system administration scripts that need storage begin their lives quite content to keep their data on the local disk. Many require no more than this over the entire course of their existence. This is bread-and-butter stuff.

Throughout this section I use a running example to give some grounding to the three different approaches discussed. In this example, we've been charged with implementing a script that will keep an eye on computer usage in a busy lab. This script will run periodically, checking to see how long a given user has been logged in. This information will then be committed to disk so that some other watchdog process can use it to decide whether or not to boot off the user.

Obviously, how we store this data is going to change between each subsection—providing some illustration of the differences between the solutions. A summary comparison of performance between the methods is at the end of the section.

Inspection Time

By now you will be more than familiar with the ability to invoke `some_object.inspect` to return a string representation of that object. You've likely used the shortcut `p some_object` to print out such inspection strings on many occasions. Let's think for a moment how that could be useful in storing data.

If the inspected form of an object is identical to that which you would write to create it in Ruby, we have an interesting possibility. Consider an ordinary array consisting of three usernames:

```
names = ["ne1", "4ab", "jfk"]
```

If I were to write `p names` on the next line of a script, the output would be as follows:

```
["ne1", "4ab", "jfk"]
```

Thus for an array of strings, the inspected form is identical to the Ruby needed to construct it. This is what we would expect, of course. It makes sense to have `Array.inspect` (and `String.inspect`) work this way for consistency's sake if nothing else.

Not everything can be expressed as an array of strings. What about something more complex:

```
scores = {:adam => 15, :brett => 12.2, :chris => [-5, 8.5]}
```

This little beauty is a hash using symbols as keys and an integer, a floating-point number, and an array of both of these as values. Let's try inspecting this with `p scores`:

```
{:adam => 15, :brett => 12.2, :chris => [-5, 8.5]}
```

Is there no limit to the usefulness of `inspect`? Well, let's try a much simpler example: `p Time.now`.

```
Mon Mar 26 15:31:02 +0100 2007
```

Self-evidently, if I were to write `the_time = Mon Mar 26 15:31:02 +0100 2007` in a script, I'd get a very loud complaint from the interpreter. For objects of class `Time`, the symmetry between the forms for instantiation and inspection is lost.

Before we proceed, then, it's important to identify which built-in classes do hold such symmetry. The list of common ones is short and rather obvious:

- `String`: `"hello"`
- `Symbol`: `:joust`
- `Integer`: `5` or `-2`
- `Float`: `3.8` or `-22.7`

- Array: `[1, 2, 3]`

- Hash: `{:a => "apple", :b => "banana"}`

There are a couple of others (like `Rational`), but you probably won't need them much. In any case, the point is that if you have an arbitrarily complex data structure, as long as it contains objects only of the listed classes and is not fraught with values that are inherently impossible to serialize (like Π), its inspected form will be a valid constructor for it.

Storage

From the previous discussion, it shouldn't be hard to see how easily we might store a highly structured object on disk. All we need to do is `inspect` it and write the resulting string to a file:

```
ug = {:users => some_array_of_hashes, :groups => likewise}
File.open_safely("/tmp/users_groups") { |f| f.puts ug.inspect }
```

Note the use of `File.open_safely`, which we built in the previous chapter. When dealing with the reading/writing of one file by multiple processes, as we will be in our example, the use of safe file operations is non-negotiable.

Speaking of our example, we'll write out the list of currently logged-in users together with how many minutes they've been logged in as a hash. For auditing purposes, the file path will contain a time component so that there is a distinct, recoverable set of data each time we run the check:

```
login_times = {"roger" => 17, "dodger" => 69, ...}
path = File.join("reports", Time.now.strftime("%Y%m%dT%H:%M:%S"))
File.open_safely(path) { |f| f.puts login_times.inspect }
```

If the methods used to construct the `path` are unfamiliar to you, I suggest looking at `ri File.join` and `ri Time.strftime`.

Retrieval

At this point, we have a file on disk that contains the pure Ruby needed to encode for our `login_times` data structure. Now we need to know how to read it back into memory. In order to do so, we want a method in Ruby that will take a string and run it as though it was part of the script.

`Kernel.eval` provides this highly useful behavior. Equipped with this method, recovery of our object could not be simpler. For each file created by our storage method, we just read the string in and evaluate it:

```
Dir["reports/*"].each do |path|
  login_times = eval(File.read(path))
  # do something with login_times
end
```

Pros and Cons

This pure Ruby approach to object storage is obviously quite convenient. The storage and retrieval go as fast as the inspection methods of the objects and the Ruby interpreter's own parser. In addition, the file produced will be readable by anyone who can understand (or quickly interpret) basic Ruby syntax.

This approach does have a couple of downsides, however. The contents of the file are basically being executed as though they comprised a first-class Ruby script. What's more, this is happening in the application context of our own script. Unless care is taken over permissions and data integrity, this is a potential security nightmare.

The other obvious problem is the limited (although admittedly still useful) range of classes that can be stored in this manner. The most obvious missing class in the case of our login example is `Time`. You can easily imagine wanting to track the session instantiation time for a particular user, but as you have already seen, `Time` is not symmetric under inspection.

What we need, then, is an approach that allows for more classes and that (if something goes wrong) leads to unreadable data rather than a compromised program.

Marshaling Your Thoughts

Ruby ships with a library that is able to convert collections of Ruby objects into a stream of bytes. The `Marshal` class provides both serialization and recovery of trees of objects, including those of classes you create yourself.

Almost all of the built-in classes "just work" when marshaled. The obvious exceptions to this rule are those classes it just wouldn't make sense to be able to serialize (bindings, procedure or method objects, instances of class `IO`, or singleton objects).

In addition, `Marshal` is quite clever about serializing classes it ostensibly knows nothing about. It accomplishes this by storing the name of the class of an object together with its attribute data, which covers the serialization needs of most simple classes.

Storage

If you were to guess the syntax for how to dump (serialize) a Ruby object with `Marshal`, you'd probably venture one of two possibilities: `some_object.dump` or `Marshal.dump(some_object)`. The first one is wrong (although not completely, as you will see). The second form is the right one, so in the context of our running example, we store the `users` and `groups` information like this:

```
ugt = {:users => some_array_of_hashes_including_times, :groups => likewise}
File.open_safely("/tmp/users_groups") { |f| f.puts Marshal.dump(ugt) }
```

Since marshaling is the more canonical approach to storing objects, `Marshal.dump` can take an additional argument of the `IO` object to write out to. Hence the second line of our code becomes slightly simpler:

```
File.open_safely("/tmp/users_groups") { |f| Marshal.dump(ugt, f) }
```

For completeness, I will just mention that a third argument can be supplied to `Marshal.dump`. This is an integer controlling how many levels deep to go in the object tree when serializing. The default value (-1) signifies limitless recursion.

Retrieval

Having seen how we store objects, it is not a particularly fiendish challenge to work out how we get them back again. Marshal.load is the ticket. This method takes one required and one optional argument. We'll start with the mandatory one first: the specification of the source data.

Just as there were two forms of dumping (returning a string or writing to a file), so too are there two forms of loading. Thus the first argument can be

- Any object that responds to to_s (which obviously includes strings)

- An IO object to read the marshaled data from

Since we will be retrieving objects from the disk in our example, it makes sense to use the second approach. Borrowing the code from the previous subsection, we can load up an array of reports in just one line:

```
Dir["reports/*"].map { |path| Marshal.load(File.open(path)) }
```

I referenced a potential second argument to Marshal.load. This parameter allows you to pass in a Proc object, which will be called for each object loaded, which can be useful if the objects need a bit of tweaking or indexing before use.

Customized Marshaling

During the guessing of the syntax for serialization, I mentioned that the form some_object.dump wasn't completely wrong. I also referred in the introduction to the fact that Marshal will have a pretty good stab at wrangling objects you've created even if they don't inherit from String or Array or something.

There are occasions, however, when you need to override the default behavior of Marshal. Perhaps objects of your class have a lot of cached data that could be recalculated at recovery rather than filling up the serialization stream. If you do need to customize the marshaling process, then there are two special methods you should implement: _dump and _load.

The instance method _dump will be invoked with one argument (the integer depth limit as previously discussed) and should return a String, which sufficiently encodes all of the information necessary to recover the object (and any children/referenced objects as appropriate given the depth limit).

The class method _load will be passed the dumped contents and should return an object of this class.

Pros and Cons

Marshaling is a good storage mechanism. It is roughly as fast as the pure Ruby approach (more on this later). It is flexible enough to handle just about any class you might throw at it while still being quite space efficient.

This efficiency does come with some strings attached, however. The format is not human readable unless you are doing at least geek factor 8. In fact, it's worse than this; you have to know something about the classes you're deserializing before you do so, or you might never be able to recover an object. At least with the pure Ruby approach, the classes are well understood and could be reconstructed without much difficulty.

Additionally, because the binary serialization strategy for the built-in classes might well change (and has been known to), the `Marshal` library places a version specifier at the front of any serialized stream. You can get more detail on this by reading `ri Marshal`, but suffice it to say that `Marshal` can occasionally be very sensitive to version changes in Ruby.

Having said all this, it is apparent that what's needed is a happy medium that is easy to parse with a good standard set of notations for common classes. It should be human readable but every bit as extensible as `Marshal` (following the same general usage pattern if possible). This is where YAML steps up to the plate.

YAML Ain't Markup Language

The intent of the YAML project (`www.yaml.org`) was to provide a simple and human-readable data storage format without sacrificing efficiency. Its data types also closely model those of the various common scripting languages, making it rather easy to implement in Ruby, Python, and Perl. Here's a sample:

```
---
john:
  male: true
  age: 22.3
andre:
  logins: 5
  last-login: 2006-04-15 20:50:43.394148 +01:00
```

What I was most struck by when I saw a YAML document for the first time was its brevity. In the same way that Ruby acts like executable metacode, YAML data feels like something I might jot down in a text editor if I were making quick notes.

It is a testament to a great piece of language design that I don't need to explain any of what's written in the sample for you to instantly see that it represents a hash of hashes or that it contains strings, an integer, a floating-point number, a Boolean value, and a timestamp.

Indeed, I often feel that XML documents, when compared with equivalent YAML files, demonstrate all the grace and calm reserve of a Pee-wee Herman chase scene (complete with rope swing, speedboat, sleigh, and man in a Godzilla costume).

Storage and Retrieval

Since the syntax for using YAML is basically identical to that of `Marshal` (and purposely so), I need only show the two relevant lines from our running example to demonstrate serialization:

```
File.open_safely("/tmp/users_groups") { |f| YAML.dump(ugt, f) }
```

and recovery:

```
Dir["reports/*"].map { |path| YAML.load(File.open(path)) }
```

The only real difference between YAML and `Marshal` with respect to these basic methods is that `YAML.dump` does not accept a recursion limit parameter. It should be noted as well that an alternate form for dumping objects exists. A quick look at `ri Object` will tell you that all objects have a `to_yaml` method, which does exactly what you think it does.

Customized YAMLing

Just like `Marshal`, YAML can do a pretty good job of serializing your custom classes, including collections (even coping with cyclic references). If you ask YAML to cope with a class for which there is no corresponding native data type, it uses a cute little construction to name the class for later recovery (i.e., just like `Marshal`, only with added cuteness). Imagine a `User` class like this:

```
class User
  def initialize(name, login)
    @name, @login = name, login
  end
end
```

If we were to instantiate one of these users and then ask YAML to dump it (`User.new("Andre Ben Hamou", "andre").to_yaml`), the resulting data would look like this:

```
--- !ruby/object:User
login: andre
name: Andre Ben Hamou
```

The simplest bit of customization you can achieve with YAML is specifying exactly which attributes are to be serialized/restored. This is accomplished by adding a `to_yaml_properties` instance method to your class:

```
class User
  def to_yaml_properties
    ["@login"]
  end
end
```

This modification ensures that only login names survive the serialization process. More substantial customization requires understanding of the YAML concept of domains together with a more in-depth appreciation of the serialization and recovery processes. This is beyond the scope of the chapter, so I encourage you to visit the YAML for Ruby site (`http://yaml4r.sourceforge.net`) for more detail.

Pros and Cons

YAML provides easily one of the "friendliest" serialization mechanisms available in Ruby. The output is eminently readable yet extremely flexible. It has enough built-in types that storing common/simple objects leads to output that is instantly recognizable and unambiguous. It is also supported in a wide range of languages (and has the extra bonus of being essentially a superset of JSON, `www.json.org`).

YAML's main disadvantage is that it is (currently) much slower than the other two approaches discussed in this section. Thus I always tend to err on the side of using YAML except where vast amounts of data are in play.

Benchmarking the Alternatives

We've seen pure Ruby, Marshal, and YAML all doing their thing. All of these methods offer (arguably slight) advantages over each other depending on one's emphasis. The one comparison we haven't yet made is that of performance.

In order to perform such a comparison, we need to be mindful of the restrictions placed upon us by the pure Ruby approach. Thus we need an example dataset that is composed of simple data types and is sufficiently large to give a meaningful sample time on modern hardware. This dataset also needs to have some structure so that it doesn't fall to a competition between reading a couple of paragraphs of text.

Let's benchmark the storage and retrieval of a hash where the keys are the first 25,000 words in the system dictionary and the values are the integer lengths of the corresponding keys. Listing 6-1 shows a script to do just this.

Listing 6-1. *Benchmarking the Storage Mechanisms*

```
require "benchmark"
require "yaml"

data = {}
IO.readlines("/usr/share/dict/words")[0..25000].each do |line|
  line.chomp!
  data[line] = line.size
end

Benchmark.bmbm do |b|
  serialised_data = nil
  b.report("rb_write") { serialised_data = data.inspect }
  b.report("rb_read") { eval(serialised_data) }

  b.report("ms_write") { serialised_data = Marshal.dump(data) }
  b.report("ms_read") { Marshal.load(serialised_data) }

  b.report("ym_write") { serialised_data = YAML.dump(data) }
  b.report("ym_read") { YAML.load(serialised_data) }
end
```

In this listing we grab the words from the dictionary and build the hash (data). We then invoke Benchmark.bmbm, which as you will remember from Chapter 3 performs the benchmark twice (a rehearsal followed by the main run). We then perform serializations and restorations for each storage strategy. The results, as shown in Listing 6-2, demonstrate the relative speeds of the storage mechanisms. As discussed, pure Ruby and Marshal are pretty much on par, while YAML is way behind (particularly for serialization).

Listing 6-2. *Pure Ruby and Marshal Running Laps Around YAML*

```
Rehearsal -------------------------------------------
rb_write   0.110000   0.020000   0.130000 (  0.138682)
rb_read    0.240000   0.020000   0.260000 (  0.299074)
ms_write   0.110000   0.000000   0.110000 (  0.133449)
ms_read    0.080000   0.010000   0.090000 (  0.095195)
ym_write   5.740000   0.160000   5.900000 (  6.493976)
ym_read    0.800000   0.040000   0.840000 (  0.934086)
------------------------------ total: 7.330000sec

              user     system     total       real
rb_write   0.110000   0.000000   0.110000 (  0.125638)
rb_read    0.120000   0.000000   0.120000 (  0.137981)
ms_write   0.110000   0.000000   0.110000 (  0.132280)
ms_read    0.090000   0.010000   0.100000 (  0.100199)
ym_write   5.930000   0.090000   6.020000 (  6.601733)
ym_read    0.400000   0.010000   0.410000 (  0.459951)
```

Network-Aware Storage

As systems develop and their reach increases, so too must the data that is drawn upon by the scripts that manage them. At some point there is a clear need to decouple this data from any one host and instead present it across the network in a consistent and reliable manner. In practice, there are two main approaches to choose from. The central question governing this choice concerns the lifetime of the data.

In the case of short-lived information (perhaps used to coordinate power consumption or system shutdowns), we really just need a cloud of data. There is no permanent record to be kept; no logs to keep safe. We simply have a large distributed process relying on a common state recorded in the cloud. To provide such a service, we will look to memcached.

If our data is long-lived and (perhaps more important) needs to be in a highly consistent state, then we need a network service providing fine-grained access to permanently stored data. This means a database and, for the purposes of this chapter, specifically points to an SQL database.

General Design Principals

I'm going to take a few lines to describe some of the things to be aware of when implementing network storage. The reason it's important to do so is that information stored in a remote/distributed fashion is often accessed by many different systems created by lots of creative and enthusiastic programmers who may never have even met.

Thus this subsection engages in a fairly high-level discussion of the considerations that can be important when venturing into the world of network-aware storage. If you are already familiar with concepts like system scaling, complexity, and basic database theory, then you should feel free to skip ahead.

Know Your Audience

It may seem like an obvious point, but it is imperative to know who/what is going to be interacting with your data, in what manner, and how often. Any nontrivial requirements are going to involve distributed access. Connections will be coming at your system from every which way, and it will be up to your chosen interface and storage mechanism to cope.

Get a sense for the range of complexity of operations. Any data store you use will allow you to structure that data in some way. However, some structures are more suited to simple object-style queries: "Give me the name and number of every person." Other queries might force you to read the data store completely multiple times and provide higher-order relationships: "Give me the name of every person who has at least one friend who is a member of the clergy." Consider whether your operations will be mostly reads, writes, or a mixture of both: "Set the imprisoned flag of every person who has at least one friend in the Communist party."

Get clients to be honest about the number of such operations they'd expect per minute or per hour. You will not be able to serve 20 million write queries a minute using YAML-marshaled object files on a single Mac Mini (no matter how much your manager wishes you could). At the same time, deploying a cluster of state-of-the-art servers with a massive distributed memory architecture to power an online survey of the members of the over-50s peanut butter appreciation society would be nothing short of the shock-and-awe approach to system deployment.

Not all of the third parties accessing your data may have been enlightened as to using Ruby, so they may find it difficult to adapt to new protocols quickly. For example, if you are planning to provide a CORBA interface, but none of the target programmers (being under 30 years of age) have even heard of it let alone know what it is, it may be too much of an uphill struggle to get them to adopt it.

To many businesses, availability is the number one concern. It doesn't matter if the apocalypse itself is going on three cubicles down, the data must remain accessible. It takes a lot of effort to design such a service, and trying to roll one from scratch yourself might occupy a great deal of the rest of your life. Thus it is important to choose technologies with well-understood mechanisms for peering and backup in environments that require them.

Above all, remind your colleagues and overlords that open standards exist for a reason. This is the same reason that train-track gauges and screw heads are standardized: to make our lives easier and allow more people to take advantage of common interfaces to add useful functionality (think screwdriver).

Databases

It's amazing to think that one of the highest paid jobs in the IT sector is that of a database administrator (DBA). As I understand it, their raison d'etre is to create a few database accounts every so often and massively slow down deployment of new data stores by arguing endlessly about relational schema design.

I must say that I have many good friends who are DBAs, and the ones who have ended up filling this role of IT's grouchy old men certainly didn't start out meaning to. It is all because of the pressure that comes with a centralized data-storage philosophy. If you hammer it into an administrator that he holds the keys to the golden city and that the slightest misstep that occurs within its walls is his ultimate responsibility, he is going to become understandably paranoid about every change and fastidious about formal design processes to the point of lunacy.

As administrators, we yearn for rapid deployment followed by a fast iteration process. For a lot of administrators, the moment they hit the word "database," they can almost smell the quagmire ahead. There seems to be this perception that databases are for people with nothing better to do. It takes way too much time to learn how to use them properly, so we'll just make do with a few flat files here and there and hope for the best.

As you might anticipate, I'm going to argue that it is the interface's fault. I don't mean SQL, which is brilliant (not to mention the only popular, mathematically complete programming language on earth). It is the business of shoehorning database interaction, transactional awareness, and multiuser logic into an existing script that seems so daunting. This process of wrangling things back and forth between variables in your code and data in some DB tables gets cumbersome very quickly. As you will see before this chapter is finished, when you have a language like Ruby to play with, all of the gruesomeness of this kind of task melts away.

At a more technological level, when most people think of databases they almost always picture something like MySQL, PostgreSQL, Oracle, and others. These are all relational databases that accept and process queries written in SQL. They are not the only type of database. There are a small number of object-oriented database management systems (DBMSs) available, of which a couple are open source. The community hasn't really embraced OO databases in a big way, preferring to rely on middleware for object-relational mapping. For this reason, I will not provide specific examples of their use.

That said, relational databases are an extremely popular way (some might say the de facto standard) for storing data in a canonical manner. Why is this? Modern databases provide particular features that are essential for a data store you wish to rely on. These features are summarized by the slightly worrying acronym ACID and have been pillars of database theory for some time now:

- *Atomicity*: Each modification either succeeds or fails (there can be no partial writes).

- *Consistency*: Any modification that would lead to a breach of some internal rule (such as a field value not exceeding 32) must fail in a manner that rolls back an entire transaction.

- *Isolation*: Each transaction should operate in a manner that means other transactions see a consistent state (transaction A shouldn't have to care that transaction B exists and may even be trying to operate in parallel on some of the same data as A).

- *Durability*: Once a transaction is committed, there should be nothing on earth short of complete annihilation that can cause it to be lost.

In addition to all of these, relational databases place an emphasis on both the relationship of logical entities in the data cloud and the accessibility of every atom of data, both for retrieval and query construction. This renders them a potent means for organizing huge volumes of structured information. Combine this with the fact that two of the most popular DBMSs are open source, provide tools for peering and backup, and offer bindings for myriad languages, and you begin to see why they are so widely used.

memcached: A Great Big Hash in the Sky

Many of the data structures we create on an informal basis are pretty flat. A person could be the collection of a name, an age, and a favorite color. When they aren't flat, we like to be able to use familiar programming conventions to model something belonging to something else. In Chapter 4, we got used to the idea of using hashes in method signatures to provide an informal data structure for passing in parameters. Hashes as structured buckets for data are something that users of just about any scripting language should be familiar with. As the data becomes more structured, it isn't uncommon to find hashes of hashes, hashes of arrays, arrays of hashes, and so forth. Listing 6-3 carries an example of this.

Listing 6-3. *Mixing Collection Classes to Create Structure*

```
zoo = { :tigers  => ["Ralph", "Michael"],
        :lions   => ["Missy", "Sherbert"],
        :donkeys => ["George", "Richard", "Tony", "John"] }

puts "There are #{zoo[:tigers].size} tigers in our zoo"
puts "The premier donkey is #{zoo[:donkeys].first}"
```

Of course, as our program grows in size, there comes a point where all this informality starts to catch up and we should move to proper classes for managing the data. However, this kind of construction will always be useful. Wouldn't it be nice if there were some sort of technology that allowed us to bundle up our objects and shove them into memory such that we could write the preceding sort of code but have the data reside in a network-aware cloud rather than our own little corner of RAM? Please rise for memcached (www.danga.com/memcached).

Originally created to speed up LiveJournal.com (which it did—astronomically), memcached implements a distributed object-caching system that is entirely memory based. It is not designed to replace a database as the ultimate storage location for your data, but rather to generalize the process of caching objects in memory. As you will see in the next section, once data comes out of a database it exists as some kind of object in your program. If you don't update that object before you next try to retrieve it, you can simply grab it out of this object cloud without all of the strain of re-executing SQL queries and performing relational-to-object mapping. This applies even if you happen to be in a different thread running on a different machine from the one that originally put the object in the cache.

Before we can use it, we need to get it running. I'm not going to provide detailed installation instructions, as the previously mentioned site does a far better job than I ever could and these instructions will vary from platform to platform. Once memcached is installed, it can be run as follows:

```
$ memcached -d -m 1024 -l 10.0.0.1 -p 11211
```

which starts memcached as a daemon using 1GB of available memory bound to 10.0.0.1:11211.

Currently, the speediest Ruby library for interoperating with memcached is memcache-client, which is available as a gem. As ever, see Chapter 10 for gem installation instructions. A detailed overview of this library (as well as several other rather cute ones) is available at http://dev.robotcoop.com. Let's have a play with it.

Connecting to the Service

Connecting to your running cache is achieved with MemCache.new. It takes a list of one or more servers and a set of global options like this:

```
cache_object = MemCache.new("localhost:11211", :readonly => true)
```

The server specification is of the form hostname:port or hostname:port:weight (where the weighting parameter allows your script to declare a greater affinity for one server or another).

The server(s) can also be specified with a list of `MemCache::Server` objects, about which you should refer to the documentation for further discussion.

The options hash may contain any of the following three parameters:

- `:namespace`: A string to prepend to all keys used (`nil` by default).

- `:readonly`: A `true` value causes cache writes to raise an error (`false` by default).

- `:multithread`: Cache access becomes thread safe via a mutex (`false` by default).

There is also the ability to change the number of seconds the library will wait before timing out via the `request_timeout` attribute. To set this timeout at ten seconds, for example, we would write

```
cache_object.request_timeout = 10
```

As already implied, it is possible to run multiple `memcache` servers in a cloud for added redundancy. Thus we might want to use a primary and some backup server at the same time, specifying that the primary should be used as a matter of preference. We could do so like this:

```
cache_object = MemCache.new("mem1.example.com:11211:2", "mem2.example.com:11211")
```

Note that for `mem2`, we don't bother to specify the weight explicitly as the default weight (1) is exactly what we want in this situation.

Using the Cloud

The object returned by `MemCache.new` acts just like a hash with a couple of extra features. Imagine I was storing a list of animals at our e-zoo. A simple round-trip of relevant data might look something like this:

```
zoo = MemCache.new("localhost:11211")
zoo[:donkeys] = ["George", "Richard", "Tony", "John"]
puts "The premier donkey is #{zoo[:donkeys].first}"
```

Do you notice how both the write and the read operations completely abstract the fact that the storage is no longer local RAM? It looks like a hash and acts like a hash, therefore it is a duck . . . erm . . . hash.

You may wonder how these objects are being stored (particularly after the discussion in the first half of this chapter). It turns out that the `memcache` API really just associates keys with buckets of data so that a flat representation of our objects is required. The `memcache-client` library simply `Marshal`s the objects committed to the cloud and then automatically un-`Marshal`s them on the way back. This behavior can be overridden, and I encourage you to read the documentation for more detail.

For efficiency (as well as partially satisfying the isolation and consistency portions of ACID) it is possible to request multiple keys simultaneously as one giant transaction. This is achieved via the suitably named `get_multi` method:

```
hash_of_values = zoo.get_multi(:donkeys, :antelope)
```

There is one other pair of methods that might be of occasional use. These methods allow you to `increment`/`decrement` the value associated with a key by an integer amount. The key must already exist, and its associated value will be treated as an integer irrespective of what it actually is (taking the value of 0 in any ambiguous cases). Obviously, it is invalid to call for a decrement to below a value of 0.

Using these methods, we could count the number of web page hits in a particular day. Within our web page controller, we would have a method to be run before each page is constructed:

```
def log_hit
  key = Date.today.strftime("hits-%Y%m%d")
  CACHE[key] = 0 unless CACHE[key]
  CACHE.incr(key, 1)
end
```

This method constructs a key based on today's date, ensures that key exists within the cloud, and then increments it to reflect the hit. This approach to monitoring web hits is useful as it can provide administrators with interesting load statistics on a daily (or other timely period) basis without leaving logs behind to be retrieved, processed, analyzed, and ignored.

(Auto)Removing Data

So far, we've used the hashlike getting and setting methods. If we were to use the more explicit cache_object.set, we would be granted an extra piece of functionality. The memcache protocol supports the notion that any particular key can be set to autoexpire after a given period of time. Thus we might use this system to maintain temporary session data, which should always disappear after an allotted amount of time:

```
sessions.set("andre", session_data, 3600)
```

With this code, after an hour my session would simply cease to be. Given that the whole point of memcache is to provide a cache, it makes sense that we would want to be able to specify the useful lifetimes of things that should (after all) be temporary in nature.

If you need to decouple the expiration process from the point of setting the key, but you still need a fire-and-forget mechanism, the delete method is your friend. Ordinarily, deletion operates immediately like this:

```
sessions.delete("andre")
```

However, delete accepts an extra parameter specifying a period of deferment before the deletion should take place:

```
sessions.delete("andre", 3600)
```

Other Activities

The library provides a few metafunctions that allow you to perform some basic monitoring of the general health of the data cloud. The most basic of these is a method called active?, which runs a check to ensure that an object is present on at least one of its designated servers:

```
raise "our parrot has joined the bleedin' choir invisible" unless parrot.active?
```

A more comprehensive set of statistics is available using the `stats` method. This method returns a hash containing an entry for every server associated with a given object. These statistics include byte limits, process information, uptime, and a plethora of other information.

There isn't much else to cover as, by its nature, the core `memcache` API is simple to understand, yet its implications can be profound. If you need true enterprise-grade performance and your data is largely throwaway, it is a real contender. However, a lot of your data will need to be stored for a more serious amount of time and will simultaneously mandate more solid adherence to the ACID principles. Yep—it's time to look at databases.

Databases

In this subsection, we will be discussing something of great import to many administrators. Databases (particularly the relational kind) are at the heart of so many back-end systems that it is vital to be at ease with the path of least resistance where their use is concerned.

We will first cover the more traditional way to (ab)use a database—the DBI approach. This will be eminently familiar to those with a Perl background, and it was where the Ruby community was before Rails came along.

The arrival of Rails changed everything in the field of Ruby and databases. Thus the main chunk of this subsection is devoted to the piece of Rails named `ActiveRecord`, which makes database usage easy and just a little bit fun.

Old-School Database Access: Raw SQL Queries and DBI

Just the thought of having to remind myself of this style of database access gives me a queasy feeling. I'm glad it doesn't do the same to the thousands of PHP programmers who code like this every day or we'd run out of vomit bags.

Back when relational databases were really starting to get popular, people had already pretty much stopped writing CGI programs in C and switched to Perl and PHP. Hence, there were bindings for both of these covering just about every SQL DBMS there was. Pretty soon, it became obvious that a common interface was needed so that programmers could worry less about which specific DBMS was being used. Thus the infamous Perl database independent interface (DBI; `http://dbi.perl.org`) module was born.

The idea was to create an abstraction with methods, variables, and conventions that were independent of the underlying database. You see, one DBMS might ship a language binding whereby the method for executing an SQL query on the server would be called `execute` and return some sort of structure. By contrast, another DBMS might call this method `exec` and return a plain old hash. Changing the DBMS was close to unthinkable once a lot of code had been written.

DBI was the answer to this problem in the Perl world. As for PHP, there was also a DBI implementation, but most novice coders (very nearly the universal set where PHP is concerned) seem to have settled upon the direct bindings from MySQL as a de facto standard. We'll use the abstraction that resulted from all of the hard work put in by the DBI team.

Ruby DBI is available from `http://ruby-dbi.rubyforge.org`, which also carries detailed installation instructions. In particular, DBI has the concept of DBDs, or modular bits of code that essentially map the abstracted method space of DBI to a given DBMS's calls. Ensure you enable the DBD appropriate to your current database setup. I'm going to assume this is MySQL.

As with most network libraries, we start by acquiring a *handle*—an object that gives us access to the database:

```
require "dbi"
dbh = DBI.connect("DBI:Mysql:test", "username", "password")
```

Perl users should feel quite at home at this point. The `connect` method specifies the DBMS handler and the DB name all in one and takes the appropriate access credentials. Now let's put some data into a `sweetmeats` table with Listing 6-4.

Listing 6-4. *Inserting Our Sweetmeats*

```
["fudge" => 12, "praline" => 32, "crispy-frog" => 1542].each do |name, stock|
   dbh.do("INSERT INTO sweetmeats (name, stock) VALUES (?, ?)", name, stock)
end
```

Clearly, this executes the given SQL query and does some safe value substitution from particular variables. This kind of substitution is essential in avoiding SQL injection attacks. Given that this has run, our `sweetmeats` table should now look like Table 6-1.

Table 6-1. *The Sweetmeats Table After the Initial INSERT Operation*

Name	Stock
fudge	12
praline	32
crispy-frog	1542

Next we'll retrieve and inspect some of this important data:

```
query = dbh.prepare("SELECT * FROM sweetmeats")
query.execute
p row while row=query.fetch
query.finish
```

Finally, we'll close the database connection with a `dbh.disconnect`.

The funny thing is, being Ruby enthusiasts, the people who re-created this library for Ruby quickly saw how to make it feel more easy-to-read and obvious than the approach it had been forced to take by the limitations of the Perl language. Remember `File`'s approach to handles is to encourage the use of blocks that only end up running if the handle is opened successfully? Here's what we can do with Ruby DBI:

```
DBI.connect("DBI:Mysql:test", "username", "password") do |dbh|
   # code from listing 6-4
   dbh.select_all("SELECT * FROM sweetmeats") { |row| p row }
end
```

With this more Rubylike approach, we don't have to care about the structure of the result of a query. We can merely treat it as a black box that implements an iterator.

Even though this is better from a readability perspective, it's still pretty noisy. What we actually want to do is say, "Here are three sweetmeats—shove them into the database, please" and "Give me all the sweetmeats." Instead, the majority of code here is either SQL to perform these very simple operations or the bookkeeping needed to support those queries—and this is a painfully simple example.

Of course, all this code to grab the relevant data and then instantiate objects based on that data belongs inside the objects themselves, encapsulated rather than saturation-bombed all over our code. What we need is a system that automatically maps between relational records on one hand and pure objects on the other.

Object-Relational Mapping with ActiveRecord

Rails is hugely popular and one of the main reasons for this is the suite of functionality provided by the `ActiveRecord` module. Even though it is almost always seen as part of the Rails framework, `ActiveRecord` is an entity unto itself and can be downloaded as a gem (see Chapter 10). Having said that, I will assume you have installed Rails in its entirety. The reason for this is that Rails projects are structured nicely in terms of configuration and convenience methods. Also, if you get stuck, there is a raft of documentation out there to help you, but it is written with the assumption that you are talking about a Rails project.

In order to explore the object-relational mapping (ORM) capabilities of `ActiveRecord`, I am going to invent a pet project. This project is skewed toward not needing any of the other parts of Rails so that we don't get distracted. You will not be serving up a web page at any point in this walkthrough.

The project brief is to design a system that will record changes in disk drive usage, taking snapshots every 15 minutes and placing the results in a database for later analysis. It should model the relationship between a host, its disks, and a timestamped disk space report.

Before we go any further, then, let's create a Rails project folder called `diskmon` with the following command (to be run in whatever directory is most appropriate to your setup):

```
$ rails diskmon
```

which will dump a flotilla of messages to the terminal confirming that various directories and files have been created and stowed away in their proper places.

The next step is to configure your database access. I'm assuming that you have a DBMS of some sort running, and this example is specifically geared toward MySQL. Within the `config` directory of your newly created project folder is a file named `database.yml`. This is where the access details for your DBMS are held. Assuming you have a database called `diskmon` and one called `diskmon_dev` (for production and development, respectively), then your file would look like Listing 6-5.

Listing 6-5. *Configuration of Database Access Details for ActiveRecord*

```
development:
  adapter: mysql
  database: diskmon_dev
  host: 10.20.30.40
  username: uname
  password: pwd
```

```
production:
  adapter: mysql
  database: diskmon
  host: 10.20.30.41
  username: uname
  password: pwd
```

Now that `ActiveRecord` knows what to connect to and how, it's time to think about schema design. In any database modeling, my first step is always to determine the various types of objects involved and how they relate. Fortunately the design brief spells this out explicitly. Hosts can have many disks and disks can have many reports (see Figure 6-1).

Figure 6-1. *The system's objects and their one-to-many relationships*

`ActiveRecord` provides a Ruby way to specify the schema of your database tables rather than keeping a collection of SQL files hanging around. This approach also allows for smooth migration between different versions of the schema (see the documentation for more details). Within the `diskmon` project we execute this:

```
$ script/generate migration InitialSchema
```

This creates a skeleton migration file located at `db/migrate/001_initial_schema.rb`. A quick inspection of this file will show you that it is just a class definition with two class methods (`up` and `down`). Unsurprisingly, these methods are meant to contain all the instructions for migrating up to this revision of the database schema (i.e., to version 1) and the corresponding tasks for rolling back down (i.e., to version 0, the empty schema). With that in mind, Listing 6-6 shows a sample migration file for our database.

Listing 6-6. *Initial Schema Definition for the Disk Monitoring Project*

```
class InitialSchema < ActiveRecord::Migration
  def self.up
    create_table :hosts do |t|
      t.column :name, :string
    end

    create_table :disks do |t|
      t.column :host_id, :integer
      t.column :dev_name, :string
      t.column :mnt_point, :string
      t.column :mb_available, :integer
    end
```

```
    create_table :reports do |t|
      t.column :disk_id, :integer
      t.column :created_at, :datetime
      t.column :mb_used, :integer
    end
  end

  def self.down
    drop_table :hosts
    drop_table :disks
    drop_table :reports
  end
end
```

I'm certain you will be familiar enough with database schema to understand the code in this listing without further comment, save for a quick note that since reports belong to a disk and disks belong to a host, the corresponding tables have to have foreign keys (`disk_id`, `host_id`) that point to records in the parent tables. On this basis, shouldn't we specify the creation of columns named `id` to give each record a table-unique number? Because this is the fundamental basis on which ORM is built, `ActiveRecord` automatically adds such a column to every table created.

In addition, the `created_at` column is "magic." That is to say that when a record is first created in that table, its `created_at` value will be set automatically by `ActiveRecord` to the then-current time. This is rather nice as it means we get timestamping for free.

Armed with this schema, we can create the database with a simple invocation of one of Rails' built-in tasks:

```
$ rake db:migrate
```

Remembering that the whole point of ORM is to make a relational database feel like a cloud of objects, we come to defining our classes formally in Listing 6-7 (which contains the code for three files named `host.rb`, `disk.rb`, and `report.rb` to be located in `app/models`).

Listing 6-7. *Class Definitions for the Disk Monitoring Project*

```
class Host < ActiveRecord::Base
  has_many :disks
end

class Disk < ActiveRecord::Base
  belongs_to :host
  has_many :reports
end

class Report < ActiveRecord::Base
  belongs_to :disk
end
```

There are three things to recognize about this code. First, all the classes inherit from the base `ActiveRecord` class, which is an abstract class that does all the heavy lifting. Second, notice the `has_many` and `belongs_to` directives, which are completely self-explanatory DSL macros (see Chapter 4) that add various methods to the classes (more on this in a moment).

Third, sit down before I tell you that Listing 6-7 is the entire amount of object/class definition code we need to write for this project. Don't believe me? In the project's `lib` directory, create the script (named `demo.rb`) as shown in Listing 6-8.

Listing 6-8. *A Quick Demonstration of the Functionality Acquired for Free from ActiveRecord*

```
host = Host.create(:name => "slarti")
disk = host.disks.create(:dev_name      => "/dev/disk1s1",
                         :mnt_point     => "/",
                         :mb_available => 80 * 1024)
disk.reports.create(:mb_used => 20 * 1024)
disk.reports.create(:mb_used => 25 * 1024)
```

This script creates a sample dataset (see Figure 6-2) and can be run with the following command:

```
$ script/runner "require 'demo'"
```

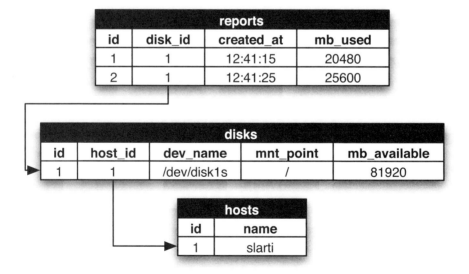

Figure 6-2. *Database contents after running the script from Listing 6-8*

Notice how we never had to specify table names or write a single chunk of SQL? Instead, we were able to write naturally readable code that concentrated on the data and structure rather than the DBMS bookkeeping. This is just the beginning, of course. The data isn't of much use to us if we can't get at it. Let's assume that we want to generate a list of disks for each host. Nothing could be simpler, as demonstrated in Listing 6-9.

Listing 6-9. *A Script to Produce a Report of Disk Deployment*

```
Host.find(:all).each do |host|
  puts "***#{host.name}***"
  puts host.disks.map do |disk|
    [disk.mnt_point, disk.dev_name, disk.mb_available].join("\t")
  end.join("\n")
end
```

This chunk of code first grabs every Host out of the database and then iterates through them. Notice how the subiteration through each host's set of disks simply treats disks as an array belonging to host. This is functionality provided by the has_many directive (as was the disks.create construction in Listing 6-8).

ActiveRecord provides a whole host of convenience macros like these. For example, suppose we decide that valid device names have to start with /dev/. We can add a regular expression check to that particular field like this:

```
class Disk
  # previous code
  validates_format_of :dev_name, :with => /^\/dev\//
end
```

With that precaution in place, should anyone try to create a new Disk or update an existing one with a nonconforming device name, such an operation would have no effect and the object itself would track the associated errors. Adding an exclamation point to the create statement as employed in Listing 6-8 will cause an exception to be raised in the event of validation problems.

ActiveRecord is way too fully featured to cover in detail in this section, but it has one more style of method that I wish to discuss, as it is yet another good example of metaprogramming in action. Imagine that we wish to calculate the average size of all the root hard disks in the database. In other words, we need to filter out any entries that do not pertain to an mnt_point of /. This would be easy enough in SQL, but ActiveRecord makes it even easier:

```
root_disks = Disk.find_all_by_mnt_point("/")
total_size = root_disks.inject { |sum, disk| sum + disk.mb_available }
puts "Average root disk size: #{total_size / root_disks.size}"
```

■**Tip** If you are performing numerical calculations, take a look at the ActiveRecord Calculations feature, which can provide this sort of functionality with much greater efficiency than the rather academic approach under discussion in this section.

Before diving into how that first line works, it's worth pointing out the use of inject, which is a really useful function that comes as part of the Enumerable module. Its most common use is for keeping running totals and other calculations of that sort. I encourage you to look at ri inject as you'll wonder how you lived without it once you start using it.

Now, how on earth did ActiveRecord manage to run a method called find_all_by_mnt_point? There is no way the Rails developers (smart though they are) were forward thinking enough to include exactly that method in anticipation of the day that we would need it. If you recall, in Chapter 4 we explored the use of Object.method_missing to create dynamic methods. Underneath, ActiveRecord implements the method_missing call and actually parses a command from our method call, dispatching a dynamic SQL finder built according to our specifications. Furthermore, this dynamic method is then stored for future use by the interpreter so that the parsing hit happens only once. This is one of the single greatest examples of the flexibility and customizability of Ruby providing a simpler and more intuitive way to interact with objects than is found in almost any other language.

Thinking about our Disk class, we're going to need some method that will extract the current usage for a particular disk. Given the structure of our database, that figure is defined as the mb_used value of the most recently created Report attached to a given Disk or nil if there are no such Reports yet attached. This is a prime candidate for a judicious bit of SQL, as demonstrated in Listing 6-10.

Listing 6-10. *Extending the Disk Class to Include a Current Usage Method*

```
class Disk
  # previous code

  def usage
    r = reports.find(:first, :order => "created_at DESC")
    r ? report.mb_used : nil
  end
end
```

In many ways, usage as defined in Listing 6-10 is a virtual field. Its value is calculated on the fly, but to the outside world it is just another parameter associated with a Disk. This sparks yet another idea. Let's make it so that when we want to add a new usage report we can do disk.usage = 15 * 1024 instead of disk.reports.create(:mb_used => 15 * 1024). I think you'll agree that the first form feels more natural and uncoupled from the details of the database structure than the second. The code for this method is in Listing 6-11.

Listing 6-11. *Adding a Setter to Complement the Getter Added in Listing 6-10*

```
class Disk
  # previous code

  def usage=(value)
    reports.create(:mb_used => value)
  end
end
```

Now that we have a proper set of accessor methods for usage, it is apparent that this approach will not scale particularly well. As discussed, to the outside world usage is just another field belonging to a Disk. The problem is that programmers might start to treat it as such, even though our implementation actually requires a separate SQL query every time it's called. We need to find a way to cache the value.

One alternative would be to create an instance variable that caches the value intelligently based on when it's updated/read. However, this would be available only to people using our library and is quite a bit of effort for what is, in the end, a simple integer. In particular, ActiveRecord already has intelligence for caching real field values and updating them in memory without having to reload them from the database. It does the work so we don't have to. Thus a better approach in our hypothetical scenario might be to add a column to the disks table.

Just as the schema was defined using an initial migration, we will create yet another to add our usage cache column. As before, we generate the skeleton migration with the following:

```
$ script/generate migration AddDiskUsageCache
```

As this is the second migration you've generated, you should end up with a file named 002_add_disk_usage_cache.rb. To this migration, we want to add a column to a particular table; the mechanics of this are shown in Listing 6-12.

Listing 6-12. *Migration for Adding a Disk Usage Cache*

```
class AddDiskUsageCache < ActiveRecord::Migration
  def self.up
    add_column :disks, :usage, :integer, :default => 0
    Disk.update_all("usage = 0")
  end

  def self.down
    remove_column :disks, :integer
  end
end
```

There are two items of interest in this listing. First, note the :default directive on the column definition. We could have used this in the original schema definition, but I thought I'd save it until now. If the underlying DBMS supports default values for columns, this directive will ensure that such values are set appropriately. Second, as setting this default doesn't help any existing records, we use another of ActiveRecord's convenience methods, update_all, to populate such entities. To execute this migration, once again run the command

```
$ rake db:migrate
```

As Orwell observed, the destruction of words is a beautiful thing, and in that vein it is now time to undo our handiwork from Listing 6-10. From now on, usage is a first-class field—there is nothing virtual about it. It will always contain the mb_used value of the most recent usage report. Thus the whole of our usage method can be erased, as ActiveRecord will provide it for us. The setter usage= is a different matter, however. This method needs to be modified as shown in Listing 6-13 so that, in addition to creating a new Report, it updates the cached value.

Listing 6-13. *Modifying the usage Setter to Support Caching*

```
class Disk
  # previous code

  def usage=(value)
    Disk.transaction(self) do
      reports.create(:mb_used => value)
      self.update_attribute(:usage, value)
    end
  end
end
```

Notice that we've wrapped the two operations (adding the Report and updating the cache field) in a transaction. This is for the obvious reason that we need to treat both operations as a single atomic whole. If the database crashes in between creating the Report and updating the cached value, it would be left in an inconsistent state. Thus the use of a transaction block forces the database to do both operations or neither.

You may be wondering why we passed self to the transaction command. ActiveRecord's transaction system allows for nominating objects that will be changing within the transaction so that the in-memory state of those objects can be rolled back in harmony with the database in the event of some failure.

Doubtless you will be unsurprised to discover that ActiveRecord has convenience methods for cached-value fields like usage, so we needn't even have written the paltry amount of code in Listing 6-13. Take a look at the documentation online for more details.

For completeness, we should probably finish the project so that it meets the design brief. Listing 6-14 contains the complete script to be located in an appropriate subfolder of the diskmon project folder (such as lib) and to be run by a cron job (or your platform's equivalent) every 15 minutes using the following:

```
$ script/runner "require 'collect_stats'"
```

Listing 6-14. *Complete Disk-Monitoring Script to Be Run Every 15 Minutes*

```
hostname = `/bin/hostname`
host = Host.find_or_create_by_name(hostname)

`/bin/df -lm`.each do |line|
  next unless line =~ /^(\/dev\/\S+)\s(.*?)$/

  dev_name = $1
  total, used, available, capacity, mnt_point = $2.split(" ")

  disk = host.disks.find_or_create_by_dev_name_and_mnt_point(dev_name, mnt_point)
  t = total.to_i
  disk.update_attribute(:mb_available, t) unless disk.mb_available == t

  disk.usage = used.to_i
each
```

Stepping through, we derive the hostname from the command tool of the same name—remember, the backticks mean "Run this command and give me the string of its standard out." Using the hostname, we try to match against an existing `Host` in the database or create a new one if none exists using the sublime `find_or_create_by_` construction.

Another in-place command grabs the disk data for the local machine (`-l` implies local volumes only; `-m` requests values in 1MB blocks). `String.each` as just used will iterate through the string, finding every substring separated by the default record separator, which is a UNIX line feed. We only execute the block for a particular line if it starts with a device name of the form `/dev/blah`.

From our regular expression match, the first bracketed term is the device name and the second bracketed term is a whitespace-separated list of values in a given order (which may be platform specific, so watch out). We split up the list of values and assign them to some appropriately named variables.

Just as we did when we found/created `host`, so too do we attempt to match against an existing `Disk` by device name and mount point, creating a new one if none such exists. In addition, we have allowed for the total size of the volume to change and so update the database if this is the case. Finally, we use our fantastic setter method to create a new usage report.

It's important to recognize that we could go on for an entire book's worth of chapters growing this example as a way to explore the vast, guilty pleasures of `ActiveRecord`. We could learn about how easy it is to adapt its idioms to match legacy databases or how to trap and observe the various methods of an `ActiveRecord` object. We could see how expressive its DSLs are for dealing with joins, sets, lists, and other tasty treats. We could even explore the wonders of transactions, aggregates, and single-table inheritance. Alas, we must move on.

Playing with the Big Boys

The motivation of this chapter was to inspire and guide your thinking when looking to deploy new solutions whereby decisions on data storage were yours to make. You've seen the possibilities for rapid storage and retrieval of objects on disk, whether it be via pure Ruby, `Marshal`, or `YAML`. As well, you played with a great big hash in the sky via `memcached` and saw how `ActiveRecord` makes database-backed object storage a breeze.

Sadly, the corporate world is one where only infrequently do we as administrators get the final say in choosing the way our objects will be stored. The enterprise is an immense information monster, sucking data in and spitting it back out again with equal brutality and chaos.

Years of accumulated, often contradictory data policies and forgotten technology deployments lead to the inevitable task of trying to cram the useful bits back together and present them in a decent manner. The following chapter will hopefully nudge you in the right direction as you embark on your enterprise information safari.

Working with Enterprise Data

Ruby's value in a corporate environment is not to be underestimated. In this chapter, we'll cover how to perform some of the most common parsing tasks found in daily enterprise life, manipulating delimited values and XML documents with ease. The second half of the chapter is devoted to the vital requirement of being able to interact with business information systems over LDAP, XML-RPC, and SOAP, and using the increasingly popular REST principals.

RUBY'S ROLE IN THE ENTERPRISE

The Ruby community has had its share of flame wars about the readiness of Ruby for the enterprise. I have said that I can think of no modern language that matches Ruby's versatility and expediency. That means that I'm always keen to see whether it can be applied to whatever I'm working on. However, the more intense Ruby-philes have circulated the impression that something as general as a high-level programming language can be deemed universally fit for every task of every business.

This kind of thinking is a natural by-product of the fervor that surrounds any engaged and enthusiastic community. The problem is that it leads to entirely the wrong kind of argument. When dealing with big business, touting a few days of productivity gains per development cycle is not enough. Corporations have long-standing ties with existing vendors and technologies that provide certain processes and guarantee certain standards are met (for better or worse).

Corporate culture often appears to have the unswerving momentum of a triceratops on a bobsled. The bigger and more important the corporate system under review, the more Sisyphean the task of selling Ruby as a viable alternative seems to be. Whatever the reason for this, poking big business with a stick because it seems slow to try new things is utterly pointless. If you want to address managerial concerns about the risks associated with a cool, new technology, then actions speak louder than words. It's been my experience that speeding up all those little jobs that never seem to get automated in the enterprise is a great place to get Ruby in under the radar. Start a revolution the way it's meant to start—from the bottom up.

Parsing Data

In the previous chapter, we discussed easy ways to commit and retrieve objects. There was little or no work associated with the data storage mechanism, as it was being handled for us transparently. Oftentimes in the enterprise, other people make choices about data formats so that we are not given the luxury of choosing the one that would present us with the least work.

On many of the occasions that my role as an administrator has veered toward that of a systems engineer, the projects concerned have invariably had some facet of data coercion at their core. I suspect this is a hallmark of being a code monkey in even a modestly sized organization—you repeatedly get asked to glue disparate systems/processes together by creating software that can intermediate between them. The obvious first step in such conversion operations is that of reading in the data.

There are a palpably obscene number of ways of formatting information out there, but mercifully I've found that most of the files I've ever been asked to convert or otherwise process have tended to be in the form of either delimited records (e.g., comma- or tab-separated values) or markup-encoded tree structures (e.g., XML and friends). This section discusses the parsing of both of these stalwarts.

Separation Is Such Sweet Sorrow: Delimited Values

Let's start with a quick reminiscence from Chapter 2. We saw that the pervasive nature of record-oriented processing as encountered by administrators lead Ruby to adopt Perl's convention of the -n and -p flags. Such records (and the fields they contain) tend to be separated by some common character/string. This concept is systematized through the presence of the global variables $/ and $;, which modify the default behavior of the pertinent string and file handling methods.

In Chapter 2 we wrote a command that I promised to expand upon later. Here it is again:

```
ruby -a -ne 'open("/tmp/user_#{$.}", "w") { |f| f.puts $F }' user_info
```

To begin, we need to examine the structure of the file user_info. I indicated that this was a classic whitespace-delimited, record-oriented file. Here's a snippet of user_info with all invisible characters explicitly marked:

```
Anthony [TAB] Burgess  [TAB] ab152 [TAB] 500MB [LF]
Marcus  [TAB] Aurelius [TAB] ma841 [TAB] 150MB [LF]
...
```

In parsing this data, we need know only three things:

- By what character/string records are separated ([LF] (ASCII: 10))

- Likewise for fields within those records ([TAB] (ASCII: 9))

- Whether it is safe to assume that these delimiters will not appear anywhere as actual data (*yes*—for this simple example, a tab or a line feed within a field would be considered illegal data)

The one-liner under discussion copes with these constraints with basically no direct specification of them. In fact it cheats a little. As stated in Chapter 2, -n wraps the to-be-executed code in a while gets ... end block. So a call is being made to Kernel.gets in order to grab the next line for processing until there are no lines left. Listing 7-1 explodes the one-liner into a more readable form.

Listing 7-1. *A More Digestible Yet No Less Magical Form of the One-Liner*

```
while gets
  $F = split
  open("/tmp/user_#{$.}", "w") { |f| f.puts $F }
end
```

The first thing to say is that, now that we're no longer in one-liner territory, there is way too much magic going on here. For Ruby-ists, maintaining code with this level of implicit behavior is akin to a man with a kumquat lodged in an unfortunate orifice—it does not sit well. It might be useful to analyze the implicit bits quickly to get a feel for what's going on. From there we can deduce how to make this script more concrete.

Retrieving Each Record (Line)

`Kernel.gets` retrieves the next line from each file specified in `ARGV` (or from standard in if no such files are specified). Thus this code has neither mention of the file to be opened nor logic to determine it explicitly. On each loop, the next line including the newline character is placed in a variable called `$_`.

You may wonder how `gets` knows that the record separator in `user_info` is a line feed. After all, due to the impressively tedious history of teletypes and other such mechanical savagery, there are at least three conventions for indicating a new line in a block of text. Without explicit specification, the default input record separator `$/` is used, and Ruby defines this to be the UNIX-style line ending: a line feed. Why, it's almost as though my example was contrived to take advantage of that fact.

This behavior is actually encoded using the default value of the only argument taken by `gets`. Thus it can be overridden by explicitly writing something like `gets("\r")` for old Macintosh text and `gets("\r\n")` for Windows text and things like HTTP headers. As to why the line feed (`"\n"`) is the default, I would have to be considerably less sober than I currently am to want to discuss that.

Retrieving Each Field

As discussed previously, the `-a` directive used in the one-liner autosplits each line of text into an array called `$F`. We reproduce that behavior in Listing 7-1 with a call to `split`. The fact that there is no indication of what is being split is another bit of magic. In this case, a quick check with `ri` confirms that `Kernel.split` is absolutely equivalent to `$_.split`. This relies on `$_` being populated with the data of concern—something we've already covered with `Kernel.gets`.

As with the enclosing lines, it's not obvious what criteria are being used to determine where each field begins and ends. I briefly mentioned `$;` in the introduction to this section and, sure enough, this global variable is to `Kernel.split` what `$/` is to `Kernel.gets`. By default, `$;` has the value `nil`, and when `String.split` is invoked with either `nil` or a single space as its argument it will split on all whitespace, ignoring any leading or contiguous runs of whitespace characters.

I mentioned that the code was cheating slightly and now it should be clearer why I said that. The definition of the format for `user_info` did not make space characters illegal in fields, so technically this splitting-on-all-whitespace approach is overly voracious and could lead to problems. These problems are almost guaranteed to be of the sort that don't bite you where it hurts until a year has passed and you've forgotten about everything you've written—which is precisely why the kind of implicit variable handling and parsing decisions embodied by the one-liner should not survive into production scripts.

Creating a Numbered File

The other thing that `Kernel.gets` accomplishes is the maintenance of a whole slew of state information about its operation. One of the bits of data that can be accessed is the current line number of the file being read. This variable is called `$.` and is used in Listing 7-1 to build the name of the file to be written to.

The first thing I wonder when I think about this proposition is how the Ruby interpreter will cope with input that isn't from a file. Will it still autonumber the lines for me (is `$.` just a counter incremented by `gets`)? Also, what happens when we move to a new file because more than one was specified on the command line? Does `$.` get reset? It wouldn't take much effort to find out, but separation of concern between how input is retrieved and how it is processed mandates that we shouldn't be using a naming mechanism open to such questions.

The Output Behavior

If you run the code on the sample data, you'll find that each numbered file in `/tmp` contains the field values from a particular user split onto multiple lines so that

```
Anthony [TAB] Burgess [TAB] ab152 [TAB] 500MB [LF]
```

becomes

```
Anthony [LF]
Burgess [LF]
ab152   [LF]
500MB   [LF]
```

Clearly, `Kernel.puts` is engaging in some implicit behavior. The code in Listing 7-1 asks for the output of something that isn't a string but rather an array (`$F`). We get a string anyway and one that is separated in a manner that reflects its origins as an array. `Kernel.puts` is really just `$stdout.puts`, which has some distinct behaviors. The one everyone knows is that if you give it a single string argument, that string gets dumped to the console and will get a newline on the end if it doesn't already have one.

Additionally, if `puts` is passed multiple arguments, each of these get printed out with a newline after it as though `puts` had been invoked once for each argument. This also applies to arrays that are passed as arguments; thus `puts([1, 2, 3], 4, [5, 6, 7])` yields each number by itself on a separate line as though they'd all been passed as individual parameters. Suffice it to say that this is handy in a one-liner but a little obscure when trying to deal with predictable text-file formats on a systematic basis.

The Explicit Version

In considering all of the previous facets, we are now ready to construct a less magical version of Listing 7-1 that doesn't use ethereal variables or arduous-to-remember behavior. That less magical version is Listing 7-2.

Listing 7-2. *An Explicit Version of Listing 7-1*

```
file_names = ARGV.select { |name| File.exist?(name) }
fail "no existing files were specified" if file_names.empty?

count = 0
files_names.each do |name|
  IO.readlines(name, "\n").each do |line|
    count += 1
    output = line.split("\t").join("\n")
    File.open("/tmp/user_#{count}", "w") { |f| f.puts output }
  end
end
```

The first thing to recognize is the addition of specific file-handling logic to support the multiple-file specification allowed for by Listing 7-1. We've used a simple selection procedure that tests for the presence of at least one file. Of course, more detailed checking could be performed depending on the sanity requirements of the script.

Following on from this file presence detection, we define a variable, count, that will be used to track the unique numbering of each file in /tmp. This gets around the problem we had with $. whereby it might not have coped with multiple input files.

For each name in our list, we read in all the lines as an array, splitting explicitly on a line-feed character. Note that reading all the lines into memory is usually (although not always) less efficient than reading them one by one as gets did. I'm adopting this approach anyway on the basis that the dataset is probably a few thousand rather than tens of thousands of lines, and the greater code clarity is worth the likely tiny performance hit. We could use IO.gets but then we'd have to open and deal with each file handle explicitly, leading to more code.

For each line of each file (which will include the line feed, remember), we increment the counter and build an output line based on the splitting operation. In the case of Listing 7-2, our split is now only based on the presence of the tab character as a delimiter. Note that the output is a string due to the explicit join operation, which allows us to define precisely how the output is to be built.

A reasonable criticism of this code might be that the split and join operations could be accomplished in one step by using String.tr to replace each instance of "\t" with "\n". I tend to resist such optimization because it belies the semantics (breaks the abstraction) of the job at hand. We are splitting a line into fields and then joining them back together. This process occupies one line only because the two operations are trivially simple. If we needed to update this script in the future to split and recombine conditionally (e.g., omitting or altering individual fields), it could be less obvious where and how to make such a change if we took the tr approach.

At the end, the output is dumped to a file in /tmp whose name is based on the current value of count. Note that the fact that we haven't chomped the line is not a problem because puts only appends a line feed if one is not already present at the end of the string being dumped.

CSVs vs. TSVs

Two delimited formats represent *some-made-up-number-over-95* percent of all the field/record style files you'll ever parse. These two formats are tab-delimited and comma-delimited. As we've seen, a lot can be accomplished with IO.readlines and String.split in parsing delimited files—especially with the use of regular expressions. Unfortunately, whereas tab-separated values (TSVs) are values separated by tabs (a concept almost painfully elegant in its simplicity), comma-separated values (CSVs) are a whole other ball game.

It all comes back to the third assumption made in parsing user_info. Namely, we took it as read that no delimiters could appear in field values. Thus it was always safe to assume that finding a tab meant that we'd found a field boundary. Somebody decided this was awfully limiting, and so the proper CSV standard was born.

CSV provides an escaping mechanism so that not only can commas appear in fields but also other things like newlines, which would break our line-reading logic as well as the naïve splitting operation. Thank goodness somebody shipped a library for handling CSV with Ruby. Listing 7-3 shows a simple example of its use.

Listing 7-3. *Some Batch Processing Using the CSV Library*

```
require "csv"

file_name = ARGV[0]
fail "no existing file specified" unless File.exist?(file_name)

records = []
CSV.open(file_name, "r") do |record|
  records << record.values_at(0, 1, 3)
  records << record.values_at(2, 4, 5)
end

# some global data-checking here, perhaps

CSV.open("#{file_name}.new", "w") do |output|
  records.each { |record| output << record }
end
```

Briefly, this listing includes the CSV library, checks for a supplied filename, and reads in each record from the file specified, breaking that record's six fields into two groups (by index) and shoving those groups onto the end of an array (records). The final operation is to write out a second CSV file that encodes the structure of that array.

The operation described by Listing 7-3 is largely incidental. The important point is that the CSV library abstracts away the nature of the data formatting and presents the records of fields as an array of arrays, which is a much nicer representation.

The bundled library used in Listing 7-3 is formally correct; it should parse any valid CSV file no matter how convoluted. However, it can be a little slow due to all the work it's doing and a fairly liberal approach to things likes row endings. A more recent alternative exists in the form of the FasterCSV gem, which is faster and works with every file I've ever thrown at it. As usual, more detail on gems can be found in Chapter 10.

XML

I refuse to open this section with the same old interminable regurgitation of the history of XML you get almost everywhere. Nobody cares about SGML or the theory of marking something up.

You know exactly what XML is or you probably wouldn't be reading this book. Additionally, unlike in the delimited values section, we are not going to be writing an XML parser, as I am fondly attached to the notion of having enough time left to do other things before I die.

XML is utterly ubiquitous. Somehow it has become the standard by which we are all supposed to exchange data. Why it became so popular is an interesting debate in itself (and rather outside the remit of this book). Suffice it to say that vast swaths of institutions now consider it the de facto standard for data storage and communication. One need only examine the number of business process–related patents that purely cover some tiny application of XML to convince oneself of its importance to corporations and indeed government agencies.

Thus, being familiar with the Ruby tools that exist to parse XML is essential for enterprise work. Now that we seem to have decided to be ruled, found, brought, and in-the-darkness-bound by this one format, it is imperative that we know how to wrestle with it in Ruby and have some chance of winning. Let's start with what you get in the box.

REXML

As you might expect, Ruby ships with an XML library as standard. It has a few nice features:

- It's implemented as pure Ruby so it is always as cross-platform as Ruby itself.

- It passes the Oasis nonvalidating XML test suite (a godsend in a world of malformed XML documents).

- It has a simple-to-use API.

- It has full XPath support.

Most important, as the author himself describes (`www.germane-software.com/software/rexml`), it was created in the spirit of good Ruby code everywhere in keeping the common cases simple and the uncommon ones possible. Let's dive right in with Listing 7-4, which grabs XML from a file and shoves it in memory.

Listing 7-4. *Parsing an XML Tree into Memory from a File*

```
require "rexml/document"

filename = ARGV[0]
fail "specify an existing XML file" unless filename and File.exists?(filename)

file = File.open(filename)
doc = REXML::Document.new(file)
file.close
# do something with doc
```

Listing 7-4 performs a complete tree parse of a valid XML file specified on the command line and creates an object of type `REXML::Document` to hold that tree. We'll see how to access the elements of the document in a few moments. The `REXML::Document` constructor is kind of cute in that it automatically does the right thing whether it is passed a file handle (as in Listing 7-4) or a string (as in Listing 7-5).

Listing 7-5. *As for Listing 7-4 But with a String As Input*

```
require "rexml/document"
include REXML

string = <<EOF
  <enctext encoding="to_i_32">
    <word>14476545457114006</word>
    <word>604</word>
    <word>16155</word>
    <word>764273404</word>
  </enctext>
EOF

doc = Document.new(string)
# do something with doc
```

Just as a reminder, the `include` directive places entities from the REXML namespace into the global namespace. The consequence of this in Listing 7-5 is that we do not need to fuse the somewhat ungainly `REXML::` to the front of the various items we'll be dealing with. Note also in this listing is an example of the string block (*heredoc*) syntax, whereby a block delimiter (`EOF`) is defined at the beginning and the consequent string deemed to be everything up to the point where that delimiter appears by itself at the start of a line.

Having parsed the XML, we are left with a document object (`doc`) that has various methods allowing for its exploration. The one you'll likely use most often is an XPath-based iteration as in the following snippet, which continues on from Listing 7-5:

```
doc.elements.each("*/word") { |element| puts element.text }
```

Rather unsurprisingly, this bit of code iterates through each `word` element and dumps the text out to the console. What about determining the encoding mechanism for our document?

```
encoding = doc.root.attributes["encoding"]
```

Notice that we are able to specify the root node of the XML tree (in this case the `enctext` node) as well as treat its attributes as an ordinary hash. If we wanted only the first `word`, we could use this shortcut:

```
puts doc.elements["*/word"].text
```

which performs the same XPath search as before but returns only the first result. It is a fairly obvious point but it is worth stressing that an unsuccessful search of this kind would return `nil`—something to be aware of when writing code that might have to cope with such an eventuality:

```
first_word = doc.elements["*/word"]
puts first_word.text if first_word
```

Another subtlety to be aware of is the need for specifically invoking the `text` method of an element. The standard `to_s` method of an element produces the XML necessary to encode it so that the following cases are different:

```
puts doc.elements["*/word"]      # gives: <word>14476545457114006</word>
puts doc.elements["*/word"].text # gives: 14476545457114006
```

Elements can also be accessed based on their absolute position relative to their siblings. This approach has always seemed rather fragile to me so I've used it only when I've had no other choice (i.e., depressingly often):

```
puts doc.root.elements[1].text
```

It's important to note that such numbering starts from 1 rather than 0. The XPath standard defines element relationships in this way, so REXML wisely keeps the numbering scheme consistent whether searching or referencing.

There are lots of other features that are nice to have in certain cases, but I could fill the rest of the chapter with them unless we move on now. You can explore these features more fully by referring to the API documentation at the REXML website. Also, I will refrain from discussing how to construct an XML document using REXML as this section is purely about parsing and, in any case, the approach you'd almost always use is really very simple (basically `element.add_element(name, attribute_hash)`).

The Streaming Approach

For improved performance (particularly in large and complex documents) it is possible to use a more stream-oriented callback technique. This approach renders tools like XPath unavailable for reasons that will become obvious.

Under such a scheme, we ask REXML to parse the document bit by bit and pass each item to the relevant method of an object we supply. Listing 7-6 contains a simple example employing this process.

Listing 7-6. *A Simple Streaming Class in Action*

```ruby
require "rexml/document"
require "rexml/streamlistener"
include REXML

class Streamer
  include StreamListener

  def tag_start(name, attributes)
    puts "[start] #{name}: #{attributes.inspect}"
  end

  def tag_end(name)
    puts "[end] #{name}"
  end

  def text(string)
    p string
  end
end
```

```
# assume the contents of 'string' are as for Listing 7-5
streamer = Streamer.new
Document.parse_stream(string, streamer)
```

The delegate object in this listing is one of a class we define called Streamer. It implements two out of a number of possible callback methods that are invoked by REXML's streaming API. REXML::StreamListener, which we include in our class, is a template module containing every method that could be called under these conditions. It basically provides do-nothing stubs for our class so that we don't get a method_missing error the first time the parser encounters something that isn't either a start or an end tag (i.e., a text field or a document type definition). More detail on all the other methods you might want to trap for can again be found in the REXML documentation.

With the class defined, we then simply instantiate an object from it that is then passed to REXML::Document.parse_stream along with the source XML. As before, this source can be a file handle or a plain old string. Running Listing 7-6 (with the definition of string properly filled in) gives output that looks like Listing 7-7.

Listing 7-7. *Output from Running Listing 7-6*

```
"     "
[start] enctext: {"encoding"=>"to_i_32"}
"\n\t\t"
[start] word: {}
"14476545457114006"
[end] word
"\n\t\t"
[start] word: {}
"604"
[end] word
"\n\t\t"
[start] word: {}
"16155"
[end] word
"\n\t\t"
[start] word: {}
"764273404"
[end] word
"\n\t"
[end] enctext
"\n"
```

As you can see, the streaming parser is running the methods we defined in Listing 7-6 and we're getting output just as we specified. What should be immediately apparent is the fact that text areas seem to be anything not inside a tag (that isn't quite true, but it will hold for our purposes). When parsing actual data, it's important to be aware of all the useless whitespace that can and does float around inside XML documents.

When parsing XML documents to create data structures in memory, using a streaming approach necessitates maintaining some sort of state. Which objects are responsible for this is entirely a matter of project-specific design. As a general rule, however, the principle of maximum laziness should be ever present when making such decisions. As you'll see in the next section, built-in classes often have everything we need.

Taking the PList

We're going to create a parser for a now very common XML format: the property list. Of course, I say "common" because I happen upon them regularly as I skate happily through an Apple-dominated working week. They can be found doing a number of jobs on quite a few platforms, but overwhelmingly they flourish as the storage format for Apple's system-managed preference files.

The property list (PList) format is actually quite good for generalized storage of primitive data types (integers, floating-point numbers, strings, arrays, hashes, dates, and Booleans). What's nice is that Ruby has every one of these data types accounted for as a class, which makes this example reasonably simple to follow.

To start with, Listing 7-8 is a copy of something in my home folder called `com.apple.desktop.plist` that I suspect is responsible for the nice picture of Saturn on my desktop.

Listing 7-8. *A Copy of a PList File*

```
<?xml version="1.0" encoding="UTF-8"?>
<!DOCTYPE plist PUBLIC "-//Apple Computer//DTD PLIST 1.0//EN"➥
  "http://www.apple.com/DTDs/PropertyList-1.0.dtd">
<plist version="1.0">
<dict>
  <key>Background</key>
  <dict>
    <key>default</key>
    <dict>
      <key>BackgroundColor</key>
      <array>
        <real>0.0</real>
        <real>0.0</real>
        <real>0.0</real>
      </array>
      <key>Change</key>
      <string>Never</string>
      <key>ChangePath</key>
      <string>/Users/andre/Pictures/Desktop Pictures</string>
      <key>ChooseFolderPath</key>
      <string>/Users/andre/Pictures/Desktop Pictures</string>
      <key>CollectionString</key>
      <string>Desktop Pictures</string>
      <key>ImageFileAlias</key>
      <data>
      AAAAAADiAAMAAAAAv1gJBQAASCsAAAAAAgQjQBUBBcAAMG6p54A
```

```
            AAAACSD//lBOR2ZHSo9O/////wABABAACBCNAAXUOgAF1JwAAGuF
            AA4AJgASAFMAYQBOAHUAcgBuACOAQwBhAHMAcwBpAG4AaQAuAHAA
            bgBnAA8AGgAMAE0AYQBjAGkAbgBOAG8AcwBoACAASABEABIAOFVz
            ZXJzL2FuZHJlL1BpY3R1cmVzLORlc2tOb3AgUGljdHVyZXMvU2FO
            dXJuLUNhc3NpbmkucG5nABMAAS8AABUAAgAM//8AAA==
```
```
         </data>
         <key>ImageFilePath</key>
         <string>/Users/andre/Pictures/Desktop Pictures/Saturn-Cassini.png</string>
         <key>Placement</key>
         <string>Centered</string>
         <key>TimerPopUpTag</key>
         <integer>6</integer>
      </dict>
   </dict>
</dict>
</plist>
```

What is evident from this listing is how the various data primitives are represented. The global structure is that of a hash (more properly a `dictionary`). Each key-value pair within the hash exists as a pair of tagged entities, where the first is always a `key` and the second is a simple data type such as `array`. The array appears to be a simple ordered set of tagged objects (again of primitive data types). That covers the structured data and every other type is flat in that it cannot contain discrete child objects.

Taken together, this should be enough information to create a broadly correct parser that will take in a PList and yield a hash full of the pertinent Ruby objects. We'll use the streaming-parser method as it's much more efficient for this kind of parse-a-whole-file job. This does mean that we need to consider how to maintain state as we go. Thinking about it, there are really only three callback methods we need to implement, and these are exactly those we employed in Listing 7-8: start tags, end tags, and the text they contain. Hence the skeleton class definition will look like Listing 7-9.

Listing 7-9. *A Skeleton PList Parser*

```
require "rexml/document"
require "rexml/streamlistener"

class PListParser
  include REXML::StreamListener

  def initialize
    # declare initial state variables
  end

  def tag_start(name, attributes)
    # handle a start tag
  end
```

```
  def tag_end(name)
    # handle an end tag
  end

  def text(string)
    # handle some text
  end
end
```

The first thing to think about is that we'll need to get some sort of output from this process—implying that the parser object needs to maintain a variable holding the parsed tree. Since it will be the root of the tree, we'll call it @root. One important property of the object referred to by @root is that it must be a collection (an array or a hash), as the preference file could never contain more than one value otherwise. Enforcing this constraint will provide some useful, basic sanity checking.

On my first mental pass through this exercise I supposed that all of the object creation was going to occur in tag_start, and then it struck me that (apart from array and dict tags) the contents of the object are not known until the subsequent text data is fed in. Hence, with the exception of the collection classes, the process of instantiating flat objects like integers is a two-stage aim-and-fire process. The aiming is done by tag_start, which somehow has to note the type that's coming up next. The firing is then done from within text, using the type information collected in tag_start.

Note that, in theory, we could actually create the object in tag_start and give it a 0 value, awaiting the text logic to fill that value in, but that just means extra work for the interpreter. Hence, we will maintain a state variable that tracks the type of thing that is about to be read (or is nil if we are not parsing a flat object). This variable will be called @to_read.

The only other piece of information that might have a bearing on how we react to each callback would be the version number of the PList format. As you can see in Listing 7-8, this version number is given as an attribute of the plist tag. Conceivably, future versions of the format might introduce new data types or even modified structural semantics, so it is probably worth keeping track of the version number. Our complete initialize function is shown in Listing 7-10.

Listing 7-10. *The Completed Initializer for the PListParser Class*

```
def initialize
  @to_read = nil
  @root = nil
  @version = 1.0
end
```

We've taken the liberty of assuming that, absent any information to the contrary, the PList being parsed is of version 1.0 (which is the prevalent current version). If we wanted to be stricter, we could set @version to nil and then fail unless it had been set correctly by a plist tag before any other tags or text were encountered.

It should be apparent that @root is useless if it remains forever stuck inside the parser object with no means for its access. Thus we'll also shove the following accessor macro into the top level of the class definition:

```
class PListParser
  ...
  attr_reader :root
  ...
end
```

Looking at Listing 7-8, a well-formed PList will have `plist` tags at the top and bottom. Aside from this, all other tags encode data and fall into the two camps previously discussed: collections and flat data, or what might be referred to as vectors and scalars by Perl users.

In designing the code for the `tag_start` method, we can see that we will be doing one of four things:

- Reading `@version` out of the `plist` tag

- Adding a hash or an array to the current parent object in response to a `dict` or `array` tag

- Priming the parser to read one of the flat data types in response to a `data`, `integer`, `key`, `real`, or `string` tag (which are the only other tags we know about from Listing 7-8)

- Whining very loudly if we encounter any other tag

This leads to the implementation shown in Listing 7-11.

Listing 7-11. *The Completed Open Tag Callback Method for PListParser*

```
def tag_start(name, attributes)
  case name
    when "plist" then @version = attributes["version"]

    when "array" then add_object(PListArray.new)
    when "dict" then add_object(PListHash.new)

    when "data", "integer", "key", "real", "string" then @to_read = name

    else raise "unknown tag: #{name}"
  end
end
```

You probably spotted the sneaky deployment of `add_object`. We haven't defined such a method yet, but the need for it should be pretty obvious. We know, both in `tag_start` and in whatever we end up writing for the `text` method, that there will be an eventual need to add a new object to the tree. Given that this occurs in multiple places and will not be trivial, it needs to be abstracted away.

This brings us to a discussion of how we will maintain context as the PList moves up and down the tree. Adding something to an array is trivial, but what about determining the array's parent collection? We could try and maintain some list of parent-child relationships, but there is an easier way: subclass `Array` and `Hash`. This is something you might have guessed at given the presence of `PListArray` and `PListHash` in Listing 7-11.

By adding a `@parent` variable to these classes, they can keep track of what object (if any) contains them. In turn, we will be able to use this variable to navigate back up the tree in an obvious manner. We needn't stop there, however.

The way to add an item to the end of an array is `Array.push` or its synonym `Array.<<`. The method for adding an object to a hash is `Hash.[]=`. These are very different invocations for obvious reasons. What's interesting about the PList parsing process is that, within a `dict`, we get the key a couple of steps before the value. In other words, the value is parsed in the context of a previously read key.

We could modify our hash subclass to have some notion of the key to use when the next object is added. With such an approach, the mechanism for adding an item to the hash would become the equivalent of a simple `push` as long as the key had already been set. With this in mind, we could standardize the API for adding objects to either collection.

With all this reasoning applied, our subclasses look like those in Listing 7-12.

Listing 7-12. *Custom Array and Hash Classes to Standardize Tree-Parsing Operations*

```
class PListArray < Array
  attr_accessor :parent

  alias :add_object :push
end

class PListHash < Hash
  attr_accessor :next_key, :parent

  def add_object(object)
    raise "no key set" unless @next_key
    self[@next_key] = object
    @next_key = nil
  end
end
```

Now that both classes have an `add_object` method, `PListParser.add_object` should be simpler. Note the way that `@next_key` is handled. It guarantees that each specified key gets used only once and that an exception will be raised if the whole key-value-key-value rhythm is broken for some reason.

With theses subclasses in place, it is now possible to see our way through to the mechanism by which current tree position is tracked. There are three possible motions within the tree:

- *Move down into a new collection*: `tag_start("array")` or `tag_start("dict")`

- *Remain at the current level*: `tag_end(...)` when `@to_read` is primed

- *Move back up to the parent collection*: `tag_end(...)` when `@to_read` is not primed

Put more succinctly, we only ever move down the tree when a new collection is specified. We only ever move up when we reach an end tag and the state of `@to_read` indicates that we weren't just reading a flat value.

Because of the presence of @parent in our custom collection classes, we can use @root to track the current tree position. Thus PListParser.add_object will override @root if the object being added is a collection and tag_end will set @root to its own parent (if it has one). Hence @root will end up pointing to the root collection if the PList is well formed. We'll start with tag_end in Listing 7-13.

Listing 7-13. *The Completed Close Tag Callback Method for PListParser*

```
def tag_end(name)
  if @to_read then @to_read = nil
  else @root = @root.parent || @root
  end
end
```

This method could explicitly check that the tag name was one of the flat data types in the case of @to_read not being nil and vice versa. Such checks would make the method less terse but equally more able to identify badly formed documents—increasing its usefulness in the long term. It is with a sense of levity that I have opted for brevity over longevity.

Let's jump straight from here to the implementation of PListParser.add_object in Listing 7-14, which completes the tree manipulation logic.

Listing 7-14. *The Abstracted Object-Adding Method for PListParser*

```
private
def add_object(object)
  @root.add_object(object) if @root
  if object.is_a?(Array) or object.is_a?(Hash)
    object.parent = @root
    @root = object
  end
end
```

Since this add_object method is strictly for use during parsing and makes no sense outside that particular occupation, we have made it private. Implemented like this, it has a couple of interesting behavioral side effects. If a PList had a flat data value at the top level, it would be ignored (something we discussed earlier). In addition, note how the collection classes are handled in such a way that @root is able to track the current position in the tree for future objects (also something we've already discussed).

You might wonder why I chose to write object.is_a?(Array) rather than object.is_a? (PListArray) and similarly for hashes. Either would do (since is_a? returns true when handed a superclass) but I wanted to emphasize that the outside world can treat these objects as though they were the standard collection classes shipped with Ruby—an essential requirement of our design.

All that remains is to implement the text method, which will be responsible for the actual parsing of values. Remember that this method will add an object to the tree in all cases except for that of a key. In this case, it instead assumes that the current collection is a hash and sets the next_key value of that hash. Thus we are left with Listing 7-15.

Listing 7-15. *The Completed Text Value Callback Method for PListParser*

```
def text(string)
  return unless @to_read

  if @to_read == "key"
    raise "cannot use key as not within hash" unless @root.is_a?(Hash)
    @root.next_key = string
    return
  end

  object = case @to_read
    when "data" then string.strip
    when "integer" then string.to_i
    when "real" then string.to_f
    when "string" then string
  end

  add_object(object)
end
```

The first thing to note in this listing is the immediate `return` from `text` when `@to_read` isn't primed with a type to be read. The motivation for such behavior is pure cynicism. We will assume that any amount of junk/whitespace might creep into an XML document where it shouldn't be (e.g., outside a tag pair). Thus if such detritus exists, it is ignored completely.

As stated, the handler for `key` data insists that it can only operate if the current tree position is within a hash. For all other known types, the string is coerced appropriately. Once again, we've used the remarkably useful syntax of `variable = some_block`, making the code very easy to follow.

Where the `data` type is concerned, it was important to decide how much work to do in the parser. The text from Listing 7-8 would seem to imply that binary data streams are stored in PLists as some sort of base-64 encoded string (doubtless to make them ASCII safe). That means that leading and trailing whitespace are not significant and we can safely `strip` them.

The stripping is not particularly costly as operations go and it means that just the encoded data ends up stored in our tree. However, we could go further. Why not perform the decode operation in the parser so that clients using our library are saved the bother?

This is an issue of scale. We have no idea how many such streams will be in the PList being parsed or their total size. We also have no clue which ones will be of interest to the client application, if any. Thus we deploy the awesome power of laziness and let clients specifically decode only the ones they care about.

Listing 7-15 completes the class with one minor quibble. We were very good in Listing 7-9 in not polluting the namespace of our client script through a global `include REXML` statement. This is not just a question of good manners, however. The whole point of building this parser class in the first place was to abstract away the XML nature of the PList so that client applications could concentrate on the data.

As it stands, using this class would involve something like this:

```
parser = PListParser.new
REXML::Document.parse_stream(File.open("com.apple.desktop.plist"), parser)
root = parser.root
```

In the spirit of complete abstraction, let's add a class method as Listing 7-16 that takes in the XML string or file handle and does these three lines internally, returning the root.

Listing 7-16. *A Convenience Class Method for One-Step Parsing*

```
def self.parse(source)
  parser = new
  REXML::Document.parse_stream(source, parser)
  parser.root
end
```

Listing 7-16 leaves us able to parse a PList like this:

```
root = PListParser.parse(File.open("com.apple.desktop.plist"))
```

Alternative Parsing Libraries

In order to conclude this section on XML parsing, I just wanted to mention a couple of alternative XML libraries that each improve on REXML in particular ways but are not bundled with Ruby as standard (yet). They are both available as gems, so jump to Chapter 10 for a more in-depth discussion.

Libxml-Ruby (`http://libxml.rubyforge.org`) addresses speed concerns that naturally arise from not using a parser written in C. Its use requires the presence of the GNOME Libxml2 library (or something API compatible) on your system, and it still has a few outstanding bugs, but the speed benefits it offers can be dramatic in the extreme. For example, an XPath query from the project's benchmarks enjoyed a speedup of nearly 200 times compared with the same test run with REXML.

The other library is fairly recent and is actually focused on HTML parsing (but will do equally well for well-formed XML). It's called Hpricot (`http://code.whytheluckystiff.net/hpricot`), and it provides a really succinct and rather cute API for common document operations.

Network Services

Just as there are a bewildering number of data formats swirling around the corporate vortex, so too are there a frankly stupid number of different service mechanisms for vending data and functionality across the network. We did SQL storage to death in the last chapter, so I won't reprise any of that. Instead, we will focus on a handful of the data-wrangling technologies/approaches most commonly found in the enterprise: LDAP, XML-RPC, SOAP, and REST.

Lightweight Directory Access Protocol

According to what I've absorbed over the years, directories in the context of the enterprise are basically special-purpose databases that are read from far more than written to. They track a hierarchy of objects with some sort of standardized schema for what the categories should be and what attributes each object should have.

Probably the most common directory service used by corporations is Microsoft's Active Directory, which tracks all of the network policy information you'd expect about users, groups, printers, and others. In addition, many similar LDAP-based directory information services are provided by other vendors (Novell's eDirectory, Apple's Open Directory, Oracle's Internet Directory, etc.).

Because administrators so often end up gluing systems together in such a way that they particularly need to wrangle such network policy information, being able to interact with a company's canonical LDAP service is a frequent requirement.

In the last chapter, we saw the conceptual advantages to be gained by mapping SQL relations to Ruby objects with ActiveRecord. Given that LDAP is ostensibly a system for wrangling objects anyway, shouldn't there be an equivalent object-oriented library for Ruby? Enter *ActiveLDAP*.

Available as a gem (`ruby-activeldap`), ActiveLDAP maps objects in a directory to Ruby objects with dynamic accessor methods for LDAP attributes. As the name implies, this library is written in pure Ruby, but it does depend on the Ruby/LDAP library, which binds to a number of common low-level LDAP libraries. As usual, installation instructions can be found in Chapter 10. Let's walk through a potted example that should give you a feel for the style of the library.

Examining the Schema

First, we'll look at the structure of our sample LDAP schema. Because of the hundreds of competing schema designs, I'm going to keep this very generic rather than consciously basing it upon a particular standard. Figure 7-1 shows the top of the schema for ImaginaryCorp.

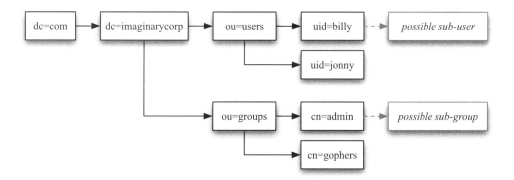

Figure 7-1. *LDAP schema section for ImaginaryCorp*

As should be evident from this figure, we basically have a domain called `imaginarycorp.com`, which contains user and group subdirectories. In turn, these subdirectories contain the various objects appropriate to them, and so on.

Tip If you have to deal with LDAP a lot and find yourself permanently confused by what actually constitutes an organizational unit (ou) versus a common name (cn) or a domain component (dc), then you are not alone. LDAP terminology has acquired its near-artistic levels of mess from a history of legacy solutions and misunderstandings stretching back so far that the first specifications may have actually been brought ashore at Mount Ararat. I recommend the following two-step plan, which I adhere to at all times:

1. Keep the LDAP Wikipedia entry bookmarked in your browser: `http://en.wikipedia.org/wiki/Lightweight_Directory_Access_Protocol`.

2. Whenever anyone suggests continuing use/support/deployment of LDAP solutions, laugh in their face with such explosive force that your response may be easily interpreted as an act of war.

Connecting to the Service

Just as all the database mapping classes were subclasses of `ActiveRecord::Base` in the previous chapter, all of the relevant LDAP mapping classes will inherit from `ActiveLdap::Base`. This class encapsulates all the basic functionality of the library. In particular, it handles the connection.

ActiveLDAP has an entire configuration subsystem that mirrors the features found in ActiveRecord. This means that configuration can be held separately and connection to the LDAP service established automatically when the first method call is made that requires one. Since this is meant to be a reasonably quick and self-contained review of the library, I will eschew this configuration approach in favor of establishing a connection explicitly as shown in Listing 7-17.

Listing 7-17. *Connecting to an LDAP Service*

```
require "active_ldap"

ActiveLDAP::Base.connect(
  :host => "directory.imaginarycorp.com",
  :base => "dc=imaginarycorp,dc=com"
)
```

The code in this listing attempts to establish an anonymous connection to the indicated host on the default LDAP port (389). As you might guess, `connect` accepts many more arguments than those indicated in Listing 7-17. Table 7-1 has a summary of these arguments.

Table 7-1. *Arguments Accepted by ActiveLDAP::Base.connect*

Key	Description	Default Value
host	Server's hostname	`"127.0.0.1"`
port	Service's port	389
method	Connect using :tls, :ssl, or :plain	:plain
base	Domain's base DN	N/A

Table 7-1. *Arguments Accepted by ActiveLDAP::Base.connect*

Key	Description	Default Value
bind_dn	Server's expected bind format	"cn=admin,dc=localdomain"
logger	A Log4r logging object	A logger that prints fatal messages to standard error
user	Username to use in binding	ENV["user"]
password	Password to use in binding	nil
password_block	Proc that returns binding password	nil
store_password	Call password_block only once	true
allow_anonymous	Whether to try anonymous binding	true

Also worth a mention is the try_sasl parameter (which is set to false by default) and associated settings like sasl_quiet. With the appropriate extra software, this switch asks the library to try Kerberos (GSSAPI)-based authentication—which is very handy for Active Directory and others. The mechanics of the more advanced connection options such as SASL and retry/timeout settings are beyond the scope of this section, so I encourage you to read the ActiveLDAP documentation for more detail.

Creating a Mapped Class

With the connection in place, we can now turn our attention to writing a class that encapsulates one of the object types from our schema. Let's say that we want to create a User class that maps to the set of user entries. All we need to do is produce a small chunk of code like that shown in Listing 7-18.

Listing 7-18. *A Basic Mapped LDAP Class*

```
class User < ActiveLdap::Base
  ldap_mapping :dn_attribute => "uid", :prefix => "ou=users",
               :classes => ["top", "posixAccount"],
               :scope => LDAP::LDAP_SCOPE_ONELEVEL
end
```

This listing instantly allows us to do things like this:

```
all_users = User.find(:all, "*")
billy = User.find("billy")
uid = bill.uid # and similarly for any other attributes
```

The ldap_mapping directive is the thing allowing ActiveLDAP to understand the particulars of the relationship between LDAP items and Ruby objects. In Listing 7-18, we tell the library that the distinguished name attribute of each user is uid. We also describe the fact that users exist inside the users organizational unit.

The `classes` parameter (which overrides the default value of `["top"]`) lists the LDAP structural classes associated with an object of this type. This part of the picture is essential to object creation. The list of classes determines the set of attributes an LDAP object may have.

The scoping parameter ensures that any searching is performed only one level deep (e.g., so that subusers couldn't be found by a user query). In other words, only direct children of `ou=users,dc=imaginarycorp,dc=com` would be found by a search. This behavior is the default, but it is worth being explicit about it, particularly for complex schemas.

Establishing Relationships

Just like ActiveRecord, ActiveLDAP has the class macros `belongs_to` and `has_many` for indicating interclass relationships. So in the case of our users and groups, we'd have code like that shown in Listing 7-19.

Listing 7-19. *Relationship Definitions Added to the User and Group Classes*

```
class User < ActiveLdap::Base
  # ldap_mapping line
  belongs_to :groups, :class => "Group", :many => "memberUID"
end

class Group < ActiveLdap::Base
  # ldap_mapping line
  has_many :users, :class => "User", :wrap => "memberUID"
end
```

Starting with `User`, the `belongs_to` macro adds the `User.groups` method (named according to the symbol passed as the first argument). The object returned by this method is a proxy providing all sorts of related functionality. The `:class` specification obviously specifies the class of objects returned as members of the `groups` proxy.

The `:many` parameter specifies the local attribute of each group to be matched against the user to determine membership. The fact that it is called `many` is not an accident. The `belongs_to` relationship can specify either a one-to-many or a many-to-many relationship (the latter being described by our `:many` directive). This makes sense in our example, as a user can belong to many groups and a group can have many users.

In fact, there is an extra parameter that `belongs_to` accepts and that is `:foreign_key`, which identifies the key to use from a user entity to match against the respective key in the related class. More specifically, in a many-to-many relation, `foreign_key` defaults to the `dn_attribute` of the declaring class (`uid` in this case). In a one-to-many scenario, the default would be the proxy name with `_id` tagged on the end (`groups_id`, were our example one-to-many).

In summary, then, our `belongs_to` declaration specifies that the proxy method for the related class will

- Be called `groups`

- Be populated with objects of class `Group`

- Be a many-to-many relationship with the common key referred to as `uid` in a user and `memberUID` in a group

With the semantics covered, you're probably interested to know what methods you get out of all this. To start with, this library is another good example of the practice of mixing-in modules. The proxy object returned by groups is a collection class that implements the each method. Hence, the author was able to include the Enumerable module with all of the methods implied thereby. The following sorts of operations are available:

```
billy = User.find("billy")
billy.groups << Group.find("admin")
billy.groups.each { |group| p group }
group_names = billy.groups.map { |group| group.cn }
billy_is_admin = billy.groups.any? { |group| group.cn == "admin" }
```

Moving on to Group, the has_many declaration is extremely similar to the belongs_to declaration we've just covered. We end up with a Group.users method returning a collection proxy that's very much the same as that returned by User.groups. The methods work just as you'd expect (i.e., Group.find("admin") << billy).

The only real difference lies in the name of the :wrap parameter, which performs the same duty as :many in the belongs_to declaration: identifying the attribute storing the user IDs within a group. In addition, just as the :foreign_key could be specified but was automatically established previously, the same entity is referred to as :primary_key in the has_many declaration. It defaults to the dn_attribute of the related class (uid, once again).

CRUDding Objects

Just as with ActiveRecord objects, there are only a few core methods to learn in covering the spectrum of creation, retrieval, update, and destruction (CRUD) operations. The easiest way to introduce the creation methods is with a demonstration via Listing 7-20.

Listing 7-20. *A Simple Use of the User Class to Create a New User Called "Fred"*

```
fred = User.new("fred")
user.uid_number = 1014
user.gid_number = 550
user.home_directory = "/Network/Users/fred"
raise fred.errors.full_messages.join(", ") unless fred.save
```

User.save is clearly doing the heavy lifting in this listing. It triggers an attempt to create the object on the server and returns true on success. Cases that might lead to failure include the following:

- The object already exists.

- Strong authentication is required but not in use.

- Required attributes (as defined by the object's LDAP classes) are missing.

We can also check to see whether an object exists with User.exist?("fred") or to see whether it would fail a validation test with fred.valid?. Note that the way the validation errors are recorded (in an errors proxy object) is an exact match for ActiveRecord. This is nice, as it means there's a much smaller barrier to entry when attempting to use ActiveLDAP objects in Rails projects.

We've already seen how to retrieve an object (either via a `find` or a related retrieval through `has_many` or `belongs_to`). Updating the objects we find couldn't be simpler: just take Listing 7-20 and replace `User.new` with `User.find`. `User.save` automatically copes with whether the appropriate operation is a creation or an update (just like ActiveRecord). You can actually check for this explicitly using `User.new_entry?`, which obviously returns `true` in the event that a save will mean a creation and `false` otherwise.

All that's left from out of the CRUD operations is the satisfaction that comes with an act of pure destruction, and—that's right—the method is called `destroy`. It exists in both class and object forms: `User.destroy("fred")` and `fred.destroy`.

Beyond what we've covered, there are a number of exposed functions such as `User.search` that allow you to override the behavior laid down by the `ldap_mapping` directive in each class. Check the documentation for more examples of these. With that, let's move on.

XML Remote Procedure Call

As the granddaddy of the "web services" protocols, XML-RPC enjoys a unique popularity, which arises from two properties that it has in common with an amoeba: it's been around for ages and it's really simple. Indeed in just the same way that XML has become so prevalent, XML-RPC has proven to be a popular way to vend an API across the network, being used in a number of popular blogging engines (probably including the ones used in your institution), financial services, and other, more casual hookups like weather information. In short, it is an easy approach to providing a remote interface to both data and processes.

Given that a fairly complete specification of XML-RPC could probably be written on a single side of A4 paper, it will not surprise you to learn that this will be a rather short section. Ruby comes with a built-in XML-RPC library, which has classes for both client and server operations. We'll start with the client.

Client Functionality

In the spirit of simplicity, Listing 7-21 holds a complete client application in three lines. This code creates an XML-RPC connection to a particular service and then makes a call to a method vended by that service.

Listing 7-21. *A Very Simple XML-RPC Client Script*

```
require "xmlrpc/client"
server = XMLRPC::Client.new("www.cookcomputing.com", "/xmlrpcsamples/math.rem")
p server.call("math.Multiply", 23, 14)
```

The basic client object is of class `XMLRPC::Client`. It establishes a connection to the RPC server at instantiation time and accepts a number of parameters to tune the nature of the connection. There are three variants on the `new` method:

- `new(host, path, port, proxy_host, proxy_port, user, password, use_ssl, timeout)`

- `new2(uri, proxy, timeout)`

- `new3(options_hash)`

Obviously, all three eventually lead to the same place. The first and third can be called with zero or more arguments. The third method is simply a more modern version of the first in that it provides a `:key => value`-style flexible method signature. The second takes an entire URI like `https://www.example.com:8081/xmlrpc/fish.feed` and uses it to decide the `host`, `path`, `port`, `user`, `password`, and `use_ssl` values. Every setting has a default value, as listed in Table 7-2.

Table 7-2. *Default Instantiation Values As Used by the XMLRPC Library*

Key	Value
host	"localhost"
path	"/RPC2"
port	443
proxy_host	"localhost" (if proxy_port is set)
proxy_port	8080 (if proxy_host is set)
user	nil
password	nil
use_ssl	false
timeout	30

With the connection established, the next step is to make the remote procedure `call`. The `call` method exists in two variants: `call` (raises an exception or returns a result) and `call2` (returns a `success, result` pair). Thus when writing code that deals with errors, we have two approaches:

```
begin
  p server.call("math.Multiply", 23, 14)
rescue XMLRPC::FaultException => e
  STDERR.puts "XML-RPC error code #{e.faultCode}: #{e.faultString}"
end
```

or

```
success, result = server.call2("math.Multiply", 23, 14)
if success then p result
else STDERR.puts "XML-RPC error code #{result.faultCode}: #{result.faultString}"
end
```

In addition, the library provides a proxy object that dynamically dispatches any method call as an RPC. This proxy object is created with either the `proxy` or `proxy2` method, which correspond to the first or second call styles from the preceding listing. Here's a quick example using `proxy`:

```
math = server.proxy("math")
p math.Multiply(23, 14)
```

I think you'll agree that this mechanism feels more Ruby-like. That said, we would probably avoid this kind of dynamic dispatch if performing large numbers of calls, just to avoid the overhead.

Server Functionality

It is particularly important to appreciate how an XML-RPC server could be of use for a humble administrator. As seen throughout the book, one of the biggest systems-related tasks we engage in is to glue disparate systems together—we unify interfaces. It is conceivable, for example, that the power systems in a machine room are controlled via three separate protocols (due to the differing ages of the equipment).

In such a scenario, it is useful to be able to create a single procedural interface on top of those three so that we can issue high-level commands like "list your voltage statistics for the last hour" or "shut down rack 2 in five minutes" without caring about the underlying implementation. An XML-RPC approach is ideal for rapid deployment of such a system.

In order to keep the example shown in Listing 7-21 going, we will implement a server in Listing 7-22 that satisfies the interface seen (in just four lines of code).

Listing 7-22. *A Very Simple XML-RPC Server Script*

```
require "xmlrpc/server"
server = XMLRPC::Server.new
server.add_handler("math.Multiply") { |a, b| a * b }
server.serve
```

Here we create an instance of XMLRPC::Server, add a handler block for the method of interest, and then instruct the server to start serving. As you might well anticipate, new accepts a number of arguments. The ones of principal interest are the first four (with their defaults indicated):

```
new(port = 8080, bind_host = "127.0.0.1", max_connections = 4, stdlog = $stdout)
```

■**Note** All of these arguments to XMLRPC::Server are in fact being passed straight through to the underlying server—an instance of WEBrick::HTTPServer, which we first met in the previous chapter.

As the server gets more complicated, you may find that you prefer the handler methods to be provided by actual objects. This approach scales better from a code-maintainability perspective, as shown in Listing 7-23.

Listing 7-23. *An Object Handler–Based XML-RPC Server*

```
class MathHandler
  def multiply(a, b)
    a * b
  end
end
```

```
require "xmlrpc/server"
server = XMLRPC::Server.new
server.add_handler("math", MathHandler.new)
server.serve
```

This approach has one major problem. The `add_handler` statement makes every method of `MathHandler` invokable over XML-RPC. This includes methods inherited from Kernel and Object—a very bad thing indeed. Overcoming this flaw requires the use of an *interface specification*. The simplest of these is a convenience object that will only ever expose the directly declared public methods of the handler class. This approach requires one minor change to the previous listing:

```
server.add_handler(XML-RPC::iPIMethods("math"), MathHandler.new)
```

The last thing to cover with respect to server methods is how to raise an XML-RPC fault if it becomes necessary to do so. What's cool about trappable exception mechanisms is that they allow the server code to raise the same exception the client will eventually receive:

```
raise XMLRPC::FaultException.new(15, "I don't like your shoes")
```

Topics that are outside the scope of this section but are covered in the library documentation include the following:

- The ability to swap out the underlying XML parser for a faster (non-pure-Ruby) one

- The availability of asynchronous calls

- More powerful service interface definition functionality

- Server classes for use in CGI and mod_ruby environments

Simple Object Access Protocol

SOAP arose as the horrific mutant offspring of XML-RPC. It is one of the least simple things ever invented by the fiendish mind of man and doesn't require object orientation at either end of the communications channel—so quite where the name came from, I'm not sure. In addition, the voluminous SOAP 1.1 specification contains one of the most brilliantly deranged sequences of words ever constructed:

Using SOAP for RPC is orthogonal to the SOAP protocol binding (see section 6).[1]

Google deprecated its SOAP API in December 2006, giving me further hope that this standard will die a horrible death relatively soon. Nonetheless, parts of the corporate world are still rather SOAPy. Just as with XML-RPC, SOAP-based interfaces have permeated networks throughout the world, providing access to everything from corporate accounting data and employee event information to hardware monitoring statistics and generalized sensor networks. Thus Ruby-wielding administrators would do well to familiarize themselves with Ruby's built-in SOAP functionality.

---

1. See www.w3.org/TR/2000/NOTE-SOAP-20000508.

It also follows that if we need to write SOAP clients as system administrators, then sooner or later we will be asked to provide a SOAP interface to something we're responsible for. Thus this section contains details on writing both client and server applications in SOAP.

Client Functionality

To keep things easy to follow, we'll start with an informal client and then move on to one that uses a Web Services Description Language (WSDL) file. As with some of the other networking libraries, operations are carried out using a proxy object, which is referred to in the Ruby SOAP world as a *driver*. The specific class we're interested in is called SOAP::RPC::Driver and is shown off by Listing 7-24.

Listing 7-24. *A Simple SOAP Client*

```
require "soap/rpc/driver"

tiddles = SOAP::RPC::DRIVER.new("http://www.marthascattery.com:4761/tiddles",
                                "http://cattery.example.com/ws")
tiddles.add_method("spay")
tiddles.add_method("feed", "flavour", "weight_kg")

p tiddles.spay
p tiddles.feed("asparagus_and_lentil", 55)
```

At creation time, SOAP::RPC::Driver.new is passed both the host URI and the namespace of the web service. Once initialized, the available methods are defined individually using add_method(method_name, first_parameter_name, second_parameter_name, ...). Once defined, these methods can then be called from the proxy object.

Just as with the XML-RPC library, the return value of each method call is an unmarshaled object derived from the SOAP response. Asserting that spay and feed both return report strings, running Listing 7-24 would result in output of this form:

```
"Tiddles is decidedly vexed"
"Tiddles has exploded"
```

Most web services supply a WSDL file that specifies the endpoint URL, namespace, and method information necessary to automate a client's construction. To use such a file, we turn to the SOAP::WSDLDriverFactory class, which will build our RPC driver for us. This is demonstrated in Listing 7-25.

Listing 7-25. *A Simple SOAP Client Using a WSDL*

```
require 'soap/wsdlDriver'

wsdl_url = "http://www.marthascattery.com/tiddles.wsdl"
driver_factory = SOAP::WSDLDriverFactory.new(wsdl_url)
tiddles = driver_factory.create_rpc_driver

p tiddles.stroke
```

Server Functionality

Now the real fun starts. A basic SOAP server can be constructed from scratch with two classes: a server class derived from SOAP::RPC::StandaloneServer and a class containing the methods the server will vend. Listing 7-26 has both of these goodies.

Listing 7-26. *A SOAP Server Implementation Supporting the Previous Client Script*

```
require "soap/rpc/standaloneServer"

class Cat
  FLAVOURS = ["crunchy_frog", "asparagus_and_lentil"]

  def initialize(name, weight_kg)
    @name, @weight_kg = name, weight_kg
    @last_stroked, @spayed = nil, false
  end

  def feed(flavour, weight_kg)
    return "#{@name} is confused" unless FLAVOURS.include?(flavour)
    @weight_kg += weight_kg
    if @weight_kg < 10.0 then "#{@name} now weighs #{@weight_kg} kilos"
    else "#{@name} has exploded"
    end
  end

  def spay
    @spayed = true
    "#{@name} is decidedly vexed"
  end
```

```
  def stroke
    @last_stroked = Time.now
    "#{@name} purrs contentedly"
  end
end

class TiddlesServer < SOAP::RPC:StandaloneServer
  def on_init
    tiddles = Cat.new("tiddles", 3.5)
    add_method(tiddles, "feed", "flavour", "weight_kg")
    add_method(tiddles, "spay")
    add_method(tiddles, "stroke")
  end
end
```

```
TiddlesServer.new("Tiddles", "http://cattery.example.com/ws").start
```

The server definition lives inside the on_init method, which is invoked at creation time and allows for initialization of the relevant state objects and the vending of those objects' methods. Note that the server has a shutdown method, which could be tied to a signal handler with a command like Signal.trap("INT") { server.shutdown }. This would obviously have to be run before the server is started, as server.start blocks indefinitely inside the serving run loop.

One of the nice things about WSDL files is that they completely specify the interface you would need to implement in constructing a compliant server for a particular web service. Hence it would be really useful to be able to take a WSDL file and autogenerate a skeleton server with stubs for all the relevant methods. The Ruby SOAP library currently ships with a utility called wsdl2ruby.rb that performs exactly this task.

Depending on the version and/or build of Ruby you have installed, you may find that this script is not present (e.g., it isn't under Mac OS X 10.4). If you don't want to download and build an entirely new version of Ruby, then the SOAP library is available as the soap4r gem and will run on any Ruby version in the 1.6 series or later. Once you have it, you can invoke wsdl2ruby.rb like this:

```
$ wsdl2ruby.rb -wsdl cattery.wsdl -type server
```

This will leave you with a number of files including CatteryService.rb and CatteryServant.rb. The first is the script of the executable server itself and should only need to be modified to change things like the port or network interface(s) to bind to. The second contains the class stub equivalent to our earlier Cat class. It is here that the real work is done in implementing the behavior of the server.

Beyond these basics, just as with the XML-RPC library, there is a yawning chasm filled with classes and methods to help you wrestle in SOAP. These include alternate server base classes that facilitate running under CGI or mod_ruby, fault-handling primitives, and tools for manipulating namespaces and encodings. As ever, check the documentation for more information.

Representational State Transfer

Representational State Transfer, or REST, is something of an odd one out as far as this section goes. It isn't a protocol but rather a design philosophy for action at a distance that makes the rather interesting assertion that the four CRUD verbs in combination with nouns identifying resources uniquely is all you need to accomplish the vast majority of corporate data operations.

Of course, when you think about it, this is pretty close to the proposition made by your average relational database (ignoring the extra verbs that deal with data integrity). What's nice is that the four operations needed already exist in the HTTP standard. These are listed in Table 7-3.

Table 7-3. *The CRUD Operations Available in the HTTP World*

CRUD Operation	HTTP Command
Create	PUT
Retrieve	GET
Update	POST
Delete	DELETE

This means that existing web frameworks that keep track of the HTTP command associated with a request can be modified quite simply to respond conditionally based upon that command. If we were using Rails, for example, a rudimentary approach might resemble Listing 7-27, whose behavior depends on the nature of the HTTP command issued (note that we do nothing if supplied with a PUT request).

Listing 7-27. *A Skeleton Controller Implementation for a RESTful URL*

```
class BooksController < ActionController::Base
  def unreleased
    if request.post?
      if params[:id]
        # since an ID was specified, this is an update
      else
        # no specified ID means this is a creation request
      end
    end

    if request.get?
      # render a representation of the resource
    end

    if request.delete?
      # delete the resource
    end
  end
end
```

So I could create a new unreleased book by posting HTML form data to www.beefybooks.com/books/unreleased, or update one by adding a /15 to the end. This is a nice enough concept, but having to write these conditional blocks in every RESTful method is distinctly inelegant. Also, what about client support? Most browsers can only do POSTs and GETs from forms or links (due in large part to the way the HTML specification is written).

Client Functionality

Because REST is pretty new (at the time of this writing), there are only the first stirrings of client libraries for accessing RESTful resources. The one that's had the most attention is ActiveResource, which attempts to do for REST what ActiveLDAP and ActiveRecord did for LDAP and database access, respectively. If you know how to use ActiveRecord (even if just from the last chapter), then you know how to use ActiveResource. It can provide a whole bunch of implicit functionality simply through declaring an object that inherits from ActiveResource::Base. This is demonstrated in Listing 7-28.

Listing 7-28. *A Quick Overview of the Functionality Provided by ActiveResource*

```
class Book < ActiveResource::Base
  self.site = "http://www.example.com"
end

new_book = Book.new(:name => "See Tops Ruin").save

other_book = Book.find(15)
other_book.name.reverse!
other_book.save!
other_book.destroy
```

It also has all the usual validation support you would expect from something in the ActiveThingy family. The main problem is that ActiveResource is still in its infancy. It is part of the main Rails development trunk but does not form part of the recent 1.2 release. You can grab a copy by checking out edge Rails from its Subversion repository:

```
$ svn co http://dev.rubyonrails.org/svn/rails/trunk
```

As time progresses, client-side REST will become more widely used, and that usually means a sudden influx of libraries in the Ruby community. Until then, don't forget that all we are actually talking about with REST is the moving about of HTTP traffic carrying form data and various kinds of response. With any REST client library, the tricky bit is getting the various resources' object representations dealt with.

It could be said that much blogging/aggregation software is basically RESTful—it implements retrieval of hierarchies of URL-identified pages of XML and is able to POST entries back. In this chapter we looked at parsing XML, and in the next chapter we will build a web robot. Combining these two ideas with a bit of design would leave you with an HTTP client capable of all four CRUD operations and a mechanism to parse retrieved data from a REST service. This rather neatly brings us to the server side of the equation.

Server Functionality

On the server side, I can guarantee that we'll end up talking about Rails since that is the first major Ruby web framework to introduce built-in REST support. Since a complete Rails tutorial is well outside the purview of this chapter, I'm going to assume you are familiar with the following:

- How to create and serve a Rails project

- The functionality offered by `ActionController`

- The role of `config/routes.rb` in matching incoming requests to controller methods

If you are not confident in your understanding of these items, www.rubyonrails.com has all the documentation, tutorials, screencasts, and discussions you'll need to get up to speed. Once again, the functionality we're discussing is currently available in edge Rails only, but it provides good conceptual grounding and will eventually be in general use.

In order to support RESTful server actions, Rails does two things: it introduces a new resource mapping approach for the `routes.rb` file, and it uses some hidden-field trickery to simulate the `PUT` and `DELETE` requests that you'd never otherwise be able to get from the current browser crop. Here's a resource map:

```
map.resources :books
```

From this one tiny statement in your `routes.rb` file, you get the set of mapped calls listed in Table 7-4.

Table 7-4. *The Set of Commands Available After a Simple Resource Mapping*

Command	URL	params[:action]	params[:id]	params[:format]
GET	/books	"index"	N/A	N/A
GET	/books.xml	"index"	N/A	"xml"
GET	/books;new	"new"	N/A	N/A
GET	/books/15	"show"	15	N/A
GET	/books/15;rip	"rip"	15	N/A
GET	/books/15.xml	"show"	15	"xml"
POST	/books	"create"	N/A	N/A
PUT	/books/15	"update"	15	N/A
DELETE	/books/15	"destroy"	15	N/A

Thus without any reference to how the `BooksController` is actually implemented, one simple map standardizes a whole set of CRUD calls for books as a resource—REST at its best. The `map.resources` call can take a hash of options after the object class identifier to modify the mapping behavior.

Use `:controller => "books"` to specify the name of the controller and `:singular =>` `"book"` to describe the singular name used in member routes. `:path_prefix => "/authors/`

`:author_id"` defines a prefix for the routes and may include variables to be derived from the resource object. Another way to achieve this is through nesting:

```
map.resources :authors do |author|
  author.resources :books
end
```

which automatically constructs the appropriate prefix for any book paths.

If you will be constructing multiple routes for the same kind of resource, you can specify a prefix for each route's name with `:name_prefix => "book_"` for those times when you need to refer to the route uniquely by name.

You can add extra methods to the collection path (/books) with `:collection =>` `{ :unreleased => :get }`, which will map to `BooksController.unreleased` for an HTTP GET of /books;unreleased. The hash is a list of controller-action-to-HTTP-method pairs. Similarly, methods can be added to individual members using `:member => { :award => :post }`, which would map to `BooksController.award` for an HTTP POST of /books/1;award. Note that the method could also be `:put`, `:delete`, or `:any`.

Once a resource is defined, a number of helper methods become available for linking to it that can take the place of `url_for` in your rendering code. So this

```
<%= link_to "edit", :controller => "books", :action => "edit", :id => @book.id %>
```

can become this

```
<%= link_to "edit", edit_book_url(@book) %>
```

With that, our tour of things to come (or maybe things just about here) is concluded. REST is going to make agile web development even more nimble because it standardizes another block of conventional coding. Remember that one of the Rails' mantras is "convention over configuration," and the RESTful approach is yet another step toward the nirvana of rock solid yet rapid web application development.

Back to Basics

This chapter dealt with common corporate data-parsing activities, whether that data is in delimited or XML form. We put these skills into practice building a simple PList parser. We also toured through some of the major enterprise data storage and handling protocols, and we discussed the upcoming REST approach with an eye on future development.

Now it's time to return to the roots of the network. The next chapter goes to the wire to discuss basic socket operations and build simple network client libraries. We'll build an SSH remote control system and a web scraper for a terrifying device. In short, we'll be networking for fun and profit.

CHAPTER 8

■■■

Networking for Fun and Profit

Making systems talk to one another is a fundamental task for system administrators. Often, we are called upon to provide abstraction, analysis, monitoring, and even translation of network protocols and services. Thus a grasp of how Ruby augments our network toolkit is vitally important.

In this chapter, we'll cover basic socket operations and how to deal with some of the most common problems. We'll discuss a few of the higher-level protocols and operations that can be employed quite easily from within Ruby, and we'll build a web robot and a calculation server. Finally, we'll peruse some ideas for automating command and control with SSH and sample the joys of the packet capture library.

Basic Network I/O

In this section, the focus is on raw, low-level network operations and how to achieve them with Ruby. It is often the case that a library exists to abstract away much of this detail, but it is always useful to get your hands dirty.

Almost all the network code I've ever written operates over a basic TCP/IP socket. Of course, there are plenty of other ways to abuse a network, but this kind of operation is extremely common and forms the basis for this section's discussions.

Socket to Me

Let's dive right in with a bit of Ruby to open a socket connection to a particularly fine server:

```
require "socket"
socket = TCPSocket.open("www.theonion.com", "80")
```

As you're now quite familiar with the Ruby approach, you might guess that this open method is somewhat akin to File.open in that it can accept a block, and you would be right on the money:

```
TCPSocket.open("www.theonion.com", 80) do |socket|
  socket.puts "GET / HTTP/1.0\n\n"
  puts socket.read
end
```

This snippet once again opens a connection to `www.theonion.com` on port 80 and then, upon success in this regard, requests the root path and dumps out the response. Amazingly enough, most programmers don't want to write raw HTTP in their scripts for something as common as grabbing a web page. Thus Ruby has a proper HTTP library, which we'll play with some more in the next section.

Note the double newline at the end of the request string. You may be thinking that `puts` is supposed to do an implicit newline—that's the whole point of using `puts` rather than `print` after all. In fact, `puts` will append such a line ending only if the string doesn't already have one. This is one of those examples of Ruby choosing a convention that is less strict but more helpful.

In this light, also note that `BasicSocket` and its subclasses `UNIXSocket`, `IPSocket`, `TCPSocket`, and so forth are all actually subclasses of `IO`. The basic concept of a thing-you-can-read-and-write-bytes-from-and-to behaves consistently across all domains, be they files, local sockets, or remote sockets. Hence the `puts` and `read` commands behave identically to the ones you met in earlier chapters.

The Ruby socket classes exist to make the most common socket operations require as little exertion as possible. Figure 8-1 shows these sets of classes and illustrates the sort of functionality they provide.

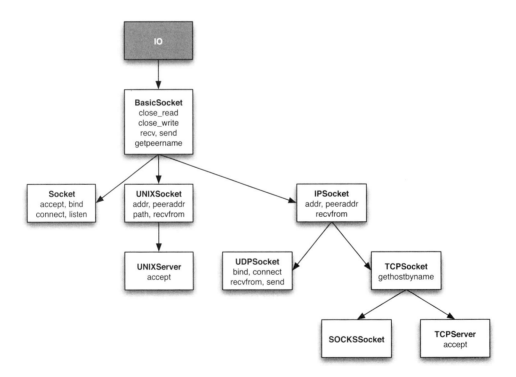

Figure 8-1. *The Ruby socket classes with a sampling of their functionality*

Socket Errors and Exceptions

The rude practicality you quickly learn to accept when engaged in network programming is that more can and does go wrong more often. Hostnames stop resolving, servers go down, links become clogged, and the whole of the Internet starts to resemble a series of tubes. Fortunately, the socket classes make enthusiastic use of Ruby's exceptions mechanism, rendering it easy to recover from such issues. Try this:

```
TCPSocket.open("www.thereisnowaythisdomainshouldexist.com", 80)
```

Unless someone has rushed out and registered this domain to spite me, you should find your script exiting with a `SocketError` exception. Similarly, if you try this:

```
TCPSocket.open("slashdot.org", 90210)
```

you'll be alerted to a refused connection, which is an exception of class `Errno::ECONNREFUSED`. The set of possible exceptions raised by sockets is vast and covers every error you'd expect from UNIX or Windows socket programming. I've found that it's safest just to think of them all as plain old `Exceptions` (remembering that all Ruby exceptions are subclasses of this), unless I have very specific requirements to do otherwise.

Imagine we have a particularly annoying web site that is so busy it refuses connections two-thirds of the time. That sounds like a job for a `begin-rescue-end` block, as shown in Listing 8-1.

Listing 8-1. *A Dogged Connection Attempt*

```
attempts = 0
begin
  attempts += 1
  TCPSocket.open("www.example.com", 80) { |socket| ... }
rescue
  if attempts < 3 then sleep 5 and retry
  else puts "I've had enough of this"
  end
end
```

Here we catch any problems that occur in relation to the socket connection and retry from the beginning if such problems occur. Each retry carries a five-second wait before it commences. After three unsuccessful attempts, we give up completely.

Clockwatching: Timing Out on Purpose

There comes a time in every script's life when it just has to accept the reality that it is stuck in a rut. Networking tends to increase the frequency of this occurrence. It is important therefore to recognize assumptions in your code as to how quickly a network operation will complete and how to react if this deadline has been missed. Ruby has a very useful library for this, as demonstrated in Listing 8-2.

Listing 8-2. *Imposing an Upper Limit on the Duration of Socket Operations*

```
require "timeout"

begin
  Timeout::timeout(5) do
    TCPSocket.open("www.example.com", 80) { |socket| ... }
  end
rescue
  puts "something untoward happened - how bothersome"
end
```

As should be obvious, the `Timeout` module has but one method (`timeout`), which takes a block to run and a number of seconds to wait before stopping it dead. When such an interruption occurs, a `Timeout::Error` is raised. I mention the specific class of the error as you might wish to handle your self-imposed timeout differently from the other socket exceptions. As discussed previously and shown in Listing 8-3, this can be accomplished by matching against the exception class.

Listing 8-3. *Rescuing Conditionally Based on Exception Class*

```
begin
  # socket code with timeout
rescue Timeout::Error
  # rescue code for our timeout
rescue
  # all other rescue code
end
```

`Timeout::timeout` takes an optional second argument that allows you to override the class of the exception to be raised upon timing out. This should give you enough flexibility to apply the `Timeout` module to a huge variety of situations. For more in-depth information on exactly how this module works, take a look at the sidebar "Time Gentlemen Please."

TIME GENTLEMEN PLEASE

The operation of the `timeout` method is actually a good example of how the application of some of the high-level features of Ruby can create very useful behavior in very little code. I reproduce here the pertinent bits of its definition as taken from /usr/lib/ruby/1.8/timeout.rb on my system:

```
# Copyright (C) 2000  Network Applied Communication Laboratory, Inc.
# Copyright (C) 2000  Information-technology Promotion Agency, Japan

module Timeout
  class Error<Interrupt
  end
```

```
  def timeout(sec, exception=Error)
    return yield if sec == nil or sec.zero?
    begin
      x = Thread.current
      y = Thread.start {
        sleep sec
        x.raise exception, "execution expired" if x.alive?
      }
      yield sec
      # line omitted as irrelevant
    ensure
      y.kill if y and y.alive?
    end
  end
  module_function :timeout
end
```

Starting at the top, we define everything that follows to be in the context of the `Timeout` module. Immediately after this, we define `Timeout::Error` to be an in-name-only subclass of `Interrupt` (which inherits from `SignalException`, which in turn inherits from `Exception`).

The `timeout` method itself is where the fun begins. As stated, we take two arguments: the number of seconds to wait and an optional override of the exception class to be raised. Note that even in the argument defaults, the current module namespace is applied so that `Error` is exactly the same thing here as `Timeout::Error`. If we are passed `nil` or `0` as the number of seconds, we simply hand control to the passed block and return its result when it's done—there is no timeout.

A `begin-ensure-end` block is used to contain the meat of this function for reasons that will become obvious in just a moment. The mechanism of this function is to spawn off a watcher thread, which will raise the given exception in the currently running thread after the specified number of seconds. Thus we first make a note of the current thread, calling it x. Then we create a new thread (y), which will sleep for `sec` seconds and then call `raise` on x.

At this point, we have two concurrent threads: the main one and the watcher. The main thread hands off to the passed block (passing it the number of seconds in the timeout) and one of two possibilities can then ensue. Either the block in question will finish inside the time limit or it won't. If it doesn't and y raises its little exception, execution of the block will stop immediately and jump to the `ensure`. If the block does finish before y does the dirty deed, we still end up in the `ensure` but without an exception condition.

The `ensure` section makes certain that the watcher thread is stopped and cleaned up before returning out of the `timeout` block. Because there is no `rescue` section, if an exception is present at the end of the `ensure`, it will then be raised on to the code that called `timeout`, and voila!

The last little `module_function` directive takes the instance method we just defined and makes it private, while creating a public class-style method as a copy. Simply put, this allows us to do `Timeout.timeout` and would make the `timeout` method available as an instance method if it were ever included in a class. Take a look at `ri module_function` for more details.

Socket-Based Monitoring

Armed with just the libraries discussed so far, it is possible to create a number of eminently useful tools. Consider a database-driven DNS system that, for certain A records, carries the notion of a backup IP address. Thus when the zone maintenance script runs, it not only checks that all the A records are current, but also checks that, for those with backups defined, the primary IP address is contactable in some way.

For such a system, we need to build a connectivity checker—something we can think of as a kind of `ping` (in a very generic sense). In this case, it will check that it can make a TCP connection to a particular port on a given IP address. Listing 8-4 shows some code to add this method to the `TCPSocket` class.

Listing 8-4. *TCP Connectivity Checker*

```
require "timeout"

class TCPSocket
  def self.can_connect?(ip, port, wait_secs = 5)
    Timeout::timeout(wait_secs) { open(ip, port) }
    return true
  rescue
    return false
  end
end
```

Note first how we're able to treat the function definition itself as an implicit `begin-end` so we only have to mention the `rescue` keyword. We perform our now familiar `TCPSocket.open` (implicitly) inside a timeout block, the duration of which can be overridden but defaults to five seconds. Quite simply, then, if any connection error occurs or the timeout is triggered, the method returns `false`. Otherwise, it returns `true`.

Continuing our DNS example, we can imagine that some `DNSRecord` class might have a `value` method for deriving the dynamic value of a web server's A record based on the `can_connect?` functionality. In order to do so, the `DNSRecord` object would need to have been initialized with an ordered list of IP addresses to try, selecting the earliest member of that list for which `can_connect?` returned `true`. Listing 8-5 shows a simple implementation of this specification.

Listing 8-5. *DNS Failover Class Snippet*

```
class DNSRecord
  def value
    return @ips.first unless @type == "A" and @ips.size > 1
    @ips.find { |ip| TCPSocket.can_connect?(ip, 80) } || @ips.first
  end
end
```

You shouldn't have any trouble following this listing, but it's worth clarifying a few points. In particular, the assumptions made by this code include the following:

- The default IP for this record is always the first IP in the defined list.

- This default IP should be used when no connectivity can be achieved.

- We always want to test on port 80 (i.e., this is not for FTP, SSH, or other servers).

- The TTL and caching behavior of the DNS system in question is conducive to this style of failover.

- The redundancy scenario is not better served by more robust IP failover methods (i.e., heartbeatd or something similar).

Even with all of these provisos in place, this sort of code can be very useful for the right kind of situation. It also demonstrates the power of Ruby for general network monitoring.

Before we move on to the next section, you may have noticed the lack of a return keyword at the end of the method in Listing 8-5. Usually I've included return for clarity (even though it is completely unnecessary). Remember that the last evaluation in a method will be returned implicitly. In this case, the line is plenty long enough already so I omitted it.

Higher-Level Network Services

Now that you have a feel for low-level socket operations, let's turn to more refined pursuits. In this section, we'll take a look at what ships with the Ruby standard library for communicating with (and providing) services over the network.

An Embarrassment of Protocols

I'm not sure whether "embarrassment" is the correct collective noun for protocols, but it feels right. Like most other high-level languages, Ruby comes bundled with a nice collection of libraries for speaking the language of common network service protocols. As you can likely predict, they are built on top of the socket libraries discussed in the previous section and provide lots of yummy convenience methods and data structures for speaking HTTP, FTP, SMTP, and more.

Once you've seen one library, you've pretty much seen them all, so I'm not going to describe them in excruciating detail but instead encourage you to consult the documentation. Briefly, these libraries are delivered as part of the Net module and are listed in Table 8-1.

Table 8-1. *Network Service Libraries in the Ruby Net Module*

Library	SSL Version
net/ftp	net/ftptls
net/http	net/https
net/imap	
net/pop	
net/smtp	
net/telnet	net/telnets

As an example of using one of these, let's build a quick web scraper. The chunk of code in Listing 8-6 will retrieve a *Futurama* quote hidden in the headers of pages from Slashdot.

Listing 8-6. *Retrieve a Futurama Quote from Slashdot*

```
require "net/http"

Net::HTTP.new("slashdot.org").get("/").each_header do |key, value|
  next if key == "x-powered-by" or not key =~ /x-(.*)/
  puts "#{$1.capitalize} says #{value.inspect}"
  break
end
```

Building a Web Robot

In my job as a system administrator, I have come to realize that new bits of kit we bring through the door might have an SSH interface or sometimes support SNMP but will almost always have a web GUI. Very often, this is all they have. Having to click the same combination of buttons in a web browser over and over again to configure a set of devices loses its novelty about 15 seconds in. As a result, one of the most common bits of code I find myself writing is one to interact with various combinations of forms on web-managed devices.

Frustratingly, the kinds of techniques described in Chapter 7 rarely apply to this problem. DSL routers, bandwidth management boxes, and proprietary firewalls don't tend to have a well-defined XML-RPC or equivalent interface. Thus we have to fall back on simulating a button-pushing monkey. More specifically, the Ruby way is to create a Net::HTTP (or SSL equivalent)-based class for each model/make of device to be administered.

Note In searching around for a good example to use here I had certain criteria. I wanted a well-defined set of operations that I could codify. These operations needed to be orderly and well understood (with no edge cases to worry about). Additionally, I needed HTML output that was reasonably easy to process so this example didn't turn into a treatise on parsing HTML.

The seven devices I tried failed these standards miserably (as—I suspect—do a broad range of commodity network appliances). The only place where four of them came through was with HTML so vile that it was easy to use typos in the output as anchors for parsing. I concluded that, in order to avoid embarrassing certain manufacturers (and probably getting sued), I should invent an HTTP-administered device with all the properties of one of these appliances but with none of the baggage.

Let's suppose a device exists called the MegaFishCannon that has the following capabilities:

- Load a fish into the hopper (specifying its name)
- Set a direction and a range
- Activate the incendiary

- Get the count of waiting fish in the hopper

- Get the current cannon status including last firing time

The actions that do something to change the state of the cannon (the first three) are all accessed via form submission (POST). The status commands (the last two) are simple URL retrievals (GET).

Before we can engage in any fish-launching fun, we need to establish a connection to the web server on the cannon, which runs on port 5000. This particular device requires a username and password to operate but doesn't support HTTPS—a malady that is as common as it is rebarbative. Also, a cookie will be returned that identifies our session to the server. This cookie needs to be used in all of our commands and so should be kept safe.

Thinking a little more deeply, the session on the cannon is a specific example of a more abstract HTTP session. Therefore, to make things easier later on, let's start in Listing 8-7 by designing a `WebSession` class.

Listing 8-7. *An Abstract Class for Tracking HTTP Sessions*

```
require "cgi"
require "net/http"

class WebSession
  def initialize(url, port = 80)
    @session = Net::HTTP.new(host, port)
    @cookies = {}
  end

  def get(path)
    response = @session.get(path, retrieve_cookies(path))
    collect_cookies(response)
    return response.body
  end

  def post(path, pairs)
    header = retrieve_cookies(path)
    header["content-type"] = "application/x-www-form-urlencoded"

    data = pairs.map { |k, v| "#{k}=#{CGI.escape(v.to_s)}") }.join("&")

    response = @session.post(path, data, header)
    collect_cookies(response)
    return response.body
  end

  private
```

```ruby
  def collect_cookies(response)
    cookie = response["set-cookie"]
    return unless cookie

    fields, cookie_path = {}, nil
    cookie.split(";").each do |f|
      raise "Unable to parse cookie from #{path.inspect}" unless➥
        f =~ /^(.*?)=(.*?)$/
      if $1 == "path" then cookie_path = $2
      else fields[$1] = $2
      end
    end
    raise "Unable to parse cookie [no path]: #{cookie.inspect}" unless cookie_path
    @cookies[cookie_path] = fields
  end

  def retrieve_cookies(path)
    cookies = @cookies[path] || @cookies["/"]
    return {} unless cookies
    return {"cookie" => cookies.map { |k, v| "#{k}=#{v}" }.join(";")}
  end
end
```

Listing 8-7 achieves all the functionality required by our skeleton definition of a web session. Most of the code is there to cope with the requirements and semantics of HTTP (storage and retrieval of cookies in particular) and so shouldn't require further comment except to point out the employment of CGI.escape, which nicely formats values for URL-encoded forms. On to the actual class for controlling the cannon, as shown in Listing 8-8.

Listing 8-8. *Method to Create a Connection to the Cannon*

```ruby
class MegaFishCannon < WebSession
  def initialize(url, uname, pass)
    super(url, 5000)
    post("/", "login" => uname, "password" => pass)
  end
end
```

Note how we use the super keyword to perform the actual abstract connection (as provided by the WebSession class) and then POST across that connection to populate the cookie jar with a session cookie. Because of the ease of use of the post method, creating the convenience methods for the first group of actions in Listing 8-9 is child's play. As normal, I refrain from wrapping any of the rest of the method definitions in the class declaration to save on space and indenting.

Listing 8-9. *Methods to Affect State Changes of the Cannon*

```
def load_fish(name)
  post("/loadfish.cgi", "name" => name)
end

def point_cannon(degrees, metres)
  post("/movebarrel.cgi", "degrees" => degrees, "metres" => metres)
end

def fire
  post("/fire.cgi")
end
```

Creating methods for the state accessors will prove a little more challenging. Ordinarily, we might grab the returned HTML document, feed it into some sort of HTML parser library, and perform a formal API-based lookup for the values we want. Unfortunately, the miscreant who wrote the pages for the cannon couldn't write standard HTML to save his life. There are mistakes all over the place. Thus we will have to try and find some uniquely identifiable string in the return that we can use as a signpost to the data of interest. Listing 8-10 contains a sample of the hopper count page.

Listing 8-10. *Extremely Stinky HTML Returned by the Cannon*

```
<html>
<head>
  <title>CANNON</tiTLe>
</head>
<body>
  <!-- immense amounts of silliness here including tables -->
  <table>
    <tr> <td> 12 </td> <TH>
  </table>
</body>
</htl>
```

It turns out that the comically inept use of TH occurs only once in this document. That means we can use it as an anchor. For those objecting to this strategy on the grounds that the next release might break our script, I can only say welcome to the real world and Listing 8-11.

Listing 8-11. *Method to Retrieve the Cannon's Fish Count*

```
def fish_count
  get("/countfish.cgi") =~ /(\d+) <\/td> <TH>/
  $1.to_i
end
```

The cannon's generic status is less problematic. The status is stored as pairs in table rows, and the CSS class of each row is `cannon-status`. Thus something like Listing 8-12 should do the trick.

Listing 8-12. *Method to Retrieve a Hash of the Cannon's Generic Status Information*

```
def status
  body, info = get("/status.cgi"), {}
  body.scan(/cannon-status"> <td> (\S*) <\/td> <td> (\S*) <\/td>/) do |k, v|
    info[k] = v
  end
  return info
end
```

Please bear in mind that the regular expressions were chosen for clarity rather than resilience. In practice, you would be far more careful to avoid delicacy in such expressions and parsing logic—especially when dealing with such badly formatted output. That said, the `MegaFishCannon` class is hereby complete and we can move on to another example.

■**Tip** There has been a recent blessing upon the world of HTML parsing in Ruby. The Hpricot library (available from `http://code.whytheluckystiff.net/hpricot`) provides a superb API for parsing documents. In particular, it copes admirably with the kind of loose formatting seen in the preceding example. If you are doing any serious amount of HTML parsing, this library is well worth a look.

Throwing Together a Server

When you originally examined Figure 8-1, the `TCPServer` class might have intrigued you. There are lots of well-known patterns for writing servers, but at some fundamental level they accept connections from clients, run given procedures possibly with supplied data, and return a result. The world doesn't have nearly enough servers, so let's make one of our own just to see how easy it is.

The `TCPServer` class does very little more than the `TCPSocket` class from which it inherits. The main functionality it adds is via the perhaps familiar `accept` method, as illustrated in Listing 8-13.

Listing 8-13. *Very Basic TCP Socket-Based Server*

```
require "socket"

server = TCPServer.new(34891)
while (session = server.accept)
  session.puts "Kindly leave me alone"
  session.close
end
```

If you run this code, it creates a new server instance bound to port 34891 on all local interfaces. The script merrily sits doing nothing until a TCP connection is made on this port, at which point it dumps an antisocial message and shuts down the connection. You can test this from another terminal with a quick `telnet localhost 34891`.

Let's try and make this server a little more functional. In order to emphasize the processes involved in creating a server, I'm going to use the rather trivial example of a simple arithmetic solver. It is not difficult to imagine how you might apply these principles to creating something like a log analysis or system diagnosis server, but the mechanics of those real-world examples are a little beyond this section.

We'll define a calculation as being composed of an operation and two numbers, the operations naturally being addition, subtraction, multiplication, and division. Thus we expect to be able to `telnet` to this server, enter `3 / 5`, and get an answer of `0.6`. Listing 8-14 shows our first attempt.

Listing 8-14. *A Simple Arithmetic Server (First Try)*

```
require "socket"

server = TCPServer.new(34891)
while (session = server.accept)
  command = session.readline.chomp
  if command =~ /^([\d\.]+) ([\+-\/\*]) ([\d\.]+)$/
    x, y = $1.to_f, $3.to_f
    result = case $2
      when "+" then x + y
      when "-" then x - y
      when "*" then x * y
      when "/" then y == 0 ? "inf" : x / y
    end
    session.puts "= #{result}"
  end
  session.close
end
```

In this bit of code, the accepted session is read up to the first line break, `chomp`ing to get rid of the break itself (remember that `readline` is actually a method of IO). The next line uses a regular expression to match against only those expressions we have deemed to be valid. We pull floating-point values out of the expression with a couple of judicious `to_f` calls and are then ready to perform the operation itself.

This kind of construction, whereby actions are performed based on some string value representing the operation, is a simple example of a dispatch table. This particular dispatch table is built around a case statement for matching against the operation and performing the calculation. Note that we have exercised care to never allow a divide by zero, which would be the only mathematically naughty operation possible with such an expression.

We finish up by dumping the result and closing the session so that the next punter can use the service, which raises an interesting point. Try connecting to the server from one terminal and (before issuing a command) connect from another terminal. In this second terminal, issue an expression and press Return. Now return to the first terminal and do the same. Notice what happened?

Unfortunately, our design is so simplistic that the queue of users waiting to vent their calculations upon the server can only gain access one at a time. There is no parallelism in our code, and so it behaves like a server a few decades behind the current state-of-the-art. Not to worry, though. We can fix it with the traditional `select` pattern as demonstrated in Listing 8-15.

Listing 8-15. *A Simple Arithmetic Server (select Based)*

```
require "socket"

server = TCPServer.new(34891)
sockets = [server]

loop do
  read_ready, write_ready, error_ready = IO.select(sockets)
  read_ready.each do |socket|
    if socket == server then sockets << server.accept
    else
      command = socket.readline.chomp
      if command =~ /^([\d\.]+) ([\+-\/\*]) ([\d\.]+)$/
        # etc...
      end
      socket.close
      sockets.delete(socket)
    end
  end
end
```

The `select` call should be familiar to anyone who has done socket programming. It takes up to three arrays of IO-like objects and an optional timeout, and then sits and waits for certain conditions to occur. In the preceding example, we specify only the first array to `select`. This array should contain one or more sockets on which we are waiting to be able to do a read-style operation. In the context of the server, this means accepting a new connection. In the context of such a connection, this means reading data.

The `select` function returns three arrays that are subsets of the provided socket arrays. The first array contains only sockets on which a read-style operation (including `accept`) would not block the execution of the script. Because we specified only that we were interested in monitoring the sockets for read-readiness, the remaining two arrays will always be empty and are only named for completeness.

If the read-ready socket is the server itself, then we accept a new connection and pop it onto the stack of known sockets. Otherwise, we perform our normal operation. Once the calculation is complete and the result has been posted back to the user, the socket is closed as before and removed from the array of known sockets.

Note that we have taken something of a liberty here in assuming that, because the socket is ready to be read from, we will be able to read an entire line and then write one as well. In serious server programming, these kinds of assumptions lead to blocked processes and worse. The problem is that the `select` approach may be traditional and well understood, but it often requires the construction of state machines so appalling in their complexity that attempts to maintain such code can render one a gibbering wreck.

Threaded servers allow for the more natural convention of state being tracked by the position in the code rather than a big data structure. Ruby provides us with a portable threading implementation (itself `select` based), so let's try that instead with Listing 8-16.

Listing 8-16. *A Simple Arithmetic Server (Thread Based)*

```
require "socket"

server = TCPServer.new(34891)
while (session = server.accept)
  Thread.new(session) do |s|
    command = s.readline.chomp
    if command =~ /^([\d\.]+) ([\+-\/\*]) ([\d\.]+)$/
      x, y = $1.to_f, $3.to_f
      result = case $2
        when "+" then x + y
        when "-" then x - y
        when "*" then x * y
        when "/" then y == 0 ? "inf" : x / y
      end
      s.puts "= #{result}"
    end
    s.close
  end
end
```

Hopefully you will notice that this is almost exactly the code from Listing 8-14 except that everything inside the `accept` has been wrapped in a spawned thread. This idea of wrapping repetitious parallel tasks in threads is applied quite commonly, particularly for network-bound operations. We might easily conceive of an operation that is very low bandwidth but takes a comparatively long time to complete, such as a five-packet ping of a host. Now imagine needing to get the ping status of each host in a list of 1,000. That operation will go much faster if we do 30–40 in parallel at any one time.

■**Caution** The Ruby threads implementation is quite good as far as completely portable user-land threading goes, but it can tend to bottom out as the number of threads increases beyond a handful (20–30 depending on the operation). In situations that require a great deal of threading, try to limit the number of threads systematically by spawning off a thread only if the number of active ones is below a certain number. Get into the habit of doing operations like `threads << Thread.new(foo) { |bar| ... }` so that you can track your threads inside a single array. Take a good look at the `ri` pages for `Thread`, as the methods it provides are simple, easy to remember, and very useful.

As a final note, it is worth mentioning that the Ruby standard library ships with something called `Webrick`, which provides a framework for building low/medium-complexity servers. If you've used Rails, you probably already know it as the built-in web server that gets run when you invoke `scripts/server` in a Rails project directory. `Webrick` can be used for more than HTTP, though. For more information, take a look at the `Webrick` project's homepage (`www.webrick.org`) and particularly the `DayTimeServer` example.

Control and Monitoring

Now that we've had a chance to get up to speed on basic server/client operations, it's time to put them into practice. If any two things could be said to summarize a system administrator's job, it would be the control and monitoring of devices on a network. In this section, we'll write code to automate both processes while showing off a couple of Ruby libraries in detail.

Taking Command with SSH

A standard control mechanism available on many systems is SSH. In particular, *nix-style machines are almost always administered at a distance with this tool. Since *nix platforms power our web servers, file servers, mail servers, and Bluetooth-aware refrigerators, it could be extremely useful to be able to automate their administration with some script-driven SSH goodness.

Consider a maintenance script that is designed to periodically empty out the `/tmp` and `/opt` directories on every host designated as a potential security risk. What if this designation is stored in a database, the access credentials to which you do not want to put on individual machines? This means that it is no good designing a script to run locally on each machine, as it will not be able to tell whether to take action.

In despair, the lonely administrator might resign herself to the fact that she will have to log in to each machine as root and perform the deletion manually. This would be very silly. Instead, she needs to create a task server with appropriate credentials to operate as root on each machine. Such a server might operate like this:

1. Examine the database of hosts and pick out those that are security risks.

2. Establish an SSH connection as root to each of these hosts.

3. Wipe the contents of `/tmp` and `/opt`.

The distinct air of panic that has set in with certain readers that we might now try to construct an SSH client from scratch is decidedly undeserved. We will instead use the excellent `net-ssh` pure Ruby SSH client library, which is available as a gem (as usual, see Chapter 10 for installation details). Let's take a look at a quick example of its use in Listing 8-17.

Listing 8-17. *Example of Net:SSH Usage*

```
require "net/ssh"

Net::SSH.start(url, user, pass) do |ssh|
  shell = ssh.shell.sync
  puts shell.ruby("-v").stdout
end
```

This chunk of code will establish an SSH session on a host at a given URL with the specified username and password, and then run one shell command (`ruby -v`) and dump the resulting standard-out data. Interestingly, the shell knew about a `ruby` method not because of some predefinition, but due to yet another example of the `method_missing` style of metaprogramming covered in Chapter 4. Specifically, the `shell.ruby` invocation actually runs `shell.send_command("ruby -v")`. This more formal method can take a second argument to be used as the standard-in for the specified command.

One of the nice things about this SSH library is that it will automatically pick up on the standard forms of cryptographic handshake available to SSH. Thus whenever I'm using it for commanding remote servers, my task server has a public/private key pair, and the public key is placed in `~root/.ssh/authorized_keys` of each host to be controlled. This allows the task server to log in as root without having to use or maintain any passwords. For more details on this style of access, take a look at `man ssh` and `man ssh-keygen`.

To continue the miniproject, in Listing 8-18 we define a class called `RemoteHost` that encapsulates the functionality we're looking for.

Listing 8-18. *Basic Class to Allow for Remote Directory Clearing*

```
require "net/ssh"

class RemoteHost
  def initialize(url, user = root)
    @shell = Net::SSH.start(url, user).shell.sync
  end

  def clear_dirs(*dirs)
    dirs.each { |dir| @shell.send_command("rm -rf #{dir}/*") }
  end
end
```

This class creates an SSH shell session upon instantiation and then allows us to perform a high-level clear operation on a specified set of directories, which can be passed as arguments to the `clear_dirs` method courtesy of the * syntax. The actual task can be constructed as follows:

```
unsafe_hosts.each do |host|
  RemoteHost.new(host).clear_dirs("/tmp", "/opt")
end
```

Of course, this is only the snippet issuing the command. Deriving the set of unsafe hosts is outside the scope of this example. Nevertheless, the preceding snippet would reside in a script to be run periodically on the task server (via a `cron` job or something similar) and in so doing would complete the specified design.

■**Tip**   There are lots of tools in the Ruby world for assisting in remote deployment or execution based on system policies. Particularly worthy of mention is the Capistrano project, which is used extensively in the Rails community and can be explored at `http://wiki.rubyonrails.org/rails/pages/Capistrano`.

Packet Monitoring

An administrator probably exists somewhere who's never used `tcpdump` or `ethereal`, but I'll probably never meet him. When all else fails, getting down and dirty with the raw packets that fly across the network can be the only viable option. In addition, the ability to roll your own tools based on raw packet data can lead to some novel applications. In this section, we'll take a look at packet capture in Ruby and use its features to build a simple bandwidth-monitoring application.

At a fundamental level, all the systems I've ever needed to do packet capture have carried the LBL Packet Capture Library (`libpcap`). The project in this section is based on this library, and since widely used programs like `tcpdump` are also based on it, we can be fairly comfortable that our monitoring application will work on a variety of platforms. This library provides a raw interface to system network interfaces allowing for the (often promiscuous) extraction of raw network frames.

A Ruby binding to this library exists, but not as a gem, so I will take a moment to walk through its setup procedure. First, download the latest version of Ruby/Pcap from `www.goto.info.waseda.ac.jp/~fukusima/ruby/pcap-e.html`. Following this, the standard build routine applies for a Ruby extension:

```
$ tar -xzf ruby-pcap-0.6.tar.gz
$ cd pcap
$ ruby extconf.rb
$ make
$ make install
```

The last line may require a `sudo` or other permission-acquiring mechanism if the installation path is not somewhere your current user can write to.

With the installation complete, it's time to flex some packets. The library we just installed has a nice little class called `Pcaplet`, which allows you to quickly create programs that accept the same sorts of flags that `tcpdump` does (for specifying which interface to listen on, among other things). It is used as shown in Listing 8-19.

Listing 8-19. *Example Pcaplet Usage*

```
require "pcaplet"

sniffer = Pcap::Pcaplet.new
sniffer.each_packet { |pkt| p pkt }
sniffer.close
```

■**Note** Because this code relies on a given network interface being in promiscuous mode, any code like that under discussion will need to be run with root (or equivalent) privileges.

The more eager among you can probably already see what the final code is going to look like. Given that we have a simple iterator that presents us with each new packet, we will be able to analyze the packet and determine where it was sent from, where it was going to, and how big it was. In turn, this information will allow us to build up bandwidth usage statistics for each host we care about. To track the bandwidth, we'll first create a BWHost class with some pertinent methods. Take a look at Listing 8-20.

Listing 8-20. *Definition of a BWHost Class for Tracking Bandwidth Usage*

```
class BWHost
  attr_reader :ip

  def initialize(ip)
    @ip = ip
    @received, @sent = [], []
  end

  def received(bytes, from, at = Time.now)
    @received << [bytes, from, at]
  end

  def sent(bytes, to, at = Time.now)
    @sent << [bytes, from, at]
  end

  def total_received(options = {})
    total(@received, options[:earliest], options[:latest])
  end

  def total_sent(options = {})
    total(@sent, options[:earliest], options[:latest])
  end
```

```
    private

    def total(events, earliest, latest)
      events.inject(0) do |sum, event|
        if ((earliest and event[2] >= earliest) or not earliest) and
           ((latest and event[2] <= latest) or not latest)
          sum + event
        else sum
        end
      end
    end
end
```

This class tracks the bandwidth usage of a particular host. It does so with two arrays (@received and @sent) that store an ordered set of bandwidth events. It also provides some basic reporting functions that allow a total to be derived both universally and with time constraints.

Note the construction of the totaling method. It uses Enumerable.inject on the array of passed events to keep a running total of the number of bytes passed. In particular, the specified time filtering is applied within the inject call, so only appropriate events are counted. The complexity of the conditional used for totaling is an artifact of the feature that an earliest time limit or a latest or both or neither can be specified.

With the benefit of this class, our bandwidth-monitoring script is easy enough to write, as demonstrated by Listing 8-21.

Listing 8-21. *Bandwidth-Monitoring Script*

```
require "pcaplet"

hosts = {}

sniffer = Pcap::Pcaplet.new
sniffer.each_packet do |pkt|
  next unless pkt.ip?
  src, dst, = pkt.ip_src, pkt.ip_dst
  size, time = pkt.size, pkt.time
  (hosts[src] ||= BWHost.new(src)).sent(size, dst, time)
  (hosts[dst] ||= BWHost.new(dst)).received(size, src, time)
end
sniffer.close

hosts.each do |ip, data|
  puts "#{ip} sent #{data.total_sent}B and received #{data.total_received}B"
end
```

Here we run through each packet received, allocating it against its source and destination hosts until we are interrupted or quit. Before exiting, we dump out a final summary of the data collected. Note the use of the ||= construction to build up the hosts hash on the fly as new hosts are defined.

This example demonstrated how to implement a basic packet-capture script. Obviously, if bandwidth statistics were needed on a real (busy) network, this approach wouldn't scale very well due to sheer volume. In practice, the approach employed in this section would be better suited to the sort of individual host/protocol analysis that couldn't be achieved with a system's generic packet counter.

End of Line

This chapter showed how Ruby makes it quick and easy to interact with network protocols and services. The idioms of Ruby (such as co-routines and easy threading) allow for much less work and confusion when writing both clients and servers. We launched some fish and sniffed some network traffic, all in just a few lines of code.

If networking is the hidden glue that binds all of our systems together, then data presentation is the polish that convinces nonexperts of the importance and effectiveness of our work. Creating graphs, figures, and tables in an automated fashion allows system administrators to provide themselves and others with useful visual summaries of everything from network traffic to server room temperature variations. The next chapter deals with this important subject.

■ ■ ■

## CHAPTER 9

Network Monitoring

Networks are full of metadata that is useful to techies and management alike. So often this data sits and rots because nobody has the time or the inclination to bring it together and use it effectively.

Processing the kinds of operational data found in a live network can most easily be broken down into three modular stages: how to gather it, how to analyze it, and how to present it. This chapter discusses all three.

In the first section, I cover how to use SNMP and SSH to pull data out of the network. In the second section, I discuss some important real-world analysis concerns. The third and final section addresses some relatively simple ways to present the data so that meaningful conclusions might be drawn from it.

Gathering Data

Butterflies can taste with their feet, crickets can hear with their legs, and a scallop has about 100 eyes around the edge of its shell. If you've never given it much thought before, you may be surprised at just how much functional data you can pull out of your network with the right data collection tools. After all, the analyses we perform and the presentations we give are only as good as the data we gather (although politicians demonstrate the flexibility of this rule on a daily basis).

This section focuses on a couple of ways (with associated examples) to get operational data out of your network. The model in both cases will be that of a centralized probe that does the actual data gathering. This isn't the only model you could employ.

So-called self-healing systems often employ a complex cloudlike structure, where each facet reports its own status and consumers of that information act locally or globally to effect repairs. The possibilities for such intricacy are beyond the scope of this book, but they are worth mentioning to ensure that network monitoring strategies scale properly.

In the previous chapter, we implemented a simple network packet grabber. We will now examine mechanisms for building more high-level monitoring systems based on two protocols: Simple Network Management Protocol (SNMP) and Secure Shell (SSH).

Simple Network Management Protocol

Now at version 3, the SNMP specification describes an extremely simple protocol for retrieving and updating bits of information in any device implementing an SNMP agent. Like its predecessor, Simple Gateway Monitoring Protocol (SGMP), SNMP is built around the need to unify the management of increasingly diverse network devices.

The designers recognized that it was completely infeasible to rely on a general command language that would need to be updated every time a new device came out. Thus they factored out all the different things you might want to do to a network device and came up with an information-oriented protocol that implements three basic abilities:

- Retrieve some data (including a mechanism for handling tables of data)

- Write/update some data

- Send information asynchronously (allowing for a more efficient alternative to polling for so-called trappable events)

Everything else device-specific is handled by a namespace approach that uniquely identifies each value that can be read or updated. This means that if a new class of device is invented, the creators need only release a Management Information Base (MIB) file pertinent to that device and any SNMP client will be able to address the values defined therein.

If this protocol strategy of putting all the flexibility in the namespace rather than the commands seems familiar, you may recall our discussion of REST in Chapter 7. It turns out that REST is merely the latest expression of this kind of information-oriented protocol.

Modularity, flexibility, and ease of implementation are all traits that such protocols aim for. Let's see how SNMP fares in Ruby.

Connecting to an Agent

Ruby doesn't yet have an SNMP library as part of the standard distributions, so we will be using the snmp gem (installation instructions can be found in Chapter 10 as usual). One of the many nice things about this library is that it ships with most of the IETF's (Internet Engineering Task Force) MIBs. Apart from being satisfying to acronym-aholics, this means that we will be able to interact with many common network devices without further MIB work.

Connections to agents are handled by the SNMP::Manager class. Just like File, this class implements both new and open methods (the latter taking a block). We'll use open in Listing 9-1.

Listing 9-1. *Opening a Connection to an SNMP Agent*

```
require "snmp"
SNMP::Manager.open do |m|
  # do something with m
end
```

It may not be immediately obvious what the code in Listing 9-1 is connecting to or how. The open method takes a hash of options, such as :Host, which are listed in Table 9-1 together with their defaults and a brief explanation of their function. The way we have invoked open in Listing 9-1 would give us a connection with all of the defaults in operation (as we would expect from a flexible method signature).

In addition to these options, there are a couple of more obscure ones. Transport allows you to select the class used to handle the underlying SNMP transport—UDPTransport being the only one currently available. MaxReceiveBytes tunes the inbound data flow profile and is set to 8000 by default. You'll almost certainly never need to fiddle with either of these.

Table 9-1. *Parameters Accepted by SNMP::Manager.open*

Key	Description	Default Value
Host	Agent's hostname	`"localhost"`
Port	Agent's port	`161`
TrapPort	Port used for notification events	`162`
Community	Community used for read operations	`"public"`
WriteCommunity	Community used for write operations	As for `Community`
Version	SNMP version	`:SNMPv2c`
Timeout	Requested timeout in seconds	`1`
Retries	Number of attempts before failure	`5`
MibDir	Directory containing MIBs	`MIB::DEFAULT_MIB_PATH`

MibModules	MIBs to use in this session	`["SNMPv2-SMI", "SNMPv2-MIB"`
		`"IF-MIB", "IP-MIB"`
		`"TCP-MIB", "UDP-MIB"]`

Retrieving Scalar Data

With a connection in place, let's grab some data from the server. There are two ways to identify the particular MIB object you'd like returned. The first is the plain old MIB object ID such as `1.3.6.1.2.1.1.6`, which corresponds to the `iso.org.dod.internet.mgmt.mib-2.system.sysLocation` object.

If that gives you the kind of stomach cramps it gives me, you'll likely prefer the more symbolic approach. The library provides simple mapping syntax from the common names (found at the end of the MIB object path) to their respective object IDs. Hence `1.3.6.1.2.1.1.6` can be referred to simply as `sysLocation.0`. In practice, this means that you end up with code like that shown in Listing 9-2.

Listing 9-2. *Retrieving and Printing Out a Couple of Chunks of Data from an SNMP Agent*

```
SNMP::Manager.open(:Host => "switch1.example.org") do |m|
  response = m.get(["sysLocation.0", "sysUpTime.0"])
  response.each_varbind { |vb| puts "#{vb.name}: #{vb.value}" }
end
```

The two pertinent methods used in Listing 9-2 are get and `each_varbind`. The get method belonging to the management session object retrieves the MIB objects listed in the array, automatically converting them into integer notation before the request is sent. Note that get can take a string if you have only one value to retrieve. For efficiency's sake, always go for the array if you have multiple values to collect.

The response that comes back from a get responds to one retrieval method and that is `each_varbind`. A variable binding can be thought of as SNMP terminology for what a MIB looks like in transit. From our perspective it's just an object that has a name and a value. As an aside, it also has a method, `asn1_type`, that will return its underlying type information.

Thus we are able to iterate through the list of objects we get back from the agent. Given that these objects will be ordered in just the same way as we asked for them, simple clients probably don't need the extra functionality of a specific variable binding. Hence, we can also do this:

```
values = m.get_value(["sysLocation.0", "sysUpTime.0"])
```

to retrieve only the values inside each MIB object returned.

Retrieving Tabular Data

The SNMP framework allows for the existence of tables of information to avoid the mess that would occur if the global namespace contained items like ifDescr1 and ifDescr2 (for the descriptions of network interfaces 1 and 2). Instead, such items can be addressed as subindices of parent "columns."

There are three ways to access such information using the Ruby SNMP library. We will discuss only the first, as the other two provide the extra power and complexity to do things that essentially sacrifice clarity for the sake of efficiency. The reason these other two methods (get_next and get_bulk) are more powerful is that they expose the raw SNMP. You can see examples of how to use these in the library documentation.

Concentrating on the approach we will discuss, how do we walk through a MIB table in an easy and systematic manner? Using the walk method, of course—as shown in Listing 9-3, which is adapted from the documentation.

Listing 9-3. *Walking Through the Interface Table of an SNMP Agent and Printing Out the Rows*

```
columns = ["ifIndex", "ifDescr", "ifInOctets", "ifOutOctets"]
SNMP::Manager.open(:Host => "switch1.example.org") do |m|
  m.walk(columns) { |row| puts row.join("\t") }
end
```

Updating Data

Updating data on the SNMP agent is accomplished with the set method. Unlike get, this method requires a little more coddling in that it only accepts variable binding objects in specifying what is to be set. Specifically, values must be specified in terms of their ASN.1 types. For example, suppose we wanted to update the system name. Listing 9-4 shows how to achieve this.

Listing 9-4. *Updating the System Name of an SNMP Agent*

```
require "snmp"
include SNMP

Manager.open(:Host => "switch1.example.org") do |m|
  vb = Varbind.new("sysName.0", OctetString.new("slartibartfast"))
  m.set(vb)
end
```

Note the use of `include` in this listing (as discussed in previous chapters) to place all of the SNMP library's functionality in the global namespace so that the classes don't have to be specified with `SNMP::` in front of them.

That really is all there is to know functionally about updating MIB objects. Of course, special attention has to be paid to object types, and more detail on this can be found in the documentation.

Handling Traps

Traps are sent when values change or move across certain boundaries (depending on the definitions in the MIB). The SNMP library includes a simple listener class that can process such events. Listing 9-5 contains a skeleton example of its use.

Listing 9-5. *Skeleton SNMP Trap Handler*

```
trap_thread = SNMP::TrapListener.new do |listener|
  listener.on_trap_default do |trap|
    # do something with trap
  end
end
trap_thread.join
```

Just as with the management class, `SNMP::TrapListener.new` can take a hash of configuration parameters. These are `:Host`, `:Port`, `:Community`, and the two equivalent obscure ones: `:ServerTransport` and `:MaxReceiveBytes`.

■Note If you stick to the default trap listening port (162), you will need to run your listening process as root on any UNIX-like system, as this is within the reserved ports range.

We used `on_trap_default` to attach our handling block to the listener. Such blocks can also be attached based on trap protocol version and even object ID using `on_trap_v1`, `on_trap_v2`, and `on_trap`. This can be handy to separate out concerns as handling complexity increases. Note that the listener executes one handler only for each trap event and that the handler choice is made in order of descending priority:

1. The handler registered for the matching object ID

2. The handler for the particular trap version number

3. The default handler

Although this section is about handling traps, it's worth mentioning that traps can also be sent from within a management block like this:

```
m.trap_v2(uptime, oid, vb_list)
```

which takes the system uptime in hundredths of seconds, an object ID for the trap, and a list of VarBind objects pertinent to the trap. For instructions on version 1 traps, see the documentation.

Using Custom MIBs

Since the design of SNMP would be sort of pointless without the ability to use custom MIBs, we'll finish off this section with a quick look at how to plug custom MIBs into Ruby SNMP sessions.

The SNMP::MIB class has a method called import_module. This method takes the path to a MIB file and processes it in order to make its definitions available to the library in future client sessions. Under the surface, what it's actually doing is storing a YAML hash that matches symbolic names to MIB object IDs.

The library does not do its own MIB parsing. Instead it relies on a tool called smidump, which you probably won't have on your system by default. Instructions on how to acquire and install it can be found at www.ibr.cs.tu-bs.de/projects/libsmi. Essentially, this tool can be made to output a Ruby-compatible hash of MIB object definitions that import_module can then use to build the simplified YAML file.

In summary, the three-stage process is as follows:

1. Ensure you have smidump on your system as part of the libsmi toolchain and that it is in your executable path (i.e., you can execute it on the command line just by typing smidump --version).

2. Write a quick script that executes SNMP::MIB.import_module(path_to_mib_file).

3. Remember to include your custom MIB in the :MibModules array passed to the SNMP::Manager.open directive.

Secure Shell

We saw in the last chapter how we can use an SSH session to execute remote commands and get data back from them. Since lots of devices implement SSH, this approach is ideally suited to network monitoring. We'll use the RemoteHost class that we started to define in Listing 8-18. Listing 9-6 describes a bare-bones version of that class.

Listing 9-6. *A Generic SSH Session Class Last Seen Lurking in Listing 8-18*

```
require "net/ssh"
class RemoteHost
  def initialize(url, user = root)
    @shell = Net::SSH.start(url, user).shell.sync
  end
end
```

Choosing the Data Source

In order to give a flavor of what's possible in collecting operational information over SSH, let's consider user logins. Imagine we were running a closed network of Linux and BSD boxes wherein each user could open as many local consoles as she wanted and could SSH into other machines (perhaps for direct control of hardware or something). Each login would leave a trace in the wtmp file on the relevant machine.

If we wanted to get a general idea of how much use the robotic arm control machine was getting, we could periodically log into it and run last to get a listing of all previous logins (at least since wtmp was last recycled). However, with an automated SSH tool at our disposal, we could collect all of this data centrally for analysis.

I'm going to come back to this example in all three sections of this chapter, so this section deals only with collecting the relevant data. The most important assumption we'll make in this respect is that none of the information we collect should be thrown away (that's what analysis is for). The output of last looks like this:

```
user1    console  fishbrain.local  Tue Jan 16 21:52 - 00:49  (02:56)
user2    ttyp4    10.0.0.10        Sun Jan 21 20:11   still logged in
user3    ttyp2                     Fri Jan 19 17:09 - 19:43 (2+02:33)
```

The structure is very simple. It's column aligned, which means we need to be a little careful when parsing it, but that aside it's really just five fields:

- The user who initiated the session

- The virtual device to which the session is attached

- The source of the session (which will likely be blank in the case of a local terminal)

- The session initiation time and date (note that there's no year indicated)

- A summary indicating whether the session is still active or (if not) how long it lasted

Collecting the Data

We should be able to parse the output from last easily by adding the method specified in Listing 9-7 to the RemoteHost class.

Listing 9-7. *Method to Grab the Login Information from the "last" Command on a Remote Host*

```
def last_logins
  logins = []
  @shell.send_command("last").stdout.each do |line|
    line.chomp!
    fields = [line[0,8], line[10,8], line[19,15], line[36..-1]]
    next if fields.include?(nil)
    logins << fields.map { |field| field.strip }
  end
  logins
end
```

The first thing to mention in the context of this listing is that we've finally found an excuse to use both forms of the String.slice invocation: offset,count and start..finish. The latter form is used to define the last field and employs a negative index, which counts backward from the end of the line.

Also, we've amalgamated the contents of the last two fields into one since it's just one big field specifying a range. Each line of the output from last is chomped to remove the trailing newline character and then split into an array of fields using the fixed column widths previously mentioned. If there are fewer fields than expected (as will happen with the final couple of lines output by last), they are ignored. Otherwise, the fieldset is added to the array of logins. For later convenience, each field has any extra whitespace stripped.

■**Note** The approach used in Listing 9-7 to derive the various field values takes advantage of the fact that last's output is column aligned. We needn't have relied on this. We could have instead parsed the line with a regular expression like /^(\w+)\s+(\w+)\s+([a-zA-Z\d\.-]+)(.+?)$/, which reads as "word, space, word, space, alphanumeric sequence with period or hyphen characters, the rest of the line up to and not including the newline character."

RemoteHost.last_logins ends up returning an array of login lines:

```
[ ["user1", "console", "fishbrain.local", "Tue Jan 16 21:52 - 00:49  (02:56)"],
  ["user2", "ttyp4",   "10.0.0.10",       "Sun Jan 21 20:11    still logged in"],
  ["user3", "ttyp2",   "",                "Fri Jan 19 17:09 - 19:43 (2+02:33)"] ]
```

Storing the Data

We will need to store the data for later analysis. Probably the simplest way to do this would be to dump it out to a file that can maintain the structure of the arrays (i.e., a YAML file). This might lead you to wonder why we would bother with all the splitting, chomping, and stripping we're doing in last_logins.

Apart from being a recipe for a great party, these three actions prepared the data in a common way for our analysis. It is conceivable that different platforms might use different column widths or field separation characters in the output of last. Maybe there are platforms that use a completely different command for accessing this data. We can abstract these differences away for the benefit of our analysis by presenting a common output from last_logins. The abstraction could go elsewhere but this placement feels right for now, as demonstrated in Listing 9-8.

Listing 9-8. *Storing the Array of Logins in a Timestamped File for Later Retrieval*

```
require "fileutils"
require "remote_host"
require "yaml"

FileUtiles.mkdir_p("data")
Dir.chdir("data")
hosts_to_monitor = ["fishbrain.local", "fishwife.local"]
hosts_to_monitor.each do |host|
```

```
  logins = RemoteHost.new(host).last_logins
  dump_file = host + Time.now.strftime(".%Y%m%dT%H%M%S.yaml")
  File.open(dump_file, "w") { |f| YAML.dump(logins, f) }
end
```

In short, the code in Listing 9-8 iterates through a list of hosts and retrieves the array of logins for each one, dumping it to a timestamped file. Note that it ensures a `data` directory is present for holding all of these files via the `mkdir_p` method. This method is also known as `mkpath`, but I use the first form to remind myself that it does the same thing as `mkdir -p` would on the command linc (i.e., it ensures that a directory exists, creating parent directories where necessary). This script would be run periodically on the monitoring machine so that the files would build up over time, hungrily awaiting the moment when they would be analyzed.

Analyzing Data

Attempting to present data without thought as to the analysis often gives rise to presentations that are nothing more than stylish gloss on a stinky foundation. It is the act of putting lipstick on a pig.

■**Caution** Under no circumstances should you put lipstick on a pig—it just isn't as funny as you might think. If you want guaranteed mirth, go for mascara on a crab every time.

It goes without saying that subjects like data mining and statistical analysis are sciences in their own right because the subjects are vast. This isn't a book on either, so we're not going to dwell on any deep theoretical background. Instead, this will be a quick section using the SSH collection example to highlight some practical challenges I often find myself facing when analyzing system data.

Marshalling the Data

In the previous section, we collected a load of login data. The way it was gathered would probably have lead to a great deal of overlap between datasets. This would have depended on how frequently the `wtmp` files on each host got recycled, how often the data collection script ran, and how many new login events occurred between runs.

Before any numerical or other structural analysis can occur, we have to sculpt the data we need out of the gigantic granite slab we've been presented with. The first step will be to rid ourselves of duplicate data. With the login example, each session is uniquely identified by a combination of its username, device, source, and starting date. We can use this fact to weed out duplicates, but there is a small wrinkle.

Recall that the dates do not have any year information. This could conceivably lead to nonunique start dates. However, even over a number of years, the chances of having two logins by the same user from the same source bound to the same device commencing at the same time on the same date where that date has the same day of the week in both cases is likely small enough that we don't have to care about it.

The other obvious assumption we're making has to do with data quality. We're supposing that usernames and system dates and times are synchronized across the entire network of monitored hosts or it would render the data virtually meaningless in aggregate.

The data was collected in files on a per-host basis. The next question to answer is whether such an approach is appropriate for our analysis data. This question is very difficult to answer in general because it has an impact on how quickly or flexibly we can analyze the data. That impact is only really quantifiable once data has been collected and analyzed for some time.

I have a default approach to answering the "How should I store that?" question, which usually works well as a first approximation in situations where data is being collected continuously. If data is time based (as it almost always is in systems analysis), split it into 24-hour chunks. These chunks may end up being too large or too small, but you'll find that out pretty quickly.

Parsing Events

That's about as much background as I can provide. Let's write some code, starting from the inside out with a method that takes a login event as supplied by the collector and turns it into a hash with more rigorous treatment of the dates. This code is shown in Listing 9-9.

Listing 9-9. *Parsing Login Fields into an Event, Particularly to Coerce the Date Information*

```
DAY_INDEX, NOW = {}, Time.now
["Mon", "Tue", "Wed", "Thu", "Fri", "Sat, "Sun"].each_with_index do |day, i|
  DAY_INDEX[day] = i + 1
end

def parse_event(login_fields, host)
  user, device, source, date_info = login_fields
  date_info =~ /^(...) (.){12}/
  wday, date = DAY_INDEX[$1], Time.parse($2)
  while wday != date.wday or date > NOW
    date = Time.local(date.year - 1, date.month, date.day, date.hour, date.min)
  end
  duration = nil
  if date_info =~ /\((\d+\+)?(\d+):(\d+)\)$/
    days, hours, mins = $1, $2, $3
    duration = mins + hours * 60 + days.to_i * 24 * 60
  end
  {:user => user, :device => device, :source => source,
   :date => date, :duration => duration, :host => host}
end
```

Starting at the top of this listing, we define two constants that will be used a great deal in the parsing operation. One is simply the current time. The other provides a lookup that matches short-form days of the week to their corresponding weekday index as defined by the Time class. The need for this will become obvious in a moment.

The method parse_event accepts an array containing the login fields originally grabbed from last. It assumes they are still in the same order in which they were collected and assigns them proper variable names. It also takes the name of the host on which the event took place.

The next chunk of code is all about parsing the start date out of the `date_info` field. Remember that this will look something like `Fri Jan 19 17:09 - 19:43 (2+02:33)`. The initial part is a short-form weekday followed by a space and then a 12-character date and time. We use the regular expression to extract these into $1 and $2.

The problem that is (mostly) solved by this bit of code is that of ensuring the date is correct given that we have no year information. First a `date` is parsed from $2. Because of how `Time.parse` works, this will always be a date in the current year. It is impossible for the same dates in two consecutive years to fall on the same day. Thus we know that if the numerical weekday of the parsed date does not equal that of the day from the login date field, the date is at least a year ahead of where it should be.

If that check somehow fails to detect the wrong year, we can always fall back on checking that `date` is not in the future (the second check). The first check also comes in handy for giving us a sporting chance of getting the right year if that turns out to have been more than a year ago. Hence the `while` loop keeps moving `date` backward a year until both constraints are met.

With good confidence in our start date, we come to the problem of determining the duration of the session. The `last` command helpfully puts the duration of a completed session in brackets at the end of the line. If the session isn't yet finished, there will be no such entity. The format of the duration is an optional number of days followed by a + and then an `hh:mm` string.

This format choice might help to explain that frankly vomit-worthy regular expression we've had to use to parse the duration out. Aside from this expression, however, the logic is clear enough. If there isn't a bracketed section, the duration is `nil`. If there is, the duration is recorded as a total number of minutes. Choosing to store it in minutes nicely sidesteps the problem of using either a convoluted duration structure or some imprecise floating-point number of days.

Finally, we are able to return the parsed event, which is a hash containing all the pertinent data. This concludes the code necessary to parse an event for analysis.

Filtering and Assigning Events

Our next task is to decide what to do with each event. If it's a duplicate, then we don't need to do anything. If it's an update, then we need to overwrite the duration time in the original event. If it's a new event, then we just need to put it in the right storage bin (based on 24-hour periods).

Ideally, it should be possible to drive all three of these scenarios from the same code. As stated, we don't need to do anything if an event is a duplicate. That doesn't mean we can't. If we were to overwrite an event with a duplicate, we'd end up with the same data, so the updated information would still be valid. If we overwrote it with an update, then we would have correctly updated an old durationless event. Both scenarios are fine as long as events are always processed in chronological order.

As for the third scenario, if we store events in bins and update them in those bins, then the solution for the first two problems will also work for the third. The collection of bins should be a hash that is keyed based on a date of the form YYYYMMDD. Within each bin, the events could be stored as an array, but we know we're going to be doing a lot of searching for duplicate events. Thus a better approach would be to use a hash as storage and then key based on the set of event-unique data (user, device, source, date, and host). Listing 9-10 contains a method that meets these requirements.

Listing 9-10. *Assigning Events to a Unique 24-Hour Event Bin*

```
def assign_event(event, bin_hash)
  date_key = event[:date].strftime("%Y%m%d")
  bin = (bin_hash[date_key] ||= {})
  event_key = event.values_at(:user, :device, :source, :date, :host).join(";")
  bin[event_key] = event
end
```

A date key is derived from the event's date and the bin assignment is determined accordingly. Note the use of the ||= construction to initialize a new bin as a hash if it doesn't already exist. The event is then placed in the bin under a key built from the various values it has.

Putting It All Together

New events need to be laid on top of those from previous runs. This can be achieved by first running through the processes already described to build a global update hash. From this hash, it will be clear which days have been updated. If files already exist on disk for those days, they can be loaded into memory and have the updates merged before being written back to disk. The code to accomplish this forms Listing 9-11.

Listing 9-11. *The Final Event Processing Script*

```
require "yaml"

data_dir = (ARGV[0] || "data")
fail "couldn't find directory #{data_dir}" unless File.directory?(data_dir)

Dir.chdir(data_dir)
Dir.mkdir("processed") unless File.directory?("processed")

# code from Listings 9-9 and 9-10 would go here
data_files, periods = DIR["*.yaml"], {}
data_files.each do |file|
  host = File.basename(file).split(".").first
  logins = YAML.load_file(file)
  logins.each do |login|
    event = parse_event(login, host)
    assign_event(event, periods)
  end
end
periods.each do |date_string, events|
  event_file = File.join("processed", date_string + ".yaml")
  if File.exist?(event_file)
    old_events = YAML.load_file(event_file)
    events = old_events.merge(events)
  end
```

```
  File.open(event_file, "w") { |f| YAML.dump(events, f) }
end
File.delete(data_files)
```

We start with four lines that check for the existence of the data directory from which we will be parsing the YAML files. This is either `./data` or a directory passed on the command line. Either way, we change directories so that we are sitting within the data folder for the rest of the script. In addition, we ensure the existence of a `processed` directory within the data directory so we have a place to keep our output.

The files of interest are defined to be any in the data directory matching the *globbing* pattern `*.yaml`. For each of these files, the pertinent hostname is determined from the filename, and the events described within are processed by the methods we previously wrote in Listings 9-9 and 9-10.

Coming out of the `data_files.each` block, we are left with a hash of 24-hour event bins full of new events specified by the processed YAML files. Taking each of these periods, we write the new events to disk, merging them with older events if they exist. Note the use of `File.join` to create a platform-independent path string.

To conclude the script, we throw away the now processed YAML files that we should no longer need. This raises an interesting point regarding concurrency. There is no systematic protection here that would prevent the processing and subsequent deletion of a half-written YAML data file. I chose not to include such measures to keep the code to a minimum.

In order to introduce better resilience in this respect, we could borrow the locked file class from Chapter 5 and use it to serialize the writing section in the original collector and reading section above.

On the subject of systematic design, it is already apparent that this script is becoming a little unwieldy due to its monolithic nature. We could have written it with `Event` and `StorageBin` classes to create greater abstraction, but it was just small and simple enough not to bother.

Aggregate Analysis

For a section on data analysis, we've talked surprisingly little about actual analysis of the data. Everything so far has been about coercing the data so that it's ready for further study. Although it's not certain, the chances are that most of the numerical or other results you might wish to glean from the data are aggregates. They will somehow summarize trends, averages, sums, frequencies, and so forth.

This is important not just for the upcoming presentation of data, but also for controlling the underlying life cycle of the data. If you're storing large volumes of data in the `processed` folder and you really need to clear some out, the fact that you can just delete the files oldest-first is one of the reasons I often choose periodic storage of this kind.

You don't have to completely destroy the data, however. If you are creating summaries as part of your analysis, they will by definition tend to take up less space than the data they summarize. Keeping the summaries around after the original data is deleted means that information doesn't just disappear but in fact degrades. It's worth remembering that this approach can keep the most pertinent bits of data around for a very long time.

As part of our login session example, we need to choose some aggregate operation that we can present later. A simple one would be a per-day analysis of the total amount of session time spent by each user across the entire network.

Such a sum is complicated by the fact that one user can have many simultaneous logins on many hosts. Integrating any session events that were coincident would be an obvious way to compensate for this, but we'll consider that a version 2 feature and proceed with the simpler example in Listing 9-12.

Listing 9-12. *Summarizing the Total Session Duration Amounts by User and Then by Date*

```
require "yaml"

source_dir = ARGV[0]
fail "couldn't find directory #{source_dir}" unless File.directory?(source_dir)
users = {}
Dir[File.join(source_dir, "*")].each do |file|
  date_string = File.basename(file, ".yaml")
  events = YAML.load_file(file)
  events.each do |key, event|
    duration = event[:duration].to_i
    next unless duration > 0
    user = (users[event[:user]] ||= Hash.new(0))
    user[date_string] += duration
  end
end
```

This script requires that the user specify the directory containing the processed YAML files. It builds a hash by username where each value is in turn a hash by date of total session duration. The logic should require little explanation, although I would just draw your attention to the use of Hash.new(0), which provides a hash whose return value is 0 rather than nil when requesting an entry that doesn't exist. This is a very handy convention that keeps subsequent code clearer.

The script does not write anything back to disk, as we've seen that code a couple of times already. This listing instead represents the first half of a script we'll complete in the next section, finally giving a script that performs analysis and then spits out some pretty charts.

Before moving on to the presentation section, I'd like to aggregate this data one other way. It might be interesting to create a graph (in the mathematical sense) in which users are related to the hosts they use by links that are weighted based on session duration totals. The script to create such a summary would be nearly identical to the previous one except that the subhashes under users would use hostnames for keys instead of dates. Basically, we wouldn't need the date_string line, and we would change the last line of the events.each block to read user[event[:host]] += duration.

Presenting Data

I was recently in London and had to buy a ticket at one of the major train stations. As usual, the queues for a teller were atrocious, so I lined up to use one of the automated ticket machines. As ATMs go, the ones at this station are pretty mundane, but (unbeknownst to me) one of them was about to do something decidedly odd.

I selected my destination and inserted my credit card. The onscreen display asked me to punch in my PIN on the keypad provided. It was at this point that an uncomfortable reality presented itself. There was no keypad and never had been. Thus I was forced to recognize that I had just met my first ATM suffering from phantom limb syndrome.

My point should be evident: presentation may be key, but the key to good presentation lies in the reality of the data. It didn't matter that the ATM was very helpful in destination and ticket selection or that each screen was a loving blend of postmodern shapes and gradients. It was asking me to pretend that it had a keypad—insisting that I play along if I hoped to complete my transaction.

The previous two sections have been leading to a point where we have good data that is analyzed cogently and ready for presentation. This section covers two distinct ways to present network data that I have consistently found useful as an administrator: charts and graphs.

Charts

We've all done it. Someone asks for a breakdown of bandwidth usage over time or average file system use per user and we follow a simple three-step plan:

1. Gather the data.

2. Export it as a tab-separated values (TSV) file (or something similar).

3. Import the data into our favorite spreadsheet application and create a chart from it.

This approach is entirely germane for creating the odd chart here and there. However, it isn't really suitable for frequent production of charts. In particular, the instant understanding of trends that comes from certain kinds of charts can be very useful in making near-real-time decisions.

If the outbound bandwidth for SMTP for a given afternoon spikes in a way you've never seen before, knowing about it while it's still going on would be great. Thus we need to be able to generate charts from data using Ruby directly, so that the process from data to chart is entirely automated.

There is a question of what output format we should use. For example, we could use a script to generate a specification file for `gnuplot` (`www.gnuplot.info`). As charting tools go, `gnuplot` is immensely powerful and would be pertinent if this were a chapter on collecting data from a particle physics experiment.

For the world of semicasual data we're exploring, there is a simple criterion for choosing the chart format. We should be able to display the chart (and any associated materials) in an unaltered web browser on any reasonably modern system. For a busy system administrator trying to get 15 things done in a single day, it is really useful to be able to center the entire world on an e-mail client and a web browser.

In that spirit, I tend to use one of two libraries: `scruffy` for bar, line, and area charts, and the CSS chart helper for Rails.

Scruffy Charts

I have to admit that I love the Scruffy Charts library. Once you get going, it is profoundly simple to create charts that boast both prettiness and clarity. The only slightly convoluted process associated with using it can be the installation (depending on your platform). Internally scruffy uses the SVG format to represent the chart, which allows it to render the graph identically at virtually any size. Unfortunately, we haven't yet reached the point where all the common browsers will render an SVG natively. Thus the chart needs to be rendered out to something more palatable like a PNG.

For rendering a graph, scruffy relies upon the RMagick library (itself a Ruby interface to the ImageMagick library). The challenge is to get this library installed and working before installing scruffy. The easiest way to accomplish this is with the package installation process for open source applications on your platform. In other words, install the RPM, DEB, or equivalent package for ImageMagick (www.imagemagick.org). For example, as a Mac OS X user I employ MacPorts (www.macports.org) so that I can simply invoke the following:

```
$ sudo port install ImageMagick
```

enter my administrative password, and have the entire installation with all dependencies handled automatically. With ImageMagick installed, the remainder of the process is mercifully simple, as both RMagick and scruffy are available as gems (as usual, more detail can be found in Chapter 10).

■**Caution** As of version 1.15.0, RMagick has a number of issues on Mac OS X 10.4 when using the gem installation process (or the ports one via the rb-rmagick package, for that matter). Download the sources directly from http://rubyforge.org/projects/rmagick. Build and installation instructions can be found within the source bundle. Alternatively, you might just decide you'd rather stick with the SVGs scruffy can produce natively and rid yourself of these dependencies entirely.

Now that we are able to use the library, the first thing to do is initialize a chart. Note that the library refers to charts as graphs, and we will stick with this convention in any source code. We start with the code in Listing 9-13 to create a chart.

Listing 9-13. *Creating a Blank Chart (with a Title)*

```
require "scruffy"
include Scruffy

graph = Graph.new(:title => "Average Flatulence per Capita")
```

As previously, we use a trusty include statement to avoid the requirement of a Scruffy:: in front of various things. Creating an empty chart is as easy as initializing a new object. The new method takes various parameters to tune the chart's appearance, as listed in Table 9-2.

All of these values can also be set individually through assignment of the form graph.title = "Average Rainfall". Take a look at the library documentation for more information on the available themes and formatters as well as details on how to build your own.

Table 9-2. *Parameters Accepted by Scruffy::Graph.new*

Key	Description	Default Value
title	Chart's title	None
theme	Theme object used in rendering	Scruffy::Themes::Keynote.new
layers	Array of layers for the chart to use	None
default_type	Symbol indicating the default type to use for layers (i.e., :line, :area, :bar)	None
value_formatter	Formatting object used in rendering	Scruffy::Formatters::Number.new
point_markers	Array of x-axis marker values	None
rasterizer	Rasterizing object used in rendering	Scruffy::Rasterizers::RMagickRasterizer.new

The next job is to add data layers to this chart (one layer per data sequence). Each layer carries not only data but also a display type (such as :bar). This means that it is possible to mix and match different display types on a single chart, which is rather spiffy and is demonstrated in Listing 9-14.

Listing 9-14. *Adding Data to the Chart (with Mixed Display Types)*

```
graph.add(:line, "Cows", [150, 200, 250, 240])
graph.add(:area, "Sheep", [100, 110, 120, 140])
graph.add(:bar, "Man", [50, 65, 78, 66])
```

The add method is used to attach a new layer of data to the chart and accepts four arguments. These are a symbol indicating the type (optional if a default_type was set), a string specifying the title of the dataset, an array containing the data values, and finally an options hash that is passed to the underlying constructor for the particular layer type.

The quickly reached final step is to render out the chart using Graph.render. This method processes the SVG structure in memory and either returns it as a string or passes it out to RMagick to render to some other format, returning a string of the resulting bytes. For convenience, it can also be made to write the string in either case out to a file directly. Table 9-3 is a list of the parameters Graph.render can be passed.

So an example for rendering our data might be as follows:

```
graph.render(:as => "PNG", :size => [500, 400], :to => "/tmp/flatulence.png")
```

Table 9-3. *Parameters Accepted by Scruffy::Graph.render*

Key	Description	Default Value
size	An array indicating [width, height]	[600, 400]
width	Width in pixels (height = 3/4 width)	600
theme	Override default theme	None
min_value	Override calculated minimum y-value	None
max_value	Override calculated maximum y-value	None
as	Format to render to (PNG, JPG, etc.)	nil (return an SVG)
to	Save data to file instead of returning it	None

As described by the documentation, the library has plenty of options for playing with themes and formats, or even adding chart types. We have all we need, however, to create a chart from our login data, as shown in Listing 9-15.

Listing 9-15. *Charting the Login Session Duration Data in a Simple Way*

```
require "scruffy"
include Scruffy

# code from Listing 9-12 would go here
exit if users.empty?

all_dates = users.map { |user, dates| dates.keys }.flatten.uniq.sort
graph = Graph.new(:point_markers => all_dates)
graph.title = "Total Login Minutes per User"
users.each do |user, dates|
  all_values = all_dates.map { |date| dates[date].to_i }
  graph.add(:line, user, all_values)
end
graph.render(:as => "PNG", :width => 1024, :to => "/tmp/user_accounting.png")
```

Here we first determine the unique ordered set of dates for labeling the x-axis and aligning the data. From the way we constructed the users hash in Listing 9-12, date-duration pairs will not appear for a user if that date had no logged session time. Hence the all_dates line grabs an array of dates from every user, flattens these arrays into one big array, reduces it to a unique set, and sorts the dates in ascending order.

We next create our chart object, set up the x-axis with these date values, and add an appropriate title. The values from the chart are in sets on a per-user basis. Thus for each user, we map every point on the x-axis to a duration logged for that user. Among other things, this means that the chart will display zero usage for any users on days when their usage data was not collected.

With the chart built, we finally render it out to a PNG. If this was inside a web application, we might render the chart and insert an image link in a page. Alternatively, we could leave off the :to parameter and simply return the stream directly as previously discussed. For complete-ness, Figure 9-1 shows a sample chart built this way.

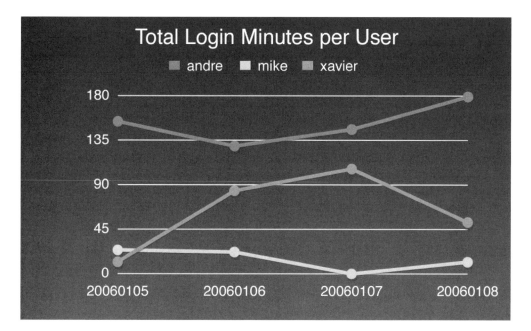

Figure 9-1. *A chart as generated by Listing 9-15*

CSS Charts in Rails

The CSS chart helper for Rails is based on a simple idea. The CSS box model allows for doing pretty basic rectangular drawing, including background, border, and alignment facilities. We can use this to build charts.

Installing the helper couldn't be easier. In the root directory of your chosen Rails application, run the following:

```
$ script/plugin install http://topfunky.net/svn/plugins/css_graphs
```

This will retrieve the latest copy of the helper and place it in your vendor/plugins directory. Included in this installation is a set of images helpful for basic chart display. These images can be added to your public/images directory with the following command:

```
$ script/generate css_graphs
```

Once the helper is available to your application, a chart may be rendered inside one of your rhtml templates using the following pattern:

```
<h2>Horizontal Bar Chart (Complex)</h2>
<%= complex_bar_graph(["Mail", 58], ["Web", 38], ["FTP", 29], ["P2P", 25],➡
  ["Other", 24]) %>
```

which will give you a bar chart like the one shown in Figure 9-2.

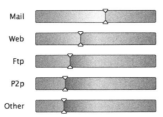

Figure 9-2. *A complex horizontal bar chart as created by the CSS chart helper*

This method populates the title field of each bar so that a rollover with the mouse will give you the value associated with each bar. The CSS helper also implements two other methods:

- bar_graph: A simple vertical bar chart with the values on the bars

- horizontal_bar_graph: A simple horizontal bar chart with values as percentages printed on the bars and bar titles available on rollover

Graphs

As previously indicated, when I refer to graphs in this chapter I do so in the mathematical sense. Put simply, a *graph* is a network of nodes interconnected by edges, which can be assigned weights or even directions. Think road maps.

Given how many things under the influence of the noble system administrator form networks (not least of which is *the network*), having a tool that allows for the quick creation of graphs can be really handy.

The Graphviz format is a well-established language for expressing networks. What we'd like to do is build a Graphviz document out of our data and then get something to render it for us. Starting with the second bit first, the Graphviz tools are available from www.graphviz.org and include a command line tool called dot. This tool can take a Graphviz document and render it out as a GIF, PNG, SVG, or PostScript file. Ensure you have the dot tool available before proceeding.

As to generating the document, a Ruby library is available for just such a purpose: ruby-graphviz. Just as scruffy used RMagick, so does ruby-graphviz sit on top of dot to do its rendering for it. The library's project page is located at http://raa.ruby-lang.org/project/ruby-graphviz, which offers a downloadable gzipped tar bundle. Once you expand it, you'll find the library and some examples.

There is also a setup file that will check for the presence of dot and ready a make-style installation for the library itself. Thus the installation process ended up looking like this for me:

```
$ tar -xzf ruby-graphviz_0.6.0.tar.gz
$ cd ruby-graphviz
$ ruby extconf.rb
```

```
checking for dot... yes
creating Makefile
```

```
$ sudo make install
```

```
/usr/bin/install -c -m 644 ./lib/graphviz.rb /usr/lib/ruby/site_ruby/1.8
/usr/bin/install -c -m 644 ./lib/graphviz/attrs.rb➥
  /usr/lib/ruby/site_ruby/1.8/graphviz
/usr/bin/install -c -m 644 ./lib/graphviz/constants.rb➥
  /usr/lib/ruby/site_ruby/1.8/graphviz
/usr/bin/install -c -m 644 ./lib/graphviz/edge.rb➥
  /usr/lib/ruby/site_ruby/1.8/graphviz
/usr/bin/install -c -m 644 ./lib/graphviz/node.rb➥
  /usr/lib/ruby/site_ruby/1.8/graphviz
/usr/bin/install -c -m 644 ./lib/graphviz/xml.rb➥
  /usr/lib/ruby/site_ruby/1.8/graphviz
```

Remember that it is almost certain that the last command will need to be issued by a user with root privileges, hence my use of sudo on Mac OS X. Once you've installed the Graphviz tools, you're ready to create a graph.

Unsurprisingly, there is a Graphviz object that holds the graph information:

```
require "graphviz"
graph = Graphviz.new("G")
```

and a way to add nodes and edges:

```
gas = graph.add_node("Atmospheric_CO2")
photo = graph.add_node("Photosynthesis", "shape" => "box")
graph.add_node("Combustion", "style" => "filled")

graph.add_edge(gas, photo, "weight" => 22)
graph.add_edge(photo, "Combustion")
```

and finally a way to produce the graph:

```
graph.output("output" => "png")
```

Note that the output method by default will dump the Graphviz file to standard out. This can prove useful if you intend to use a Graphviz viewer with the ability to change formatting and layout.

There isn't a lot more to say about this library. It does offer the ability to add subgraphs to graphs if the need should arise (via the astonishingly named add_graph method). On that subject, naming the graph G may seem odd. It is purely a referential name and has nothing to do with a title or other such human-facing concept. It exists so that we can add the graph to another by reference.

This ability aside, we have all we need to complete the examples for this chapter with Listing 9-16.

Listing 9-16. *Creating a Graph from the User Login Data*

```
require "graphviz"
# code from Listing 9-12 modified as discussed (for indexing by host) would go here
exit if users.empty?
graph = Graphviz.new("G")
users.each do |user, hosts|
  graph.add_node(user)
  hosts.each do |host, usage|
    graph.add_node(host)
    graph.add_edge(user, host, "weight" => usage)
  end
end
graph.output("output" => "png", "file" => "/tmp/user_relationships.png")
```

This is very similar to the code used to create the chart. In this case, we have to add nodes for every entity we might connect together (all users and hosts). We are able to cheat a little in adding a host multiple times (should one host be used by more than one user), as the library's internal structure stops this from leading to multiple nodes.

All That Glitters

Over the course of this chapter, we examined possibilities for collecting data over networks using both the traditional SNMP approach and a slightly more novel SSH technique. We looked at some avenues of analysis for this data, paying particular attention to data structure and retention. In the final section, we created some charts and a relationship graph in order to present the data we collected.

In the next chapter, you will discover the glittering world of gems. By understanding how to use and make them, a whole layer of modularity and abstraction will be made possible.

■ ■ ■

Extending Ruby: A Fistful of Gems

Perl has CPAN (www.cpan.org), JavaScript has JSAN (www.openjsan.org), and Python has a darkened crypt (http://py.vaults.ca). Ruby also has a unified packaging system for supplementing the available cloud of libraries on a system: *RubyGems*. Each individual bundle of functionality under this scheme is called a *gem* and contains, as you will see, all of the code and metainformation pertinent to a given library.

In exploring the world of gems, this chapter is split into two sections. We begin with a detailed run-through of how to search for, acquire, and install gems. This discussion includes guidance on using these gems in scripts and how to access documentation for the various classes and methods they define.

From here, the next logical step is to uncover the process by which we might create our own gem. In particular, we'll unpick the actual gem structure and get an understanding of how the various bits interact. We'll also look at the publishing process, both internal and global.

Managing and Using Gems

The obvious place to begin is at the RubyGems homepage (www.rubygems.org). This site is a gold mine of useful information, and I urge you to have a wander through it to both reinforce and expand upon the contents of this chapter. Of particular utility is the FAQ section, from which we may condense a couple of definitions:

- A gem is essentially a packaged Ruby application or library that has a name (like rails) and a variety of metainformation such as a version number (like 1.1.16).

- Based on the metainformation associated with each gem, the suite of tools provided by the RubyGems project allows for easy querying, installation, dependency tracking, version selection, testing, documentation, and creation of packages.

The gems system is much like any other reasonable package-management solution, providing simple tools to bolt libraries onto your scripts and install entire Ruby applications. This should be enough to whet your appetite, so let's sprint to the first hurdle: installation.

Installing RubyGems

RubyForge (http://rubyforge.org) is the de facto location for the hosting of gems. Accordingly, it is only fitting that RubyGems itself can be downloaded from this site. Point your browser at http://rubyforge.org/projects/rubygems and click the Download link to be taken to the list of available source packages. RubyGems is provided as either a gzipped tarball (.tgz) or a ZIP archive (.zip), and you should obviously choose whichever format is easiest for you.

Note As befits the subject, RubyGems itself is available as a gem. We'll get into more detail later about how RubyGems is able to update itself on your system. For now, you can safely ignore the .gem download.

Once you've extracted the contents of the archive, you'll be left with a directory named something like rubygems-0.9.1. Once you've moved into this directory, it's time to make a choice. Do you want this installation to affect the entire system or be installed in your own user-specific sandbox?

Systemwide Installation

A canonical installation couldn't be simpler:

```
$ ruby setup.rb
```

Bear in mind that this command will attempt to install the RubyGems toolchain in a system-restricted location, meaning that you will likely need to run it with escalated privileges (e.g., using sudo). From now on, I won't make this point explicitly, so remember the issue of permissions when attempting to perform gem operations.

You should also be mindful of the fact that RubyGems depends on the Ruby YAML and GZip libraries. These ship as part of the standard distribution, but on certain platforms (principally Debian and derivatives) they are extras that will need to be added before attempting to install RubyGems.

Localized Installation

Overriding the default location requires breaking the single setup step into three distinct steps to allow for configuration. Assuming that you wish to install RubyGems in /home/gerald, you will need to pass this path as the installation's prefix. In addition, you'll probably want to alter where the gem repository itself will live. This has to be done with an environment variable called GEM_HOME, for which a sensible setting might be /home/gerald/gems. Putting these steps together gives the following:

```
$ export GEM_HOME=/home/gerald
$ ruby setup.rb config --prefix=/home/gerald
$ ruby setup.rb setup
$ ruby setup.rb install
```

Naturally, the `export` command is not necessarily how you might set an environment variable on your platform of choice. Similarly, the convention of using a `/home/user` directory is pretty Linux-specific. Adapt the procedure to your system as appropriate.

The installation will end up placing the appropriate scripts in `<prefix>/bin`, so remember to add this `bin` directory to your path. Also ensure that, however you set the environment variable, it remains in effect in future sessions (otherwise, RubyGems won't have a clue where to find the repository).

The gem Command

The tool that installs, tests, maintains, removes, and provides information on gems is called gem. Before we go any further, let's just try running it and see what happens in Listing 10-1.

Listing 10-1. *The Output of the gem Command Invoked Without Arguments*

```
$ gem
```

```
RubyGems is a sophisticated package manager for Ruby.  This is a
basic help message containing pointers to more information.

  Usage:
    gem -h/--help
    gem -v/--version
    gem command [arguments...] [options...]

  Examples:
    gem install rake
    gem list --local
    gem build package.gemspec
    gem help install

  Further help:
    gem help commands            list all 'gem' commands
    gem help examples            show some examples of usage
    gem help <COMMAND>           show help on COMMAND
                                   (e.g. 'gem help install')
  Further information:
    http://rubygems.rubyforge.org
```

The output in Listing 10-1 should give you a basic flavor for how gem operates. It takes a command verb followed by appropriate arguments (nouns) and optional parameters that tweak the action undertaken. The help built in to gem is really very good, so remember that it exists and can be invoked as indicated in Listing 10-1.

Updating RubyGems

The first order of business, given that the previous section dealt with installing RubyGems, is to get a handle on maintaining the installation (i.e., keeping it up to date). You'll recall that I mentioned the availability of RubyGems as a gem—this is where that fact comes into play. The update verb accepts a special parameter that will update the installation rather than a particular gem under its care:

```
$ gem update --system
```

This command will either grab and install the latest version, providing a lot of detail in the process, or simply confirm that your installation is cutting edge. We'll look at update in more detail later on.

Searching for Gems

With a nice fresh RubyGems installation, you're ready to go shopping for gems. The key verb here is search. It allows you to search for gems in the remote (or local) repositories that match a string fragment. By default it will search only the local repository, so you'll often find yourself using the -r flag (or --remote if you prefer), as shown in Listing 10-2.

Listing 10-2. *A Simple Search of the Remote Repository for Any Gem Containing "fish"*

```
$ gem search -r fish
```

```
*** REMOTE GEMS ***

starfish (1.2.0, 1.1.3, 1.1.2, 1.1.1, 1.1.0, 1.0.0)
    Starfish is a utility to make distributed programming ridiculously
    easy.
```

Notice that there are multiple versions of the starfish gem listed here. One of the nice things about the RubyGems system is that it makes it easy to maintain parallel installation of different versions of the same gem. This can be rather handy if an API changes and you'd like to update your scripts gradually.

If you'd like to search using a regular expression instead of a simple substring match, then the query verb is for you. For example, gem query -n 'e[ds]$' will search for any gem whose name ends in either ed or es.

Installing a Gem

Once you've found a gem that you like the look of, it's time to install it. The only argument needed here is the full name of the gem (starfish). There are several options that might prove useful, however. You can set whether the local (-l/--local), remote (-r/--remote), or both (-b/--both) repositories are to be searched for the gem (the default is both). You can run any built-in tests (-t/--test) to check the gem's validity (this is not done by default).

There is also a flag to install any as yet unfulfilled dependencies automatically (`-y/ --include-dependencies`) rather than the normal behavior of prompting the user for permission to do so. The version (`-v/--version`) required can also be specified if the latest one is not what you are after. The installation of a gem looks something like Listing 10-3.

Listing 10-3. *The Installation of a Specific Version of a Gem*

```
$ gem install starfish -v 1.1.3
```

```
Successfully installed starfish-1.1.3
Installing ri documentation for starfish-1.1.3...
Installing RDoc documentation for starfish-1.1.3...
```

Note how the gem's installer has automatically generated documentation that can be accessed through the trusty `ri` command and RDoc-based documentation that can be accessed via a web browser. Precisely how to access this second form of documentation is discussed in the "Accessing Documentation via gem_server" section.

Listing the Installed Gems

It is easy to lose track of what's installed, so we are fortunate to have the `list` verb. It works exactly like `search` (particularly given that they both default to looking in the local repository only). The only real difference is that, if a fragment is provided as an argument, `list` will match it against the start of the gem names, whereas `search` will match it as a substring, as demonstrated in Listing 10-4.

Listing 10-4. *A Listing of Locally Installed Gems*

```
$ gem list
```

```
*** LOCAL GEMS ***

fastercsv (1.0.0)
    FasterCSV is CSV, but faster, smaller, and cleaner.

log4r (1.0.5)
    Log4r is a comprehensive and flexible logging library for Ruby.
```

Updating Gems

You have already encountered the `update` verb. Without the `--system` option, it will download and install the latest versions of any outdated gem. Alternatively, you can specify the particular gem you'd like to have updated if you don't want to perform this operation on all of them. It takes a number of the same arguments as `install`, so the command shown in Listing 10-5 will update `starfish`, running tests and installing any dependencies.

Listing 10-5. *Updating a Gem with Additional Options*

```
$ gem update starfish -t -y
```

```
Updating installed gems...
Attempting remote update of starfish
Successfully installed starfish-1.2.0
Installing ri documentation for starfish-1.2.0...
Installing RDoc documentation for starfish-1.2.0...
There are no unit tests to run for starfish-1.2.0
```

Remember that I mentioned the idea of being able to have multiple versions of the same library installed at once. After the update we just performed, a quick list operation reveals the following:

```
starfish (1.2.0, 1.1.3)
```

Assuming that we eventually reach the point where we no longer need the older version, we will need to uninstall it somehow. This is the purview of the cleanup verb. Once again, this command can be used on the entire repository or a specific gem, as illustrated by Listing 10-6.

Listing 10-6. *Cleaning Up After an Update*

```
$ gem cleanup starfish
```

```
Cleaning up installed gems...
Attempting uninstall on starfish-1.1.3
Successfully uninstalled starfish version 1.1.3
Clean Up Complete
```

Removing a Gem

We've searched, installed, updated, and cleaned up. All that remains of the obvious packaging operations is removal. Since it's the opposite of install, the removal verb is uninstall. The most prominent option supported by this command is the specification of the version to be removed (-v/--version).

During the uninstallation, you will be prompted to agree to the removal of any gems that depend on the doomed gem. This behavior can be overridden by instructing gem to ignore dependencies (-i/--ignore-dependencies). Listing 10-7 shows how we would remove the starfish gem.

Listing 10-7. *Uninstalling a Gem*

```
$ gem uninstall starfish
```

```
Successfully uninstalled starfish version 1.2.0
Remove executables and scripts for 'starfish' in addition to the gem? [Yn]  Y
Removing starfish
```

Notice that we were prompted to remove executables that depended on starfish. You can instruct gem to perform this step without confirmation (-x/--executables).

Other Verbs of Interest

There are quite a number of other verbs that I don't personally use nearly as often as those already discussed. Awareness of them can be useful, but you can always get a reminder (as suggested by Listing 10-1) using gem help commands. I'd like to give special mention to a few of these remaining verbs:

- Metainformation about the RubyGems installation is yielded using environment.

- The dependencies for a particular gem can be retrieved using dependency.

- The set of files installed by a gem are revealed using contents.

- A list of gems that need an update can be derived with outdated.

Using Gems in Your Code

Now that we've covered all the important bits involved in getting gems onto and off of your system, it's time to actually use the things. Because the RubyGems system allows for multiple concurrent versions of a gem to exist on your system, you can't (quite) simply use the require command as you might with the standard libraries.

Requirement of RubyGems

The first way to get gems going in your script is to require "rubygems". This overrides the default functionality of require, allowing it to perform latest-version inclusion of gems:

```
require "rubygems"
require "starfish"

# script here
```

Alternatively, it would be (slightly) easier to use a command flag to the Ruby interpreter:

```
$ ruby –rubygems script_using_starfish.rb
```

More commonly, we can encode this requirement in the environment variable Ruby reads at startup:

```
$ export RUBYOPT=rubygems
$ ruby script_using_starfish.rb
```

Explicit Versioning

If your script relies on a specific version of a gem, you'll need the gem command. Here's a basic example:

```
gem "starfish", "1.1.3"
```

Clearly, this isn't particularly complicated. It merely adds a version parameter to the normal require semantics. What's interesting is that this versioning isn't restricted to simple equality. The following version strings are also valid:

- "= 1.1.3": Equal to 1.1.3 (implied when there is no qualifying symbol)

- "!= 1.1.3": Not equal to 1.1.3

- "> 1.1.3", ">= 1.1.3": Greater than, greater than or equal to 1.1.3

- "< 1.1.3", "<= 1.1.3": Less than, less than or equal to 1.1.3

- "~> 1.1.3": Approximately greater than 1.1.3

These (in)equality statements should all be fairly self-explanatory except for the last one, which merits some small discussion. Conventional version numbering holds that at least one of the numbers in the version (usually the leftmost) will only change in the event of a major rewrite. It is entirely possible that such a rewrite could break existing code that relies on the library.

The gem statement is not limited to two arguments. You are at liberty to specify any number of constraints on the version used (at which point the version that is included in your script is the youngest one whose version number matches every constraint). So, if we were pessimistic about major version number changes, we might write this:

```
gem "starfish", ">= 1.1.0", "< 2"
```

This is cumbersome, so RubyGems provides the ~> syntax, which allows us to specify the same constraint in the following manner:

```
gem "starfish", "~> 1.1"
```

The internal logic of this is quite straightforward. The minimum acceptable version is taken at face value to be 1.1(.0) and above. RubyGems then strips the least significant number away from the given version (leaving 1), adds 1 to it, and designates that the noninclusive upper bound. This is just a convenience, and you are free to use the more specific syntax—especially if these aren't quite the semantics you're looking for.

■**Tip** Although it's probably not apparent, RubyGems uses this simple versioning syntax throughout the toolset. This includes all those places you can specify a version number within a gem command operation.

Accessing Documentation via gem_server

Another useful tool supplied as part of RubyGems is a WEBrick-based server that will vend all of the compiled documentation for the various gems in an easy-to-swallow manner. Enjoying the benefits of this utility couldn't be simpler:

```
$ gem_server
```

```
[2007-02-05 01:06:52] INFO  WEBrick 1.3.1
[2007-02-05 01:06:52] INFO  ruby 1.8.5 (2006-08-25) [powerpc-darwin8.8.0]
[2007-02-05 01:06:52] INFO  WEBrick::HTTPServer#start: pid=1860 port=8808
```

Once the server is up and running, you just point a web browser at localhost:8808 and voila—documentation abounds. The port to which the server binds (8808 by default) can be altered with a -p <portnum>. I personally have gem_server running as a permanent service on my laptop with a corresponding bookmark in my browser.

Creating Gems

There are at least three good reasons for rolling your own gems. Creating your own gems

- Forces you to think about your code in a more modular fashion

- Promotes reuse over reinvention within corporate code bases

- Enables you to give a little back to the community that makes Ruby so amazingly useful

Of these three, I would particularly emphasize the first point. There is nothing quite like trying to divide some monolithic bit of code into bits you can name individually based on what they do. For the purposes of this section, I'm going to imagine that such code division has already been undertaken and that we're ready to fashion a gem from one of the parts.

What Is a Gem, Anyway?

It's time to take the plunge and examine the format of a gem. The actual structure involved is not particularly intricate. When preparing the library and associated materials for packaging, there are a few simple rules to follow:

- All Ruby source files belong in a directory called lib.

- All tests go in the tests directory.

- Executable scripts live in the bin directory.

- Source code for extensions (e.g., in C) should be placed in the ext directory.

- The project should always have a README file in its root directory.

- Any supplementary documentation not covered by the README or autogenerated from your code should reside within the docs directory.

Once you have these entities squirreled away in their respective nests, the only thing missing is a specification file (a *gemspec*), which defines all of the metainformation pertinent to the package.

Digging deeper, a .gem is actually a tarball containing two gzipped files:

```
$ tar -tf starfish-1.2.0.gem
```

```
data.tar.gz
metadata.gz
```

The first (data.tar.gz) is a gzipped tarball of the directory in which the original resources were assembled:

```
$ tar -xf starfish-1.2.0.gem
$ tar -tzf data.tar.gz
```

```
lib/map_reduce.rb
lib/starfish.rb
lib/map_reduce/active_record.rb
lib/map_reduce/array.rb
lib/map_reduce/file.rb
bin/starfish
LICENSE
Rakefile
README
...and so on...
```

The second component of a gem is its metadata file (metadata.gz). This is produced from the specification file already mentioned. The fact that it is written in YAML makes it quite legible:

```
$ gzcat metadata.gz
```

```
--- !ruby/object:Gem::Specification
rubygems_version: 0.8.11
specification_version: 1
name: starfish
version: !ruby/object:Gem::Version
  version: 1.2.0
date: 2006-09-20 00:00:00 -07:00
summary: Starfish is a utility to make distributed programming ridiculously easy.
require_paths:
- lib
email: lucas@rufy.com
homepage: http://rubyforge.org/projects/starfish
...and so on...
```

I hope you now have a reasonably firm grasp on the nature and structure of a `.gem`. With that in mind, the rest of this section will take a brisk walk through creating one that packages a simple library.

Gathering the Files

For our minimal example, we are going to use the `WebSession` class that we built back in Chapter 8 (Listing 8-7). It has no executables, source code, or dependencies outside the Ruby standard library, so it is an ideal first gem.

Apart from the library file itself, the only other item that should really be included is a `README`. As with other gem documentation, this file should employ RDoc-style markup so that it can be compiled and deployed as part of a documentation tree when the gem is installed.

Documentation using the RDoc standard has a whole section devoted to it in the next chapter. For now, I'm just going to present the `README` as a fait accompli. Having said that, even without an introduction to RDoc, you probably won't find it hard to follow along.

The important things to include in a gem's `README` are copyright, contact, and licensing information (actual usage information and code synopses are usually reserved for documentation generated from the individual class files). Listing 10-8 contains a minimal `README`.

Listing 10-8. *A Minimal README for the WebSession Gem*

```
== WebSession

WebSession is a class that makes it easier to build web robots.
It provides a convenient interface for...

* establishing an HTTP connection
* retrieving pages via GET
* uploading information via POST
* handling cookies without fuss

== Author

Copyright 2007 Andre Ben Hamou
mailto:imaginary@example.com
http://andre.example.com

== License

This library and all associated materials are release under the terms of version 2
of the GNU Public License (http://www.gnu.org/copyleft/gpl.html).
```

When gem parses this file, a nice HTML page will be spat out at the other end. This should be the default page that a user is brought to when first selecting the documentation for the `WebSession` project as vended by `gem_server`.

At this point, we have gathered the files we need together and our file hierarchy will look like Figure 10-1. With these files in place, it is time to build the gem specification file.

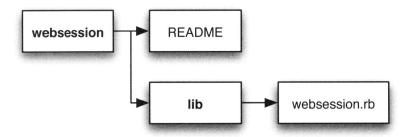

Figure 10-1. *Hierarchy of the WebSession gem ready for packaging*

Writing the Gemspec

As discussed, the gem specification file carries the metadata for the gem. In a packaged gem, `metadata.gz` is a YAML file, but the gemspec that creates it can be YAML or Ruby. In practice, you'll likely use the Ruby approach almost exclusively, as it renders the gemspecs more legible and allows for dynamically derived values in the metadata.

The `rubygems` library defines a class called `Gem::Specification` whose initializer takes a block as an argument. Within this block, individual settings can be defined as shown in Listing 10-9.

Listing 10-9. *The Smallest Possible Gemspec for WebSession*

```
require "rubygems"

Gem::Specification.new do |s|
  s.name    = "WebSession"
  s.summary = "Web automation convenience library"
  s.version = "1.0.0"
  s.files   = ["README", "lib/websession.rb"]
end
```

The first three values specified in this listing are the only required settings that don't have default values. Thus this specification (which we'll call `websession.gemspec`) is absolutely minimal. We'll get to actually building the gem in a few moments, but first let's take a look at the list of things we can specify using a gemspec in Table 10-1 (required settings are marked with an asterisk).

The only piece of metainformation not yet covered is the list of other gems that our gem might depend on. The only reason this setting is a little different is that it is specified functionally like this:

```
s.add dependency("starfish", ">= 1.1.3")
```

Obviously, the first parameter is the name of the gem upon which our gem depends, and the second parameter is a version constraint. Note that if the version specification is omitted, the constraint defaults to `"> 0.0.0"`.

Table 10-1. *Specification Options Available in a Gemspec*

Key	Description	Example Value	Default Value
author	Author's name	"Andre Ben Hamou"	None
autorequire	*See note a*	"websession"	None
bindir	Directory with executable files	"exec"	"bin"
date*	Date/time of gem creation	File.mtime("foo")	Time.now
default_executable	*See note b*	"bin/foo"	*See note b*
description	Detailed description of gem	"Very, very cool."	None
email	Author's e-mail address	"andre@example.com"	None
executables	*See note b*	["foo", "fighter"]	None
extensions	Files for building C extensions	["ext/ps/extconf.rb"]	None (*see note d*)
extra_rdoc_files	Files to add to RDoc pool	["README", "doc/foo"]	None
files	All files that make up the gem	Dir["{bin,lib}/**/*"]	None
has_rdoc	Code uses RDoc comments	true	*See note c*
homepage	Project/author's homepage	"http://example.org/"	None
name*	Gem's name	"WebSession"	None
platform*	Target deployment platform	Gem::Platform::WIN32	Gem::Platform::RUBY
rdoc_options	Options to be passed to rdoc	["--main", "README"]	None
require_paths*	*See note a*	["lib", "ext"]	["lib"]
required_ruby_version	Required Ruby version	">= 1.8.4"	"> 0.0.0"
requirements	Informal user requirements	["get a Mac"]	None
rubyforge_project	RubyForge project name	"websession"	None

Table 10-1. *Specification Options Available in a Gemspec (Continued)*

Key	Description	Example Value	Default Value
summary*	Brief description of gem	"Cool"	None
test_files	All unit test files for the gem	["test/test_all.rb"]	None
version*	Release version	"1.0.0"	None

[a] *The two settings autorequire and require_paths govern what happens when the gem is required. The require_paths array lists all of the gem-relative directories that should be added to the $LOAD_PATH of the interpreter. Specifying an autorequirement then forces a particular file to be loaded (so that the user isn't forced to use a redundant require statement once the gem has been loaded).*

[b] *The concept of specific executables (and indeed a default_executable) exists to support the idea of being able to run a Ruby application packaged in a gem in one step. The theory is that a user could download poker.gem and then run the application it contains by simply invoking gem poker.gem. The default_executable is what would be run in this case, and it gets set to the first item listed in executables as long as executables contains only that item. This inline application feature of RubyGems is not in widespread use at the moment.*

[c] *By default, RDoc documentation is generated when installing a gem. Technically, the default value of has_rdoc is false. However, this value is advisory only in that the gem command does not enforce it.*

[d] *I'm not going to cover adding C extensions to gem packages. There is an entire world of possibilities that exists based on the flexibility of using C from within Ruby (and vice versa). However, it is my contention that this topic is somewhat outside the normal focus of system administration. This is why I haven't discussed it anywhere in the book (outside of the inline snippet in Chapter 3).*

Building the Gem

With the hard work done, all that remains is to build the gem itself. To do so, we employ yet another command verb available to gem: build, as demonstrated in Listing 10-10.

Listing 10-10. *Building the WebSession Gem*

```
$ gem build websession.gemspec
```

```
Successfully built RubyGem
Name: WebSession
Version: 1.0.0
File: websession-1.0.0.gem
```

That's it. We now have a shiny new gem ready for action. Unlike most of the other command verbs, build doesn't take any optional arguments, so Listing 10-10 covers everything, really.

Many Ruby projects use the rake tool to coordinate building, testing, and other maintenance tasks. Rake is covered in detail in the next chapter, but it's worth mentioning here that there is a Rake task builder for gem packaging. Take a look at the sidebar "Building Gems with Rake" for a discussion of this.

BUILDING GEMS WITH RAKE

As described in the next chapter, `rake` combines the task-driven approach of the perennial `make` tool with the expressive power of Ruby. Just as `make` runs from a `Makefile`, so `rake` uses a `Rakefile`. When driving gem production from `rake`, the `Rakefile` is normally kept in the project's root directory (nestled up against the `README`). The file's contents end up looking like this:

```
require "rake/gempackagetask"

# insert code from Listing 10-9
# adding 'spec =' to the front of the Gem::Specification block

Rake::GemPackageTask.new(spec) do |pkg|
    pkg.need_tar = true
    pkg.need_zip = true
end
```

The extra code adds a Rake task to build a gem file in a directory called `pkg`, where the name of the gem is `project-version.gem`. We can build our package from the preceding `Rakefile` as follows:

```
$ rake pkg/WebSession-1.0.0.gem
```

Publishing the Gem

For flexibility's sake, it is important to remember that a gem is completely self-contained. We can publish a gem simply by uploading it to a web site or FTP server. In addition, `gem_server` actually makes all of the locally installed gems available over HTTP (just go to `http://localhost:8808/gems` for a listing).

If we want the `gem` tool to be able to download and search for our package automatically, we have two options. The easiest and most public way to publish the gem is at RubyForge (`http://rubyforge.org`). Simply create a new account, register a new project, and upload the relevant files.

It may not be appropriate to upload the gem to a public site. Hence the second option is to publish it internally. We've already seen that `gem_server` basically does this for us. The only missing piece is how we get the various `gem` command verbs to use our server rather than Ruby-Forge's. The answer is the `--source` flag:

```
$ gem install WebSession --source http://gemserver.example.org:8808
```

A Mouthful of Jewels

The RubyGems system vastly simplifies the modularization of code. In this chapter, we covered how useful gems can be in managing an extended Ruby library. We used the `gem` command to manipulate a glittering horde of code and the `gem` method to make that code available to our scripts. We also saw how to create and publish our own gems, both internally and to the world at large.

Of course, publishing code is the last step in a development cycle. The next chapter deals with the Ruby approach to two other important coding requisites: documentation and testing.

CHAPTER 11

■■■

Testing and Documentation

In this brief chapter, we will take a look at the tools available and conventions employed in the Ruby world for keeping one's code in order. We'll kick off with a section devoted to rake. Understanding the mechanics of this task-oriented, make-like tool can really save you time in the long run—especially where common housekeeping tasks are concerned. From here we'll move on to a section on unit testing, where we'll look at some step-by-step examples and make the case that such testing is about as simple as it can be in Ruby. Finally, we'll cover the documentation idioms and the magic of rdoc.

The business of testing and documenting code is particularly important for system administration, not least because administrators spend much of their time creating new software for use in production systems. The problem with this housekeeping is that there never appears to be enough time left at the end of a development cycle to perform it all. There's always something better to do, it seems.

In that vein, there is a particular reason that this chapter is the last major one in the book. The topics enumerated in the chapter title are vital for keeping the rising tides of chaos at bay, but that doesn't stop me from loathing them. It would be disingenuous to imply otherwise. Fortunately, as with so much else, the Ruby approach to these issues is about as painless as it gets.

Rake

As mentioned in the previous chapter, rake is a heady blend of the eponymous make tool and the expressiveness of Ruby. From its roots as a simple policy-driven file creator, it has become a popular mechanism for driving all of a Ruby project's housekeeping tasks. Rails, for example, uses rake extensively to bundle up common jobs like migrating a database schema and running unit tests. As usual, rake is available as a gem (see Chapter 10 for more details).

The Basic Task

What rake will do in a given directory is defined by the contents of a file named Rakefile sitting in that directory (the name is special and so should be reproduced exactly). Suppose we had a project with a couple of tests we wanted to have run by default through rake. A simple Rakefile that achieves this would look like that shown in Listing 11-1.

Listing 11-1. *A Very Simple Rakefile to Run Some Tests by Default*

```
task :default => :test

task :test do
  ruby "tests/test1.rb"
  ruby "tests/test2.rb"
end
```

As should be apparent, rake has the concept of a *named task* (:default, :test). These tasks contain code to be run upon invocation and can be made dependent upon other tasks. If we were to run rake (with no arguments) on the directory containing the Rakefile in Listing 11-1, it would start at the :default task, see the dependence on the :test task, and run that first. Within the :test task, two Ruby scripts are run. Unsurprisingly, the ruby command within a Rakefile runs a Ruby interpreter with the given arguments.

Way back in Chapter 4, I referred to the Rakefile syntax as a good example of a domain-specific language, or DSL. The code in Listing 11-1 is pure Ruby, but it looks like a dedicated task language (albeit one that resembles Ruby quite a bit). Again, this entire DSL approach derives from Ruby's syntactic flexibility (in allowing for unbracketed method arguments, auto-constructed argument hashes, and other such niceties).

File Tasks

As stated, rake began life as a make-alike. This implies the existence of syntax for defining which project files need to be generated and in what order. This is accomplished via the file method as used in Listing 11-2.

Listing 11-2. *A Rakefile to Rebuild an Index If Any Source Files Have Changed*

```
file "index.yaml" => ["hosts.txt", "users.txt", "groups.txt"] do
  ruby "build_index.rb"
end
```

Listing 11-2 shows a basic rake file task. As with the named tasks from Listing 11-1, it has dependencies and code to be run. In this case, the file to be built is named and the files upon which it depends are specified. Notice that the dependency can be given as a single string/symbol (as in Listing 11-1) or as an array (as in Listing 11-2).

The file task performs a basic timestamp comparison to decide whether index.yaml needs to be updated. If so, the necessary steps are performed within the code block to achieve this. This idea of tasks firing off depending on the outdatedness of files should be most familiar to users of make.

If you were to invoke rake in the presence of the Rakefile from Listing 11-2, the following error would occur:

```
$ rake
(in /tmp/project3)
rake aborted!
Don't know how to build task 'default'
```

The reason for the error that you see here is that, absent any other specification, the `:default` task is what is run . . . well . . . by default. The file task to create `index.yaml` needs to be specifically identified as to-be-done. There are two ways to achieve this:

- Specify `index.yaml` as a target on the command line: `rake index.yaml`.

- Create a default task with `index.yaml` as a dependency: `task :default => "index. yaml"`.

Ensuring That Directories Exist

Often (particularly when building target file trees from scratch), we'd like to be able to ensure that the directories exist to put them in. We could write something like Listing 11-3.

Listing 11-3. *Ensuring the Presence of Directories the Hard Way*

```
file "html" do
  mkdir "html"
end

file "html/images" do
  mkdir "html/images"
end
```

But `rake` provides a convenience method that makes the whole thing simpler, as shown in Listing 11-4.

Listing 11-4. *Listing 11-3 Made Easy*

```
directory "html/images"
```

This not only expresses the need to ensure that the `html/images` directory exists, but also implicitly ensures that all parent directories are in place, too.

Generalizing with Rules

The obvious next step is the ability to create file tasks that apply to entire sets of files. These are general rules mapping collections of path-matched files to their targets. Perhaps the simplest rules are those based on file extension. Consider the normal C compilation example as typified by Listing 11-5.

Listing 11-5. *A General Rule for Compiling C Files*

```
rule ".o" => ".c" do |t|
  sh "gcc", "-Wall", "-o", t.name, "-c", t.source
end
```

This rule declaration is very similar to an ordinary file rule and will be run anytime `rake` needs to build `something.o` and cannot find a specific rule pertaining to that file. Notice that we use an object passed to the code block (`t`). This task-related object is available inside the blocks passed to any task building method, and I refer you to the documentation for greater detail on what it can do. Also described therein is the fact that the simple extension matches in Listing 11-5 can be upgraded to full-blown regular expressions and even name-building procedures.

As discussed previously, the code in Listing 11-5 only defines what to do if `something.o` is called for. It does not suggest that this file should be built by default. It is unlikely that you would wish to specify every `.o` file you want built on the command line, so we need to explore how to bulk-specify rules and dependencies.

Synthesizing Tasks

In order to deal with files in bulk, we turn to the extremely useful `FileList` class supplied as part of `rake`. It's important to understand the mechanics of `FileList`. Essentially, it acts like an array of filenames. It uses normal shell globbing patterns to work out which files it should include. It can accept multiple simultaneous patterns and deliver files that match any of them. The simplest way to create one is with the class method `FileList.[]`:

```
files = FileList["html/**/*.html"]
```

The `files` object here would respond to all the usual array methods (`each`, `map`, etc.) but it also boasts a few interesting additions. Principal among these is the ability to perform a regular expression–driven substitution on each file path, either creating a copy of the list (`files.sub`) or making the changes in situ (`files.sub!`).

As to the files returned, these are a complete set matching any globbing patterns but excluding (by default) those that

- Contain `"CVS"` or `".svn"`

- End in `".bak"` or `"~"`

- Are named `"core"`

The documentation contains lots of detail on how to fine-tune this behavior, so let's move straight on to synthesizing a task using the magic of `FileList`. We begin with an example for making one particular file dependent on lots of others:

```
file "chupacabra.history" => FileList["suck*.story"]
```

Here, the `FileList` object is created and contains any files that are named as specified by the globbing pattern (`"suck68.story"`, `"suck69.story"`, etc.). Thus the entire line sets up the history file's dependency upon the story files. Note that we don't specify a code block. It turns out that you can make as many statements as you want about a given task and they all get mixed together properly. This aspect of the `Rakefile` DSL allows for the specification of dependencies outside the definition of the task to which they relate, which can be useful for complex build trees.

True synthesis should allow us to replicate the example from Listing 11-5. Listing 11-6 shows how we'd do it with `FileList`.

Listing 11-6. *A Synthetic Version of the Rule from Listing 11-5*

```
FileList.["*.c"].each do |f|
  file f.sub(/c$/, "o") => f do |t|
    sh "gcc", "-Wall", t.source, "-c", "-o", t.name
  end
end
```

For each .c file, we create a rule for a corresponding .o that relies upon the .c. The `rule` in Listing 11-5 was easier to read, leading one to question how useful the synthetic approach might be. The point is that such synthesis becomes more and more useful as the complexity of the rule increases. Indeed it is possible to create extremely advanced rules this way—rules that would be impossible to build using a `rule` statement.

A better example like Listing 11-7 combines rules and file lists to create a traditional bit of logic for a C project.

Listing 11-7. *A Complete Rakefile for Building a C Project*

```
task :default => "cool_app"

o_files = FileList["*.c"].exclude("main.c").sub(/c$/, "o")

file "cool_app" => o_files do |t|
  sh "gcc", "-Wall", "-o", t.name, *(t.sources)
end

rule ".o" => ".c" do |t|
  sh "gcc", "-Wall", "-o", t.name, "-c", t.source
end
```

We start by defining what `rake` should do by default: ensure that `cool_app` is built and up to date. Next, we generate a list of object files that should exist given the set of C source files. `FileLists`'s `exclude` method comes in handy here to cull the `main.c` file from the list as dictated by the project's source file naming conventions. Of notable interest is the use of `FileList.sub`, which substitutes the `c` for an `o` at the end of all the files.

We are left with `o_files`, upon which the final compiled application relies. When `rake` comes to analyze the `cool_app` task, it will realize that one or more object files either do not exist or are out of date (based on the `rule` statement). In this event, each .o is created according to the code in the second block. Once all these files are shipshape, the application itself may be compiled.

It is worth remembering that this is all just Ruby code. In Listing 11-7, the two shell commands look remarkably similar, which breaks the Ruby idiom "Don't repeat yourself." We could define a method anywhere in the `Rakefile` that would take the target name, source names, and any additional flags as arguments:

```
def compile(target, sources, *flags)
  sh "gcc", "-Wall", "-Werror", "-O3", "-o", target, *(sources + flags)
end
```

This would then shorten the shell commands to

```
compile(t.name, t.sources)
compile(t.name, [t.source], "-c")
```

■**Caution** This entire C project example is used to demonstrate a simple `Rakefile`-based project that manages tasks that most readers will be familiar with. Actually, using `rake` for building a C application is probably a bad idea, just for the sheer complexity of dependency calculation for such builds.

Documenting Tasks

To conclude our tour of `rake`, I should briefly mention that there is a method to make things easier for your inheritors. Specifically, it is possible to make a `Rakefile` self-documenting on the command line. In order to provide a list of tasks together with a description of what they do, each task should be preceded by a `desc` directive, as shown in Listing 11-8.

Listing 11-8. *Rendering a Task Documented*

```
desc "Run all unit tests"
task :test do
  # run the tests
end

desc "Build a performance profile"
task :perf do
  # build the profile
end
```

With this step taken, a list of such documented tasks may be obtained by executing `rake` with the `-T` option:

```
$ rake -T
rake test  # Run all unit tests
rake perf  # Build a performance profile
```

Testing

Midway through writing this book, my living room ceiling decided to go on its own little adventure holiday, touring various other parts of the room traditionally off-limits to a respectable over-head surface. Since the word "ceiling" derives from the Middle English word denoting the act of lining the interior of a room, I have taken to referring to the rubble as my "un-ceiling."

My domestic misadventure struck me as rather apt when I came to consider this section. In theory, a program or library should be so modular that it is possible to concoct all-encompassing tests for each minute facet of functionality (unit tests). I am almost sure that when the builders were originally installing my un-ceiling, all of the fixtures and fittings were subject to some sort of testing before being used.

Whatever testing the builders did, however, did not prevent a complete structural collapse. You see, the failure was caused by an unanticipated interaction between a handful of the individual components. It is for this reason that I despair of the common reliance on unit testing. Unit tests help to prevent the publishing of code that is downright embarrassing. They are essential for minimizing ultrasilly bugs, like having a function that is supposed to add a load of numbers but actually causes your showerhead to emit peanut butter.

Unfortunately, the really juicy, subtle, self-organizing bugs that materialize as if from nowhere are inevitably the ones that you didn't see coming and that could never have been found without the system's constant use in production. Such is life; we learn by doing. In this light, I consider the most practical piece of advice I ever received about automated testing was only to add a test each time a specific bug was found to ensure it never happened again. Beyond that, when a code passes all of its unit tests, that is when the real testing should begin.

My point is that if we are to engage in automated testing and know that it should never absorb 100% of our testing time, we need a process that makes building such tests nearly effortless. Ruby has just the thing.

Ruby's Test Library

Testing in Ruby is founded upon the excellent `Test::Unit` module that ships as part of the standard distribution. It has a very simple idiom for use and conventions that are easy to follow (and, more important, remember).

Tests are grouped into test cases. These cases will usually contain one or more individual tests on a common theme or manipulating common data. To create a test case, we forge a subclass of `Test::Unit::TestCase` in Listing 11-9 and populate it with methods whose names begin with `test_`.

Listing 11-9. *A Simple Test Case*

```
require "test/unit"

class ArithmeticTest < Test::Unit::TestCase
  def test_addition
    assert 1 + 1 == 2
  end
end
```

Listing 11-9 contains everything we need to build a simple test case. Note the use of the `assert` method. Assertions are the basic tools used in testing to describe expected outcomes. The most basic assertion is this `assert` method, which is considered to have failed unless its first argument is `true`.

A plethora of assertions are available in testing. These build upon the basic `assert` method by performing specific comparisons and dumping out a pertinent message if a given test fails. For example, the assertion used in Listing 11-9 would probably have been better written as follows:

```
assert_equal(2, 1 + 1)
```

Other assertion methods include `assert_nil(obj)`, `assert_kind_of(klass, obj)`, `assert_respond_to(obj, message)`, `assert_match(regexp, string)`, and `flunk`. Take a look at `ri Test::Unit::Assertions` for more detail.

Performing Tests

`Test::Unit` has an almost magical mechanism for running the tests: you run the class file. That is to say, if I save Listing 11-9 as a file called `test_arithmetic.rb`, I can run the tests like this:

```
$ ruby test_arithmetic.rb
Loaded suite test_arithmetic
Started
.
Finished in 0.002801 seconds.

1 tests, 1 assertions, 0 failures, 0 errors
```

Needless to say, I could also make the file executable and place a shebang line at the beginning, and then run it as a self-contained application (`./test_arithmetic.rb`). The one test is run and thankfully arithmetic still works the way I thought it did. Let's see what happens when there is a failure. We'll add another test to the test case from Listing 11-9:

```
def test_subtraction
  assert_equal(1.8, 1.9 - 0.1)
end
```

Now we rerun the test case, and lo and behold:

```
$ ruby test_arithmetic.rb
Loaded suite test_arithmetic
Started
.F
Finished in 0.052447 seconds.

  1) Failure:
test_subtraction(ArithmeticTest) [test_arithmetic.rb:10]:
<1.8> expected but was
<1.8>.

2 tests, 2 assertions, 1 failures, 0 errors
```

First, the fact that `test_subtraction` failed may have surprised you (particularly given that the failure message isn't exactly brimming with insight). It turns out that `1.8` and `1.9 - 0.1` differ from each other under standard binary floating-point arithmetic in that one can be represented exactly and the other cannot, leading to tiny rounding errors when performing the test. Let this be a warning to those who use floating-point arithmetic with reckless confidence.

We should have used a different assertion: `assert_in_delta`. This method takes three floats—the expected value, the actual value, and a delta within which the two numbers will be considered equal like this:

```
assert_in_delta(1.8, 1.9 - 0.1, 0.0001)
```

With this change made, rerunning the test case yields a final line confirming `2 tests, 2 assertions, 0 failures, 0 errors`.

Fixtures

Aside from methods with the prefix `test_`, there are two other methods that can be included in any subclass of `Test::Unit::TestCase`. These methods allow for preparation of shared data structures and their eventual decommissioning and are called `setup` and `teardown`. We may establish a connection, for example, that we will be running tests over and then close it explicitly when we're done. Code to achieve this procedure is shown in Listing 11-10.

Listing 11-10. *A Test Case with a Fixture*

```
require "test/unit"

class RemoteHostTest < Test::Unit::TestCase
  def setup
    @session = RemoteHost.new("testserver.example.org")
  end

  def teardown
    @session.close
  end

  def test_echo
    assert_equal("ping", @session.echo("ping").stdout)
  end
end
```

Rails uses fixture-based testing so that entire clouds of `ActiveRecord` objects can be instantiated out of easily constructed YAML files. Such a facility is often referred to as a *test harness*, although I must profess an aversion to this term as it puts me in mind of a rather indelicate physical process.

■**Tip** Causing your test suites to be dependent on network resources can be handy initially but often scales badly. Dependence on the presence of an external resource and predictable behavior thereof may sometimes be reasonable but can lead to confusing problems with test results. There are a couple of projects that seek to assist with mocking up such dependencies: Flex Mock (`http://onestepback.org/software/flexmock`) and Mocha (`http://mocha.rubyforge.org`).

Test Suites

As your project grows, you will inevitably end up with more than one test case. A collection of cases is referred to as a *suite*, and building such a thing is no more complicated than having a file like Listing 11-11 that includes all the individual case files.

Listing 11-11. *A Test Suite Built from Test Cases*

```
require "test/unit"
require "tc_arithmetic"
require "tc_linalg"
require "tc_diophantine"
```

We build the suite by requiring all the pertinent test cases. You'll have noticed a naming convention that is frequently used. Files containing test cases have tc_ at the beginning of their names and test suites—you guessed it—have ts_ affixed to theirs. There is no reason to stop at simple test suites. You could build suites of suites (metasuites), supermetasuites, penthouse suites, and so on. The appropriate tree structure is up to you; just try to keep it as simple as possible.

Testing from Rake

There is a test task class included with rake. Listing 11-12 shows an example of its use (it would sit in your project's Rakefile).

Listing 11-12. *Using Rake to Define a Test Task*

```
Rake::TestTask.new do |t|
  t.test_files = FileList["test/tc_*.rb"]
end
```

This listing adds a task called test to the set of tasks available to rake. It will run a test on every test case matching the globbing pattern passed to FileList. Other options that can be tweaked via the task object t include the following:

- The directories to be added to the $LOAD_PATH (the default being "lib")

```
t.libs << "extralibs"
t.libs = ["libs", "otherlibs"]
```

- The name of the task (the default being :test)

```
t.name = "longtest"
```

- Whether or not to be verbose (the default being false)

```
t.verbose = true
```

Take a look at the Rake::TestTask documentation for a more complete picture.

One scenario that is made possible by driving tests from rake in this way is to make version-controlled commits dependent on passing all the tests. This constraint may not be appropriate for larger projects but, if implemented, it would force you to ensure that your code is in a fit state before committing it back to the repository. Listing 11-13 is for a task that would accomplish this feat for a Subversion (http://subversion.tigris.org)-managed project.

Listing 11-13. *Rake Task for Committing to a Repository Only If All Tests Pass*

```
desc "Commit the current working copy if all tests pass"
task :commit => :test do
  sh "svn", "commit"
end
```

Documentation

It is fair to say that of the big three bits of housekeeping, documenting code is the task I most love to hate. There are a few things in computing (like using Windows or programming in Java) that I might do if someone held a gun to my head. Where documentation is concerned, I could not show enthusiasm for it even if I had a howitzer rammed up my nose.

Programmers long ago recognized that documenting code is the bane of all project work and that a system able to take well-written source code and automatically create the corresponding documentation is vital. Such systems exist for all the major programming languages and Ruby is no exception.

Shipping as part of the standard distribution, rdoc interprets both code and specialized comments in source files and creates nicely formatted documentation from them. It can produce HTML pages like the ones you see when running a gem_server (see Chapter 10). It also produces documentation for use by ri (rdoc prepares all of the content for the lookups you do on standard library classes). For more information on producing ri documentation, see the sidebar "Command Line Documentation."

COMMAND LINE DOCUMENTATION

The only real decision when building ri documentation is where it should live. Everything else about the standard is designed to work seamlessly, whether you choose HTML or ri output. There are three places to choose from when using rdoc: the systemwide location, the sitewide location, and your home folder.

The first location is reserved for the actual Ruby distribution itself, so it's pretty unlikely that you'd want that one. The second basically provides the documentation to all the users of the system but in a way that is separate from the canonical Ruby installation (it will still require system-level permissions). The final one should be obvious. The rdoc commands you want are as follows (in reverse order):

```
rdoc --ri user.rb group.rb ...
rdoc --ri-site user.rb group.rb ...
rdoc --ri-system user.rb group.rb ...
```

Automatic Documentation

We'll start with what you get for free. Listing 11-14 contains a skeleton class stored in a file called user.rb.

Listing 11-14. *A Skeleton Class Itching to Be Documented*

```
class User
  attr_accessor :accepts_messages
  attr_reader :age

  def User.authenticate(login, password)
  end

  def send_message(text)
  end
end
```

What the User class is for is unimportant at this stage. The main point is that it has a few of the basic things a real-world class would have (a class method, an instance method, and some attributes). In order to generate HTML documentation for this class, we would run this:

```
$ rdoc user.rb
```

which generates the documentation and spits out some statistics about it. The files are placed (by default) in a directory called docs. If we open the newly minted docs/index.html, we are presented with a basic documentation page for our class that looks like Figure 11-1.

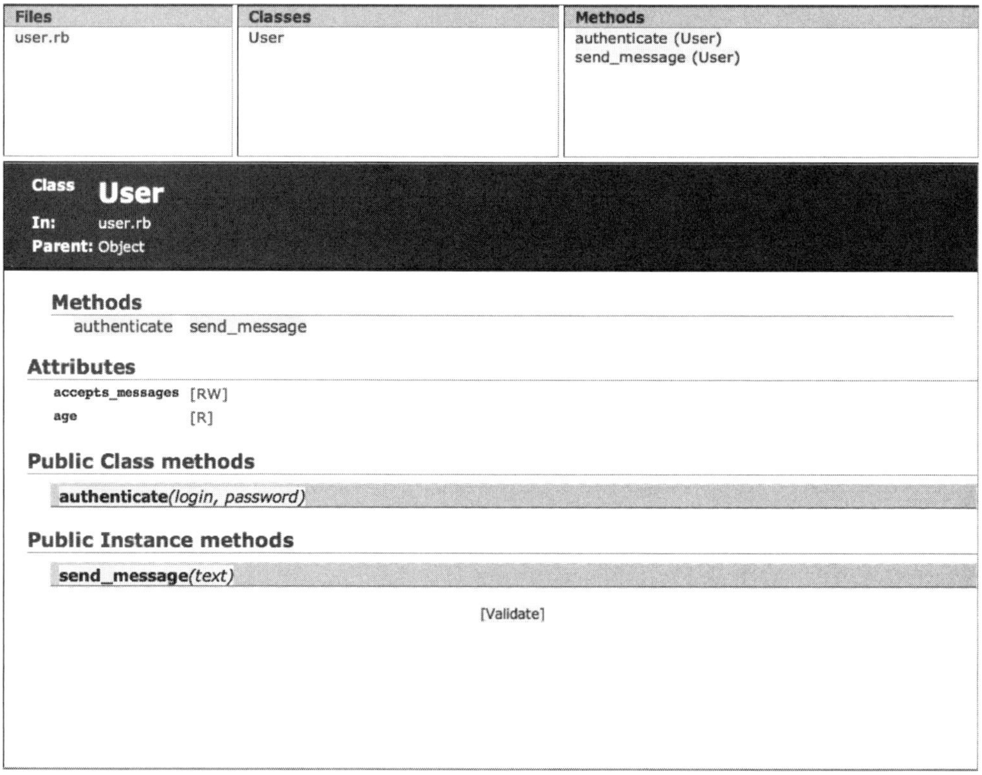

Figure 11-1. *A screenshot of the documentation generated from the skeleton class*

The rdoc command accepts lots of different command line parameters for modifying its behavior, and you can obtain a complete list by doing an rdoc --help. Some flags I commonly use include the following:

- -a (--all) to include information for all methods, not just public ones

- -d (--diagram) to generate DOT diagrams of classes and modules (see Chapter 9)

- -N (--line-numbers) to include line numbers in source code listings

- -o (--op) dir to specify the name of the output directory

- -s (--style) url to embed a particular stylesheet URL in the HTML

What is produced by rdoc is pretty much the most interactive, detailed documentation you could reasonably expect to be inferred from no information other than the source code. To go further, we need to add comments to our skeleton class.

Basic Comments

Adding comments to code is made ultrasimple by rdoc's convention that comments pertinent to a particular element should directly precede that element. Using this convention, we can add comments to Listing 11-14 to give Listing 11-15.

Listing 11-15. *A Commented Version of Listing 11-14*

```
# Models a user of our network filesystems
class User
  # A boolean determining whether the user can receive messages.
  attr_accessor :accepts_messages
  # The user's age in years.
  attr_reader :age

  # Find a User based on login.
  # Return the User if one was found and if the password matches.
  # Otherwise return nil.
  def User.authenticate(login, password)
  end

  # Send the user a message (if the accepts_messages attribute is set to true).
  def send_message(text)
  end
end
```

The resulting HTML page can be seen in Figure 11-2. As promised, each element now has its own little comment. Notice that the two instances of the word User have been turned into hyperlinks (which happen to link to the same page, but you get the idea). This is an example of rdoc once again doing its best to turn minimal code and comments into rich documentation.

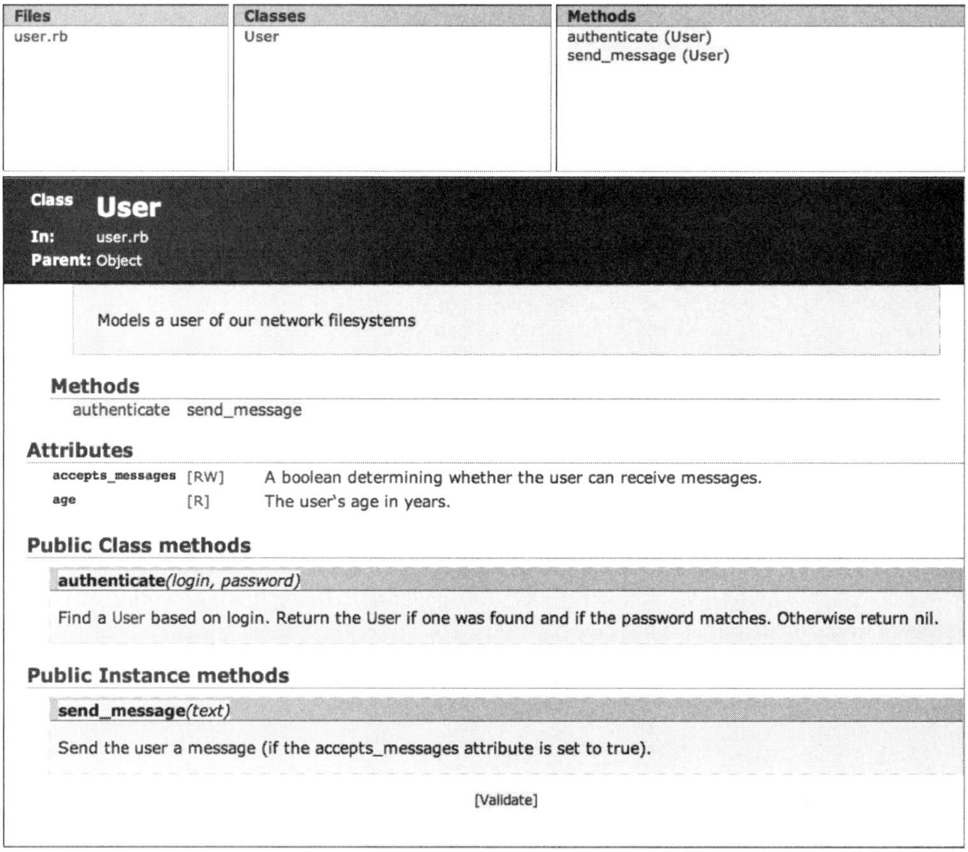

Files	Classes	Methods
user.rb	User	authenticate (User) send_message (User)

Class   **User**

In: user.rb
Parent: Object

Models a user of our network filesystems

Methods
authenticate   send_message

Attributes

accepts_messages	[RW]	A boolean determining whether the user can receive messages.
age	[R]	The user's age in years.

Public Class methods

authenticate*(login, password)*

Find a User based on login. Return the User if one was found and if the password matches. Otherwise return nil.

Public Instance methods

send_message*(text)*

Send the user a message (if the accepts_messages attribute is set to true).

[Validate]

Figure 11-2. *The documentation page with comments*

You can also see that the multiline comment for the User.authenticate method has become one line. This is due to the way in which rdoc interprets a comment block. Specifically, a single paragraph is deemed to be a sequential set of comment lines that are all right up against the left margin. Anything not against this margin is rendered verbatim.

Listing 11-16 holds an example that demonstrates this difference and introduces some basic markup abilities. Figure 11-3 shows the corresponding output.

Listing 11-16. *A Quick Tour of Some of the Basic rdoc Markup Facilities*

```
# This is an ordinary paragraph.
# It will end up on a single line.
#   There is a verbatim line here, which will end up by itself.
# This paragraph has single words in *bold*, _italic_ and +typewriter+ styles.
# It then has <b>long stretches of</b> <em>each kind</em> <tt>of style</tt>.
#--
```

```
# This text is for 007 only as the double-minus switches off comment processing.
# A double-plus switches it back on.
#++
# This last sentence appears as part of the second paragraph.
```

> This is an ordinary paragraph. It will end up on a single line.
>
>   There is a verbatim line here, which will end up by itself.
>
> This paragraph has single words in **bold**, *italic* and `typewriter` styles. It then has **long stretches of** *each kind* of `style`. This last sentence appears as part of the second paragraph.

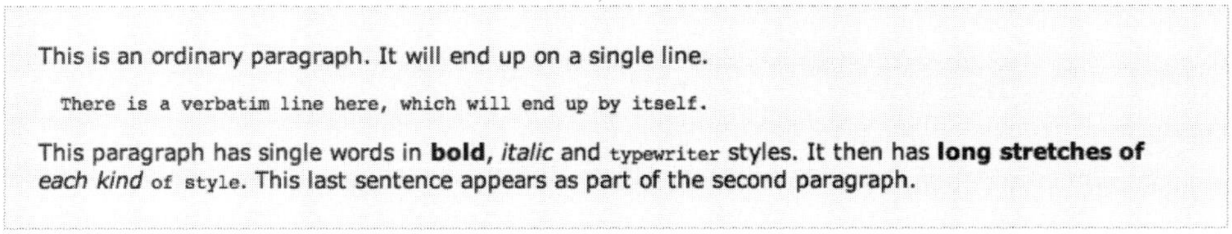

Figure 11-3. *The output produced by Listing 11-16*

Headings, Separators, and Links

A heading is signified by one or more equal signs at the start of the line. The number of equal signs indicates the relative importance of the heading:

```
# === An extremely important heading
# == A fairly important heading
# = This heading is almost feeble
```

A horizontal section break (or line, as it is sometimes called) is encoded using three or more dashes:

```
# ...and so the man says to him 'no - I asked for pop...corn'.
# ---
# There was a young girl from Nantucket...
```

Hyperlinks are automatically created anytime rdoc recognizes the name of a class, a method (containing an underscore or starting with a hash character), or a source file. These links will obviously point to the relevant section of the generated documentation. In addition, any text starting with link: will be evaluated relative to the document root.

As for external addresses, all URLs beginning with www:, http:, ftp:, or mailto: will be turned into proper hyperlinks. As a bonus, any http:-style link that points to an image is automatically turned into an <img ... /> tag, embedding the image in the page. If you want a link to have a specific label (other than the URL itself), then use the label[url] or {multi-word label}[url] syntax:

```
# http://svn.example.com, ftp://ftp.example.com
# {Send me an e-mail}[mailto:andre@example.com]
# Here's a pretty picture...
# http://www.example.com/puppy.png
```

Lists

A rather obvious syntax exists for specifying bulleted, numbered, and even alpha-enumerated lists in rdoc. Simply indent the paragraph and attach either an asterisk or a dash (for bulleted lists) or an alphanumeric character followed by a period (for enumerated lists) to the front like this:

```
# The hard disks are tracked using the following criteria...
# - capacity
# - rotation speed
# - seek time
# - mean time to failure
#
# The assessment workflow is handled in three stages...
# 1. Bob builds the chassis
# 2. Anne installs it in the rack
# 3. Malcolm takes the credit (being in management)
```

The other kind of list that is supported is one that maps specific labels to their descriptions either in heading-with-indented-paragraph form or as a table. The first form is achieved by wrapping the label in square brackets like [this]. The second is encoded by placing a double-colon on the end like this::. Both forms allow for multiline descriptions as long as they line up with either the indent caused by the label or a point just in from the label's indent starting on a subsequent line:

```
# [RAID 0] Simple data striping across entire disk pool.
# [RAID 5] Striping with a parity drive so that the pool can
#          withstand the failure of one drive.
# GIG-E::
#   Short name for gigabit ethernet. This standard has been around
#   for some time and is found with increasing frequency to run
#   all the way to the desktop in the corporate environment.
```

Processing Commands

There are a whole slew of directives that can be issued within a document to alter the processing behavior of rdoc. The documentation covers these in detail, but I want to mention a couple that can be rather handy.

A :nodoc: comment on the same line as an element that would usually be processed by rdoc will prevent that element from being documented. A modifier of all will cause this exclusion to apply to all child modules and classes:

```
module User # :nodoc: all
  class Passwd
  end
end
```

The other directive I use a lot is :include: filename, which pulls in the contents of another file. The search path for the file is either the current directory or any of those listed using the --include flag to rdoc. This directive is most useful for placing the contents of a README at the start of a class's documentation.

Documenting from Rake

We already saw the rdoc options available when building gems back in Chapter 10. Hopefully that process now makes a little more sense in the context of what we've covered in this section.

Just as there is a `rake` task for unit testing, so too is there one for `rdoc`. A section of your `Rakefile` concerned with generating the documentation for your project might look like Listing 11-17.

Listing 11-17. *Using Rake to Define an rdoc Task*

```
Rake::RDocTask.new do |t|
  t.main = "README"
  t.rdoc_files.include("README.rdoc", "lib/**/*.rb")
  t.options << "--diagram"
end
```

This listing adds `rake` tasks called `rdoc` (builds the documentation), `clobber_rdoc` (deletes all the documentation files), and `rerdoc` (rebuilds the documentation from scratch). Notice the shorthand used in specifying the files. Instead of using `rdoc_files = FileList.new.include(...)`, we are able to treat the object returned by `rdoc_files` as a file list. Other settings that can be altered via the task object `t` include the following:

- The directory in which to place the generated HTML files (the default being `"html"`)

  ```
  t.rdoc_dir = "html_docs"
  ```

- The name of the task (the default being `:rdoc`)

  ```
  t.name = "doc"
  ```

- The title of the documentation (the default being `nil`)

  ```
  t.title = "The Complete Works of Shakespeare"
  ```

Take a look at the `Rake::RDocTask` documentation for more detail.

Mission Accomplished

Testing and documentation are necessary steps in a complete development cycle. Through some clever libraries and tools, Ruby makes these tasks simple to get right and easy to integrate into your project workflow.

The dependency-tracking, task-oriented approach fostered by `rake` allows for straightforward management of all those little housekeeping jobs that accumulate like cellulite around the thighs of your code. This is particularly effective when combined with Ruby's built-in unit testing framework.

In this chapter, you saw that `rdoc` facilitates the production of documentation in both HTML and `ri` formats, leading to reference material that is presented with intelligence (although intelligibility is still the purview of the author).

The next and final chapter explores some of the exciting technologies and concepts that lie in Ruby's future.

CHAPTER 12

■■■

The Future of Ruby

As the last chapter of the book, this one's going to be a little different. I will present a very brief summary of some of the developments coming down the Ruby pipe. I feel this is important because in order to make a wholesale leap to a new programming language (as you may be), you have to be satisfied that the horse you're backing "has legs"—that it isn't a passing fad. Alternatively, if you are already sold on Ruby's credibility, I hope you will still find what is discussed here of some general interest.

One indicator of a great future for a programming language is the vibrancy and flair of the community that surrounds it. I am constantly impressed by the wit and creativity of Ruby developers. One of the best places to experience this is on the mailing lists:

- `ruby-talk` for general Ruby discussions

- `ruby-core` for core language topics

- `ruby-doc` for all documentation-related discussions

Of these three I am never without `ruby-core`, which is positively lavished with smart people discussing issues surrounding the language: standard library additions, best practices, metaprogramming, performance tweaks, and much more besides. This is one of the best places in existence to get information on upcoming changes to Ruby. Subscription instructions along with lots of other community information can be found at `www.ruby-lang.org/en/community`.

Execution Environments

It should go without saying that lots of work has been and continues to be done to improve and expand upon the execution of Ruby scripts. Two projects in particular are making big strides forward in this area: YARV and JRuby.

YARV

The most common criticism leveled at Ruby applications is that they are slow when compared with equivalent scripts in other interpreted languages. As you saw in Chapter 3, performance statements like this need to be made with care.

Nevertheless, nobody's going to object to making the Ruby interpreter faster, and this is precisely what the core team is doing. Chief among the efforts is an official migration to a new Ruby bytecode interpreter at the end of 2007. This new interpreter is called Yet Another Ruby VM (YARV).

This project (`www.atdot.net/yarv`) has but one stated aim: "to develop the fastest Virtual Machine for Ruby in the world." YARV is a simple, stack-based virtual machine (VM) with compile-time and JIT optimization, native (POSIX or Windows) threading, inline method caching, and tons of other notable additions. Compared with the current Ruby interpreter, YARV particularly improves upon programs that suffer from classic VM bottlenecks or do a lot of number crunching or symbolic processing. With typical benchmarks like the computation of an Ackermann number, YARV has been known to complete the calculation at nearly 20 times the speed of the standard Ruby interpreter. With more string-heavy tests like counting words, there is little or no difference between the interpreters.

In its current state, YARV can successfully execute most Ruby programs and libraries. To grab a copy from the Subversion repository, you need the following command:

```
$ svn co http://www.atdot.net/svn/yarv/trunk yarv
```

The build and install instructions are all on the YARV web site, together with details on what to expect when running the built-in tests.

JRuby

Wouldn't it be great if you could run a Ruby script on any platform that had Java support? JRuby (`http://jruby.codehaus.org`) is a 1.8.4-compatible Ruby interpreter written entirely in Java. Where the focus of YARV was extreme speed, the upshot of the JRuby project is extreme portability. Indeed it is quite possible that the number of current platforms Ruby runs on is far higher than for Java, especially if you omit mobile devices.

Beyond this, JRuby has added mechanisms for defining and interacting with pure Java classes from within Ruby. The interpreter also provides support for the Bean Scripting Framework (BSF; `http://jakarta.apache.org/bsf`), allowing Java application servers to use Ruby for individual JSP pages. This feature alone could prove to be a lifesaver in a busy corporate environment.

Current limitations of the JRuby implementation include the lack of continuation/binding support, the unavailability of a fine-grained timer, and some missing file operations. None of these issues should prove crippling to the average Ruby script, but they are worth being aware of.

A nice way to show off the increased portability that comes from the Java world is to try a Java Web Start-able version of `irb`. Go to the JRuby site and click the JRuby Console link. This will take you to a page with a webstart link, which you can click to automatically download and run the application.

Language Changes

The Ruby 1.9 stream is currently a testing ground for all sorts of changes to the language, some of which have been confirmed for Ruby 1.9.1 (the end-of-year 2007 release mentioned previously). In this section, I'll run through a handful of these changes.

In choosing these items, I tried to focus on the ones that will have the biggest practical impact for a system administrator. Rest assured that the complete list of changes is vastly longer and contains some fiendishly subtle revisions in behavior and semantics. Note that some of these changes might not make it into the 1.9.1 release—as ever, the future is an uncertain and slightly fishy place.

Arrays and Hashes

Throughout the book, you saw a lot of hashes that were constructed with symbols for keys. There is a new syntax for this that makes it even easier to read:

```
{:green => "house", :red => "lorry"} == {green: "house", red: "lorry"}
```

This means that all those flexible method signatures that we know and love can now look more like labeled argument lists:

```
User.create(name: "John", pass: "1234")
```

`Array.pop` and `Array.shift` will finally match the spirit of `Array.push` and `Array.unshift` in allowing multiple items to be separated from the array at once:

```
items = ["pixel", "texel", "tex-mex"]
items.pop(2) # returns ["texel", "tex-mex"], leaving items as ["pixel"]
```

Both arrays and hashes now have their canonical string conversion method `to_s` do the same thing as `inspect`, thus `puts {users: 15, groups: 12}` will now dump `{:users=>15,:groups=>12}` rather than `users15groups12`. Much better.

Strings

Strings will no longer be enumerable. This means no more using `String.each` to iterate over lines. Never fear, however—`String.each_line` will still be around. Additionally, there is the new `String.lines` method that returns an enumerator. It behaves exactly like `each_line` if passed a block. Otherwise, it is a kind of lazy-evaluated array of the lines in the string. As you would expect, both `each_line` and `lines` accept the separation character to use as an optional argument:

```
"forti \n nihil \n dificile".lines.sort # returns ["dificile", "forti", "nihil"]
```

Similarly, `String.bytes` returns an enumerator over the byte set for a given string that can be iterated through or treated like any old array.

A fundamental change is also being made to the unary operator (?). Instead of returning the integer character code of the character it is placed in front of (`?a == 97`), it will return a single character string (`?a == "a"`). This is one to watch out for, as it completely alters the semantics of this operator.

To complete the set, `String.[]` returns a single character string (`"lucky"[3] == "k"`) rather than its character code (`"lucky"[3] == 107`). To get the old behavior, use `String.ord` (`"k".ord == 107`). As a corollary to these changes, the list of `printf` format specifiers is gaining an additional entry: `%c` will encode for a single character string.

I/O Operations

The various file classes have acquired a number of convenience methods, including the most obvious one: `Dir.exist?` is now equivalent to `File.directory?`. Others include `File.world_readable?` and `File.world_writable?`.

The big news from a network and file system perspective is an entire raft of nonblocking operations:

- `IO.read_nonblock`, `IO.write_nonblock`

- `Socket.connect_nonblock`, `Socket.accept_nonblock`, `Socket.revcfrom_nonblock`

- `IPSocket.recvfrm_nonblock`, `TCPServer.accept_nonblock`

- `UNIXSocket.recvfrom_nonblock`, `UNIXServer.accept_nonblock`

All of these new functions apply the appropriate flags (`O_NONBLOCK`, etc.) to the underlying C operations being performed. It will be possible with these additions to write truly asynchronous I/O code.

Note These additional nonblocking operations are so useful that they have been merged into the current stable 1.8 stream.

Block Argument Locality

One of those little mistakes that sometimes catch out Ruby programmers is naming something in a block in a way that collides with a variable outside the block. In the future, the in-block declaration will shadow the outer variable without messing with it:

```
domain = "example.com"
["fish.fake", "fingers.fake"].each { |domain| puts domain }
puts domain
```

In 1.8, the preceding code would end up printing this:

```
fish.fake
fingers.fake
fingers.fake
```

Contrast this with the new behavior, and note how the inner declaration of `domain` does not clobber the outer one:

```
fish.fake
fingers.fake
example.com
```

Multisplatting

You've seen that it is possible to (in some sense) unpack an array and turn it into a list of arguments to be provided to a method like this:

```
def establish_connection(host, port, user, pass)
end

credentials = ["andre", "1234"]
establish_connection("www.example.com", "6969", *credentials)
```

It is not possible in 1.8 to use this *splatting* trick more than once in a given method call. That's going to change, making this sort of thing possible (continuing the example):

```
server = ["www.example.com", "6969"]
establish_connection(*server, *credentials)
```

Object Tapping

Many in-place (destructive) string functions return `nil` if they end up doing nothing, for example:

```
"line\n".chomp  # returns a copy of the string with the newline removed
"line".chomp    # returns a copy of the string unaltered
"line\n".chomp! # returns the original string with the newline removed
"line".chomp!   # returns nil
```

This behavior exists for a reason, but it can make command chaining unexpectedly hard. Consider the `chomp` operation combined with an attempt to retrieve the last character:

```
"line".chomp[-1]  # returns a new string "e"
"line".chomp![-1] # raises an error complaining that nil has no such method as []
```

Thus the destructive version of this compound operation would need to be split onto three lines (`l = "line"; l.chomp!; l[-1]`). This is manifestly ugly, so future versions of Ruby will provide `Object` and its inheritors (i.e., every object) with a method named `tap`, which both passes the object to a block and returns the self-same object. The three-liner becomes a one-liner again:

```
"line".tap { |l| l.chomp! }[0] # returns a new string "e"
```

Read-Write Attributes

Whereas currently the `attr` keyword provides a module/class with both read and write accessors for a given variable, it now only vends the reader method. The new syntax for a read-write attribute involves an extra equal sign:

```
attr :name      # provides name method
attr :age=      # provides both age and age= methods
attr :age= :name # provides all three methods
```

Enumerable Upgrades

The perennial `Enumerable` module is being shifted from the standard library into the core and so will no longer need to be specifically `required` by your libraries. In addition, a number of new behaviors are being added.

`Enumerable.first(n)` is being added and behaves just like `Array.first(n)` in that it retrieves the first n objects from the collection:

```
[1, 2, "buckle", "my", "shoe"].first(2) # returns a new array [1, 2]
{tickets: 2, rides: 5}.first(1) # returns a new array [[:rides, 5]]
```

In the case of the second example, remember that the order of a hash is undefined. For easy partitioning, `Enumerable.group_by` is really handy as it takes a block, which will generate a key for each value and then place all the values in a hash of arrays accordingly. Thus the following:

```
["acorn", "apple", "orange", "starfruit"].group_by { |name| name[0] }
```

would return a new hash:

```
{"a" => ["acorn", "apple"], "o" => ["orange"], "s" => ["starfruit"]}
```

In the searching department, we have the new `Enumerable.find_index` method, which is exactly like `Enumerable.find` save for the fact that it returns the index of the found item rather than the item itself:

```
["users", "groups", "printers"].find_index { |item| item[0] == "p" } # returns 2
```

In a similar vein, `Enumerable.count` takes either an object as an argument or a matching block and returns the number of items in the collection, either matching the object or causing `true` to be returned by the block:

```
(1..10).count(5)                # returns 1
(1..10).count { |i| i % 2 == 0 } # returns 5
```

Finally, `Enumerable.max` and `Enumerable.min` now have a couple of siblings: `Enumerable.max_by` and `Enumerable.min_by`. These methods take a block that produces a value used to assess the maximal/minimal nature of each item:

```
["52634", "22435", "4314", "22489"].max_by { |l| l.reverse.to_i } # returns "22489"
```

begin

TIOBE Software (`www.tiobe.com`) maintains an index of language popularity based on the "world-wide availability of skilled engineers, courses and third party vendors." It's an interesting way to measure such popularity, as it reflects service demand rather than lines of code written or sleepless nights per point release. This index rated Ruby nineteenth in the world in May 2006. One year later it's at number 10 and has the strongest growth rating of any programming language listed in the top 20.

From modest beginnings, Ruby has come to touch server farms and computer labs, desktops and workshops, classrooms and boardrooms. In so doing, it has made a style of programming possible that liberates the humble system administrator from the soul-sapping drudgery of spaghetti code and endless development cycles.

Over the course of this book, you explored the nature of the language and the difference it can make to those innumerable little chores that make up an administrator's day, from consistent file handling through unified data architectures to network systems analysis and administration. Throughout, I have attempted to present Ruby as I find it: a treasure that can be relied upon again and again to put a smile on my face and a spring in my step.

It is my sincere hope that you have been intrigued enough by what you've read to continue your journey through the land of Ruby—strong in will to `slice`, to `squeeze`, to `bind`, and not to `yield`.

APPENDIX

■ ■ ■

Ruby Execution

As promised in Chapter 2, this appendix takes time to introduce the general execution environment of a Ruby script. It covers the various command line options available with the Ruby interpreter as well as the many pertinent variables and constants that make very short scripts possible.

Command Line Options

Perl users should feel right at home with many of the flags that can be passed to the Ruby interpreter, as the flags were modeled very much on those used by Perl. It is my opinion that Perl's biggest strength lies in its one-liners that, while often baffling to the newcomer, provide immense power to construct unbelievably dense code. This facility stems from two things: command line modes that do very common things for you and shorthand variables for accessing/setting pertinent data and behavior.

The fact that Ruby respects the success of Perl's approach in this area often leads to the charge that Ruby is too Perl-like. This is roughly equivalent to saying a human is too much like a turkey because they've both recognized the advantages of bipedal locomotion.

With that said, I can now present a list of command line options that is complete save for four: --copyright, --version, --help (-h), and --yydebug (-y). I'm going to assume that the first three hold no mystery. The fourth basically turns on a load of debugging for the interpreter itself and is of no use unless you plan to debug Ruby.

Octal Record Separator Specification: -0[octal]

Consists of the digit 0 optionally followed by an octal value for the character to use as the default global record separator $/, which is used by methods like IO.each. Without an explicit value, NULL (000) is assumed. Passed a value of zero (-00), Ruby goes into paragraph mode, where each record is considered to be separated by two default record separators (e.g., "\n\n"). Since 511 is not a valid character code, passing -0777 will guarantee that the entire input file is read in as one record—a process somewhat indelicately referred to as *slurping*.

Auto Split Mode: -a

When used in conjunction with -n or -p, runs $F = $_.split at the beginning of each loop.

Change Directory: -C path

Causes the present working directory to be set to the specified path before the script is run.

Check Syntax Only: -c

Does exactly what you think it does (without running the script). Remember that the more sophisticated your scripts become, the less useful this flag will be, as it only invokes a simple syntax check. If all is well, you will receive the message Syntax OK. Otherwise, you will see one or more reports indicating a problem and the line it occurred on like this:

```
upload.rb:19: odd number list for Hash
upload.rb:28: syntax error
```

Debug Mode: -d, --debug

Sets $DEBUG to true, which is generally useful if you want a simple way to enable some extra tracing or differing behaviors during development. This flag also implicitly sets $VERBOSE = true.

Execute Line: -e line

Takes a line of Ruby and executes it (as you've already seen). This can be specified multiple times, in which case each instance is treated as a new separate line for bookkeeping purposes (try ruby -e 'p __LINE__' -e 'p __LINE__').

Field Separator Specification: -F pattern

Sets the global field separator $;, which is used by methods like String.split. Note that this can be a simple string delimiter or a full-blown regular expression.

Include from Additional Directory: -I path(s)

Adds to the array of search paths for the inclusion of code via the load or require statement. This array is accessible in code as $: ($LOAD_PATH). Note that many paths can be specified per -I and that many -Is can be used.

In-place Editing: -i[extension]

For each file path specified as an argument to the interpreter (in ARGV), anything written to standard out while dealing with a particular file becomes the contents of that particular file. The original file is preserved with a new extension if and only if this is specified. Obviously, this flag is pretty meaningless without the use of -n or -p. Suppose I wanted to change all instances of my name in a set of header files to my secret squirrel name. I would write something like ruby -p -i.bak -e 'gsub(/Andre/, "Nutkin")' *.h.

KCode Encoding Choice: -K encoding

Specifies the encoding of the script to support character sets like SJIS as used by our Japanese colleagues. This is equivalent to setting the $KCODE variable. An encoding of u specifies UTF-8.

Line Ending Automated Handling: -l

Sets the output record separator ($\) to the same value as the input record separator ($/) and automatically performs a chop! on each input record ($_). In simpler terms, this flag causes each record to be presented to you without its line ending or other record separator, and then adds it back once you've finished.

Nested Retrieval Loop: -n

Places an implicit while gets ... end block around your code. Note that this allows you to read each line of not only a single file, but multiple files. It is well worth having a close look at ri Kernel.gets for the rather cute behavior conventions it provides. In particular, it sets $_ to the value of the retrieved record (e.g., the next line).

Printed Nested Retrieval Loop: -p

Does the same as -n, but with an extra print $_ at the end of each loop.

Require Library: -r library

Identical to having placed require library at the beginning of your code. This is particularly useful in -n/-p situations where you don't want to require the library through every loop (although this wouldn't be disastrous, as rerequiring a library involves only a single hash lookup).

Script Search: -S

Instead of assuming a given script is in the current directory, causes the interpreter to search in the location specified in the PATH environment variable. This is mostly to allow platforms that don't support the shebang-style script header (silly as they are) to emulate it.

Smart Variables: -s

Magically removes every command flag after the script name but before any file arguments from ARGV and turns them into global variables. So ruby -s test.rb -col=blue file.c would run the test.rb script with a single argument (file.c) and give the script the global variable $col = "blue".

Taint Level: -T[level]

Turns on taint checking at the given level (or 1 if none is specified) and sets $SAFE to this value.

Verbose Mode: -v, --verbose

Activates all kinds of extra messages and warnings, sets $VERBOSE = true, and causes the version string to be printed before anything else is done (thus making a simple ruby -v do what you would expect).

Warnings Mode: -w

Does the same as -v, except that no version string is printed and the interpreter will expect input on standard in if no other code/scripts are specified.

Ignore Garbage: -x[path]

The interpreter will ignore everything it encounters until it sees a shebang line containing the string ruby, which it will interpret as the beginning of the script. It will then execute the script until it encounters an end-of-file or the keyword __END__. If a path is specified, the present working directory is changed to this path before execution commences.

Environment

Ruby provides access to its runtime environment through a set of variables that, again, should be familiar to any Perl user. First, there are the set of arguments to the script whereby the invocation

```
$ ruby count.rb 1 2 3
```

would give us

```
ARGV = ["1", "2", "3"]
```

inside count.rb. ARGV is just an Array and so supports all the methods you have/will come to love. Imagine we wanted our script to be able to take some command flags, one of which was a -r to remove something or other. One quick and dirty way to determine whether this had been passed is

```
remove_stuff = ARGV.include?("-r")
```

In practice, beyond the simplest command line options, a proper argument-parsing library tends to be a better idea.

Next on the list of most-used variables would have to be the environment itself—that dictionary of values you can see from the console by typing env (or something similar). Here's what part of mine looks like:

```
TERM_PROGRAM=Apple_Terminal
TERM=xterm-color
SHELL=/bin/bash
TERM_PROGRAM_VERSION=133
USER=andre
```

Perhaps unsurprisingly, this is accessed in Ruby using the ENV object (which acts like a Hash but isn't one). Values can be retrieved and set as you would expect:

```
terminal_type = ENV["TERM"]
ENV["USER"] = "Nutkin"
```

Beyond these two oft-used collections, a few global variables and a couple more constants are of interest.

Process Information

The following entities all relate to process-specific information such as the name of the command used to run the script and global variables for each of the command flags:

- $0: The command that originally ran the Ruby script (what C users would think of as the first argument of ARGV). On many platforms, this is writable so that how the process appears in top/ps can be changed by assigning something new to $0.

- $$: The process ID (PID) of the currently executing program.

- $:: The array of directories to check when including code via the require or load command. This array provides a programmatic alternative to using the -I flag on the command line to include new search paths. Append your chosen directory/directories as you would with any other array: $: << "/tmp/foo" or $: += ["/tmp/foo", "/tmp/bar"].

- $-<something>: Almost all of the command flags have a corresponding variable of this form—for example, $-a, which corresponds to the value passed by the -a command flag, or $-d, which is true in debug mode.

- __FILE__: The name of the currently executing file.

- __LINE__: The number of the line that is currently executing.

File Handles

These variables specify the input and output streams used by your program:

- STDIN, STDOUT, STDERR: The actual standard file handles (of class IO) for the program and the initial values of $stdin, $stdout, and $stderr

- $stdin, $stdout, $stderr: The current IO objects for the standard file handles used by methods like Kernel.puts

Magic Processing Variables

This subsection lists global variables controlling some of the more "magical" field, file, and record processing behavior we unpacked in Chapter 7:

- $/: The input record separator used by methods like Kernel.gets.

- $\\: The output record separator used by methods like Kernel.puts.

- $;: The input field separator (a simple string delimiter or a regular expression).

- $,: The output field separator used by methods like Array.join (defaults to nil).

- $<, ARGF: A special object that provides access to all of the lines of all of the files specified in ARGV (or the data from $stdin when no such files are specified). For example, $<.file returns an IO object for the current file being read, and $FILENAME is a synonym for $<.filename.

- $_: The last line read by `Kernel.gets` or `Kernel.readline`. Indeed, a number of the string manipulation functions in Kernel (such as `gsub`) operate on $_.

- $F: The array of fields as split under the `-a` command flag using $; to determine the field separator.

Other Sundries

Finally, here are some other variables (and a constant) that you might find useful in day-to-day scripting:

- `DATA`: The contents of the main program file past an __END__ directive (if such exists)

- $1 to $9: The up to nine matches from the last executed regular expression (local to the current scope)

- $!: The last exception object raised in the current context

- $@: The last exception object's backtrace

Improving Readability

Looking back over the preceding subsections, I see that I used to use a lot of these tersely named global variables (or their equivalents) when I was a Perl monkey. I'm pretty sure I've never employed most of these as a Ruby-holic, mostly because I found myself in a job where one-liners were never one-offs. Even trivial bits of code ended up getting reused, and the ease with which one can write things "properly" the first time in Ruby meant that beasts like $< never really had a chance.

If you absolutely insist on using these global variables in scripts, then you'd be well advised to check out the `English` library, which ships as part of the standard distribution. It maps many of the symbols to more intelligible variable names and can be bolted on to your script with a quick `require "English"`. Mappings include $! to `$ERROR_INFO`, $; to `$FIELD_SEPARATOR`, and $/ to `$INPUT_RECORD_SEPARATOR`.

INDEX

User.authenticate method, 206
User.groups method, 120
user_info file, 17, 100
User.new method, 122
uscr.rb file, 203
users array, 65
users hash, 172
users organizational unit, 119
/usr/share/dict/words path, 16

V
value_formatter key, 171
/var/run/myscript.pid file, 63
VarBind objects, 160
$< variable, 16
$. variable, 17
$; variable, 100
$/ variable, 100, 101
$ variable, 102
$! variable, 224
vendor/plugins directory, 173
verbose mode, 221
version command line option, 219
version key, 157, 190
virtual machine (VM), 212

W
w flag, 2
warnings mode, 222
watch utility, 19
web robots, 140–144
Web Services Description Language (WSDL) file, 126
Webrick, 148
WebSession class, 141, 187
width key, 172

word element, 106
:wrap parameter, 121
wrapper method, 28
WriteCommunity key, 157
writing servers, 144–148
WSDL (Web Services Description Language) file, 126
wsdl2ruby.rb utility, 128
wtmp files, 161–163

X
XML, 104–116
    alternative parsing libraries, 116
    building, 66–67
    overview, 104–105
    property list (PList) format, 109–116
    REXML, 105–107
    streaming classes, 107–109
XML Remote Procedure Call (XML-RPC), 122–125
    client functionality, 122–124
    server functionality, 124–125
XMLRPC::Client class, 122
XMLRPC::Server instance, 124

Y
-y (yydebug) command line option, 219
YAML, 78–79, 178
*.yaml globbing pattern, 167
YAML.dump method, 78
Yet Another Ruby Virtual Machine (YARV), 211–212
yield command, 9, 11, 12
yydebug (-y) command line option, 219

Z
ZIP archive (.zip), 178

You Need the Companion eBook

Your purchase of this book entitles you to buy the companion PDF-version eBook for only $10. Take the weightless companion with you anywhere.

We believe this Apress title will prove so indispensable that you'll want to carry it with you everywhere, which is why we are offering the companion eBook (in PDF format) for $10 to customers who purchase this book now. Convenient and fully searchable, the PDF version of any content-rich, page-heavy Apress book makes a valuable addition to your programming library. You can easily find and copy code—or perform examples by quickly toggling between instructions and the application. Even simultaneously tackling a donut, diet soda, and complex code becomes simplified with hands-free eBooks!

Once you purchase your book, getting the $10 companion eBook is simple:

❶ Visit **www.apress.com/promo/tendollars/**.

❷ Complete a basic registration form to receive a randomly generated question about this title.

❸ Answer the question correctly in 60 seconds, and you will receive a promotional code to redeem for the $10.00 eBook.

Apress®
THE EXPERT'S VOICE™

2855 TELEGRAPH AVENUE | SUITE 600 | BERKELEY, CA 94705

Offer valid through 1/08.